# Power and Responsibility in Chinese Foreign Policy

# Power and Responsibility in Chinese Foreign Policy

Yongjin Zhang and Greg Austin (eds)

E PRESS

Published by ANU E Press
The Australian National University
Canberra ACT 0200, Australia
Email: anuepress@anu.edu.au
This title is also available online at http://epress.anu.edu.au

National Library of Australia Cataloguing-in-Publication entry

Title: Power and responsibility in Chinese foreign policy / edited by Yongjin Zhang and Greg Austin.

ISBN: 9781925021417 (paperback) 9781925021424 (ebook)

Subjects: International relations.
China--Foreign relations.
China--Politics and government--1976-

Other Authors/Contributors:
Zhang, Yongjin.
Austin, Greg.

Dewey Number: 327.51

# Contents

## Abbreviations

| | |
|---|---|
| ABM | Anti-ballistic missile |
| ACME | Arms Control in the Middle East |
| ADB | Asian Development Bank |
| APEC | Asia Pacific Economic Cooperation |
| ARF | ASEAN Regional Forum |
| ASEAN | Association of Southeast Asian Nations |
| BWC | Biological Weapons Convention |
| CBM | confidence-building measures |
| CCMPO | Commission for the Comprehensive Management of Public Order |
| CCP | Chinese Communist Party |
| CD | Conference on Disarmament |
| CFA | Committee on Freedom of Association |
| CIS | Commonwealth of Independent States |
| CMC | Central Military Commission |
| CNEIC | China Nuclear Energy Industry Corporation |
| CNPC | Chinese National Petroleum Corporation |
| COSTIND | Commission for Science, Technology and Industry for National Defence |
| CTBT | Comprehensive Test Ban Treaty |
| CWC | Chemical Weapons Convention |
| DPP | Democratic Progressive Party |
| EBRD | European Bank for Reconstruction and Development |
| EEZ | Economic Exclusion Zone |
| GATT | General Agreement on Tariffs and Trade |
| GDP | gross domestic product |
| GNP | gross national product |
| GSD | General Staff Department |
| IAEA | International Atomic Energy Agency |
| IBRD | International Bank for Reconstruction and Development |
| ICJ | International Court of Justice |
| IDA | International Development Association |
| IGO | Inter-governmental organisation |
| ILO | International Labour Organisation |

| | |
|---|---|
| IMF | International Monetary Fund |
| INGO | international non-governmental organisation |
| INTERFET | International Force in East Timor |
| IRBM | intermediate range ballistic missile |
| KEDO | Korean Peninsula Energy Development Organisation |
| KRL | Khan Research Laboratories |
| MAD | mutually assured destruction |
| MFN | most-favoured nation |
| MRBM | medium range ballistic missile |
| MTCR | Missile Technology Control Regime |
| NAM | Non-aligned Movement |
| NATO | North Atlantic Treaty Organisation |
| NGO | Non-governmental organisation |
| NIEO | new international economic order |
| NMD | National Missile Defence |
| NPC | National People's Congress |
| NPT | Non-proliferation Treaty |
| OAS | Organization of American States |
| OECD | Organisation for Economic Cooperation and Development |
| PLA | People's Liberation Army |
| PLC | Political and Legal Commission |
| PRC | People's Republic of China |
| PTBT | Partial Test Ban Treaty |
| R&D | research and development |
| RFE | Russian Far East |
| RMA | Revolution in Military Affairs |
| ROC | Republic of China |
| ROK | Republic of Korea |
| SAR | Special Administrative Region |
| SCO | Shanghai Cooperation Organisation |
| SRBM | short range ballistic missile |
| TMD | Theatre Missile Defence |
| UN | United Nations |
| UNCLOS | United Nations Convention on the Law of the Sea |

| | |
|---|---|
| UNCTAD | United Nations Conference on Trade and Development |
| UNDP | United Nations Development Programme |
| UNEP | United Nations Environment Programme |
| UNGA | United Nations General Assembly |
| UNHCR | United Nations High Commissioner for Refugees |
| UNICEF | United Nations Children's Fund |
| US | United States |
| USSR | Union of Soviet Socialist Republics |
| WMD | weapons of mass destruction |
| WTO | World Trade Organization |

# Contributors

**Greg Austin** is Director of Research for the Brussels-based International Crisis Group. He has worked in other professional and academic posts in Canberra, Hong Kong and Washington. He is co-author of *Japan and Greater China: political economy and military power in the Asian century* (with Stuart Harris, 2001); and *Red Star East: the armed forces of Russia in Asia* (with Alexey Muraviev, 2000); and author of *China's Ocean Frontier: international law, military force and national development* (1998).

**Gerald Chan** is Senior Lecturer at Victoria University of Wellington, New Zealand. His latest publications include *Chinese Perspectives on International Relations* (1999), *China's International Relations in the 21st Century* (co-editor, 2000), and 'From the 'Olympic formula' to the Beijing Games', *Cambridge Review of International Affairs* (2002).

**Rosemary Foot** is Professor of International Relations and the John Swire Senior Research Fellow in the International Relations of East Asia, St Antony's College, University of Oxford. Her most recent book is *Rights Beyond Borders: the global community and the struggle over human rights in China* (2000).

**Baogang He** is Associate Professor at the School of Government, the University of Tasmania, currently on leave as Senior Research Fellow, East Asian Institute, National University of Singapore. He is the author of *The Democratic Implication of Civil Society in China* (1997), and *Nationalism, National Identity and Democratization in China* (with Yingjie Guo, 2000).

**Stuart Harris** is Professor Emeritus in the Department of International Relations in the Research School of Pacific and Asian Studies at the Australian National University. Former Head of the Australian Department of Foreign Affairs and Trade, his research interests include China's international relations and Asia Pacific economic and security cooperation. His most recent publications include *Will China Divide Australia and the US?* (1998) and *Japan and Greater China: political economy and military power in the Asian century* (with Greg Austin, 2001).

**Ann Kent** is Australian Research Council Research Fellow at the Centre for International and Public Law, Faculty of Law, Australian National University. She is the author of *China, the United Nations and Human Rights: the limits of compliance* (1999) and numerous other publications on China, international organisations and human rights. She is currently writing a book on China and international organisations.

**Gary Klintworth** has a PhD in International Relations. He was a China analyst for Australia's Joint Intelligence Organisation and a Senior Research Fellow with the Northeast Asia Program at the Australian National University. He has published several books on East Asia including *New Taiwan, New China* (reprinted 1997).

**Ji You** is Senior Lecturer in the School of Politics and International Relations at the University of New South Wales. He has published widely on China's political, military, economic and foreign affairs. Most recently, he authored the book, *The Armed Forces of China* (1999).

**Yongjin Zhang** is Fellow in the Department of International Relations, Research School of Pacific and Asian Studies at the Australian National University. His most recent publications include *China in International Society since 1949—Alienation and beyond* (1998) and 'System, empire and state in Chinese international relations', *Review of International Studies* (2001).

# Acknowledgments

The genesis of this book is an international conference on 'China at Fifty: power and responsibility' that we organised in November 1999 in Canberra. We chose the occasion of the fiftieth anniversary of the founding of the People's Republic of China to bring a number of scholars from around the world to reflect on changes and the new orientation of Chinese foreign policy. Discussions and debates at and following the conference have further stimulated our interests in looking at how the international behaviour of the People's Republic of China has been increasingly shaped by China's understanding of its growing power and responsibility in international society. We would like to acknowledge the Department of International Relations, Research School of Pacific and Asian Studies at the Australian National University for providing funding and organisational support for that conference.

This book would not have been possible without the active support and encouragement we have received from all contributors, who share strong belief in how our collective work can contribute in its own way to understanding China's sometimes erratic international behaviour. The publication of this book sees the fruition of our continuous conversation in the last two years. We would like to express our gratitude to all of them.

Finally, we are grateful to Maree Tait and Matthew May, both at the Asia Pacific Press at the Australian National University, for their painstaking efforts to see our manuscript through to print.

Yongjin Zhang and Greg Austin

# 1
# China and the responsibility of power

**Yongjin Zhang and Greg Austin**

Why does China behave as it does in its foreign policy? How and why does China behave differently from other Great Powers in international society? How does China's understanding of the responsibility associated with its rising power explain its international behaviour? In what sense can we argue that China has become more (or less) responsible in international relations? In China's search for its Great Power status, how do domestic politics and historical experience matter in its understanding of the responsibility of power? Does China think it is well served by a responsible approach to the rights and duties bestowed on it by international society? How do others evaluate whether China is living up to its obligations as a rising power? These are among a particular set of questions that individual essays published in this collection reflect on and debate. Collectively, this book explores a gap in the existing literature on the studies of Chinese foreign policy and focuses on whether and how a particular idea—the idea of the responsibility of power—helps to shape as well as explain China's changing behaviour in international relations.

The rising power of China has been one important theme in the discourse of post Cold War international relations. Recent and current debates have revolved around two important questions. What are the implications of the rise of China for regional and global international order? And how should others, particularly the United States, respond to the rise of China?[1] On the first question, a realist reading suggests that changing power relations, particularly those of a rising power vis-à-vis the pre-eminent power (that is, China vis-à-vis the United States), will inevitably lead to conflicts and even war. Further, China is revisionist and destabilising because of its historical grievances and irredentist agenda. It is bent on challenging and changing the existing international order. A realist reading is quick to point out that, historically, the rise of Japan and Germany as two have-not powers has provoked major wars. Even a liberal reading of the rise of China is likely to reinforce the realist wisdom. China is the remaining Leninist state. The Chinese Communist Party still presides over an authoritarian political system and repressive regime that is antithetical to democratic values. Naturally, Beijing continues to hold conflicting worldviews about the nature and structure of the international system. The distorted relationship and tensions between state and society and the lack of social balance of power in China's state–society complex also makes a strong China more of a threat than a contribution to peace and stability.[2] Such readings underlie the variegated interpretations of the 'China threat'.

On the second question—how best to respond to or manage the rise of China—proposed strategies in the debates differ sharply, ranging from containment to constrainment, to conditional, constructive and comprehensive engagement.[3] Realist arguments emphasise the containment and constrainment of China, whereas liberal arguments favour engagement. Either implicitly or explicitly, realist arguments in general posit that China is a classic dissatisfied but rising power like Nazi Germany and the former Soviet Union. China and the United States are therefore destined to clash with each other or become strategic rivals, or at least strategic competitors.[4] For realists, the historical lessons of the failure of the British appeasement policy in the 1930s and the success of US containment policy during the Cold War support their arguments for the containment strategy.[5] Some further argue that, as China's approach to international relations remains *realpolitik*, only concerted power can deter or constrain it. In East Asia, therefore, a new balance of power should be established for that purpose.[6]

Realists believe that liberal arguments for engaging China are based on shaky ground. It is true that economic interdependence between China and the world economy is intensifying. Economic interdependence alone, however, is insufficient to change Chinese behaviour decisively and is at the mercy of Chinese leadership's cold calculation of cost and benefit. It is also true that China's participation in regional and global international institutions is growing. Regional international institutions in East Asia, in contrast to Europe, are, however, too weak to exert any real influence in modifying China's security policy and behaviour in the region. While engagement policy may encourage the Chinese government to liberalise internally, other domestic variables such as succession politics and the vulnerability of the political system are more decisive of the future of China's democratisation.

The contributors to this volume share many common concerns with the current debates. We also believe that the rise of China is central to the future shape of the regional and global international order and China's international behaviour will change as its power grows. Further, China's growing power needs to be managed carefully to minimise its disruptive effect on the international system. We differ, however, on the assessment that the rising Chinese power is necessarily and inevitably destabilising and threatening. A crucial variable here is China's attitudes towards the responsibility of its rising power in international relations. Does China view power as a means or an end, and a means to what end? What is the conception among Chinese élites of China's responsible role in international relations? As a rising power, does China share with other Great Powers similar understanding of their responsibility for managing the international system? Where is the gap? How can international society induce a rising China to play an increasingly responsible part in the emerging international order? Answers to these questions, we argue, have important bearings on our understanding of the implications of an ascendant China for the future international order.

We seek therefore to join the debate by investigating this missing dimension in the current discourse on the rise of China and to invigorate the debate by taking us beyond the sterile discussions of a rising power vis-à-vis a pre-eminent power. Regardless of one's theoretical preferences, the role of theory is to aid in understanding and explaining. There are two additional reasons why this line of enquiry should be pursued. First, China has often been stigmatised as an irresponsible power and a 'rogue state'.[7] Evidence drawn from, for example, China's evolving arms control policy and its policies towards North Korean nuclear and missile programs, as well as its behaviour during the Asian financial crisis in 1997–98 and its missile exercise in the Taiwan Strait in 1996 is, however, inconclusive and contradictory at best. Such contradictions need to be analysed carefully. Second, unique among Great Powers, China has developed a set of uneasy and unusual social relations with global international society. Our investigations must be embedded in that social context and are to contribute to our understanding of that social context.

Power exacts responsibility. Even in the anarchical and hierarchical world of international relations, this conventional wisdom remains unpalatably true.[8] Hedley Bull once explicitly argued that it is precisely because of the embedded inequality of states in terms of power in international society that Great Powers enjoy special rights and privileges at the same time when they assume duties and managerial responsibilities for maintaining and sustaining international order. Great Powers also have a greater stake in the existing international order.[9] Bull argues more specifically that Great Powers contribute to international order 'by managing their relations with each other; and by exploiting their preponderance in such a way as to impart a degree of central direction to the affairs of international society as a whole'.[10] The persistent vitality of G7 (now G8), the uncompromising privileged status of the exclusive nuclear powers club, and recent debates over the reform of the United Nations Security Council are testimony of the continued relevance of Bull's arguments after the end of the Cold War. Two points need to be made here, though. First, the concept of the responsibility of Great Powers is fundamentally different from that of the state responsibility. Whereas state responsibility is legally and explicitly defined in international law (for example the responsibility to protect aliens and their property),[11] Great Power responsibility is politically as well as morally postulated implicitly rather than explicitly. It rests on shared understanding principally among Great Powers. Collective expectations of international society therefore underlie the conceptualisation of the responsibility of power. Second, in his discourse on the duties and stake of Great Powers in international order (largely conducted in the 1970s), Bull clearly privileges order over justice in world politics, although he is not entirely comfortable, and is sometimes ambivalent, as to where he situates justice vis-à-vis order. As Ian Harris has noted, Bull's ambiguity in his treatment of justice results from lack of an enquiry into international ethics.[12] Further, Bull's discussions suggest that the rights and duties of Great Powers are mostly, if not exclusively, structurally determined. There is little elaboration in Bull's discussions about how the domestic constitutions of individual states shape their attitudes towards power and their understanding of the responsibility associated with it.[13] Discourse on the responsibility of power which is deprived of normative content and blind to the role of domestic institutions and ideas can no longer be either justified or left unchallenged.

The responsibility of power, arguably one of the most fundamental concepts in international relations, remains one of the most underexplored in international relations theory. We are not here, however, to launch a study of the ethics of power and responsibility in international relations. Important as it is, it belongs to an entirely different enquiry.[14] Our purpose here is simply to highlight how notoriously difficult ethical considerations of power and responsibility can be and why they are likely to remain contentious and controversial. Ethical judgment of how and whether a power fulfils its responsibility is ultimately subjective. Difficulties in investigating Chinese behaviour in this kind of analytical construct are further amplified by the differences in Chinese philosophical tradition and political culture that sustain China's historical assumptions about power and responsibility.[15] Whereas a system of legal and institutional checks on the exercise of political power has been developed in the Western political tradition, the Chinese political tradition has relied more on the ethical and moral character of rulers to restrain the abuse of power.

This is not in the least the only complexity to consider. Chinese revolutions in the twentieth century and China's turbulent relations with other Great Powers have also conditioned its understanding of the responsibility of power. In particular, China's unique experience of socialisation into international life in the second half of the twentieth century has helped produce a special set of social relations between China and the changing international society. As Yongjin Zhang argued recently, Revolutionary China's relationship with international society in the 1950s and the 1960s is best characterised as alienation rather than isolation.[16] It is not hard to imagine why Revolutionary China did not feel obliged to take any social responsibility to an international society of which it was not regarded part and in which its legitimacy was tenaciously denied. In this context, it also makes perfect sense to talk about how and whether China is (re)joining the world.[17]

Yet, China's position in international society remains a curious one. China has been a declared nuclear power for almost forty years and has been one of the Permanent 5 in the United Nations Security Council for more than thirty years. It is now universally regarded as a rising power. Its membership in the Great Power club is nevertheless at best contentious. In the post Cold War international society, inference more often than direct reference is made to China being a 'rogue state'. China's full membership in international society continues to be questioned, but from a different angle. Human rights and democratisation are now the litmus test, as Rosemary Foot argues in her chapter.[18] As the lingering Westphalian system becomes less tolerant of political heterogeneity,[19] the nature of the domestic political system, democratic process and institutional set-up become increasingly significant in defining not only the domestic legitimacy but also the international legitimacy of a particular regime.

It is against this background that contributors to this volume conduct their conceptual and empirical investigations. It is in this context, we believe, that power and responsibility in Chinese foreign policy should be evaluated and understood.

## Responsibility: an evolving concept and a moving goalpost

The first two chapters analyse conceptually the issue of responsibility in greater depth than the others. Rosemary Foot and Gerald Chan identify different aspects of the question of responsibility in the international system. Their perspectives are mutually complementary in that Foot looks at the question from outside-in, that is, largely from the perspective of international society, whereas Chan examines the problem from inside-out and offers a Chinese perspective. Their analyses taken together suggest an interpretation as follows. The concept of the responsibility of power has not remained static in recent decades. It is for some purposes a highly subjective concept, and therefore it may remain difficult, if not theoretically impossible, for China to ever actually meet a benchmark of responsibility.

Foot notes the principle, which in our view is fundamental, that the privilege of statehood—being recognised as a state by the international community of states—carries with it an obligation to contribute to world order. She then sketches how the concept of responsibility in meeting that obligation evolves through three phases, from a more basic concept relating to the discourse and practice of diplomacy and embrace of international law, through a more expansive phase of not just minding one's own business, but also contributing to a series of multilateral regimes that 'make up the substance of international life' in a world marked by far more interchange and more mutual responsibility. The third phase is one marked by a new 'willingness to promote the protection of individual security, or human rights, and to foster legitimate forms of representation' of popular will.

Foot notes that determination of a particular state's level of responsibility will be in itself a political act, but suggests that some objectivity (or at least consensus) is possible in respect of China by reference to the degree to which it meets the measures of responsibility in the first two phases mentioned above. Foot suggests, as do several authors in this volume, that by these standards China has been quite responsible. She also notes appropriately a lack of scholarly consensus on the motivations for this pattern of behaviour by China. Is China a 'system maintainer' or a 'system exploiter'?

It will be much harder, Foot concludes, for China under the current system of government to meet the standards of responsibility in the third phase of evolution of international society—respect for human rights and appropriate representation of popular will. Until China meets this standard, Foot believes that 'China will remain outside global society'.

Chan takes the discussion into another dimension, proceeding from the view that, in Chinese tradition, the level of responsibility that a person is obliged to take depends on their position in a hierarchy of power. He links this to the rise in China's power, and asserts—correctly in our view—that Chinese leaders and many ordinary Chinese people expect China to be accorded a level of responsibility relative to its rising power. This is clearly different, Chan notes, from being seen or judged as responsible by other members of international society. There seems to be no evidence, in his view, that Chinese leaders have any conscious thought that China should be seen to be responsible to the world when they make foreign policy decisions. Chan also makes an interesting distinction that he thinks does exist in the minds of the Chinese leaders that the type of responsibility a state possesses is linked to whether it disposes of soft power (cultural appeal) as well as hard power.

Chan concludes that it is indisputable that China is more responsible now than it was two decades ago. Second, he concludes that if we want to analyse how responsible China is, then this must be a comparative exercise: how does China's level of responsibility compare with other powers?

## Domestic changes and the Party–state: international implications

The next two chapters address the internal foundations of the power of the Party–state. In Chapter 4, Greg Austin focuses broadly on leadership perceptions of the government's power against the backdrop of a rapidly changing society, whereas You Ji addresses in Chapter 5 the gradual but inevitable divorce of the armed forces from the Party. Both chapters identify important implications of these significant domestic changes for China's international power and responsibility, though these are deliberately asserted rather than elaborately argued. These assertions are quite justified in both cases, however, since any in-depth analysis of the very complex relationships emerging in domestic political power does not leave room for much analysis of the international implications.

Austin sketches the political and social effects of the whirlwind of economic reform in what he sees as a weak state. The Chinese Communist Party (CCP), he argues, is facing mounting discontent on too many fronts and, on the basis of recent evidence, seems to be losing in Western Xinjiang. Austin sees the Chinese state as weak not only because of these mounting challenges, but also because the political system itself is fragile. The Communist Party has withered on the vine and no new substitutes for it have been found, though neo-authoritarianism has surfaced, in rhetoric at least, as a possible alternative. The strike-hard campaigns might lead some to conclude that this choice has been made, but Austin contends that the strike-hard campaigns are a reflection of the weakness of the state and the nervousness of its leaders, and not evidence of a post-Communist transition to a stable form of authoritarianism.

Austin concludes that the 'very foundations of domestic governance, and therefore of China's international position, remain fragile'. In his view, the battle for the future of Chinese politics will be fought between more radical, more liberal minded reformers and less radical, less liberal reformers in the Communist Party and by the supporters of both camps in the armed forces and security services (such as the Ministries of State Security and Public Security). He also concludes that the scale of disadvantage and disaffection in China is so great and growing so quickly that major social and political turmoil seems inevitable. It will be in the response to such outbreaks of disorder that the future of the Party–state and its policies will lie. If the more liberal reformist elements of the Party come to dominate these decisions, coercion will be avoided in favour of spreading democracy (and the blame) and by patching up regional welfare problems on an ad hoc basis. If the less liberal, though still reformist, elements in the leadership dominate decisions, then sustained resort to coercion and a deterioration of the social contract are inevitable. If the discontent is not defused more quickly and more effectively than it has been so far, the outcome will almost inevitably be more consistent resort to force and fragmentation of the society.

You Ji reviews the slowly changing 'marriage' between the People's Liberation Army (PLA) and the CCP—a direct consequence of the fundamental nature of the authoritarian state, where the armed forces must serve an internal security role. He predicts an eventual divorce or, more interestingly, 'widow' status for the PLA, since the CCP may well simply die. Under either scenario, he sees a much more 'normal' constitutional relationship between the PLA and the Chinese government. That is, however, his longer-term prediction. Whatever happens, he notes, each side in the relationship has become weaker, and the military in particular now has to vie for influence alongside a larger number of other interest groups with increased influence.

You Ji's assessment of the shorter term is based on his view, with which it is difficult argue, that for the last two decades the two sides have been getting on quite well. He complements the civilian government for its performance in striking a good balance between allowing the military to feel that it occupies an important place in the political order while at the same time advancing a broader development agenda and denying the PLA undue influence in domestic politics. At the same time, he concludes that the PLA is 'still the most awesome political institution' in the country because of its size and physical power, because of its popular support, and because of its 'constitutional status' established through the highly autonomous Central Military Commission of the CCP. The main trend though has been towards professionalisation and depoliticisation of the armed forces, and this trend has been strong.

You Ji sees the PLA and the CCP leaders as being in general agreement over the strategic threats to the country, but says there has been visible discord about relative priorities in two important policy areas—military posture (more or less defence expenditure) and Taiwan (more or less military pressure). He sees a continuation of the dominance of the line of the civilian leadership on both counts—except perhaps in the event that a crisis is forced on China, in which case the civilian leadership may be forced to side with a more aggressive military posture demanded by the PLA in order to avoid being tarred with the brush of betraying national interests.

## Towards a responsible power? Practice and evidence

Chapters 6–9 provide brief case studies and offer accounts of how China's recent international behaviour in specific issue areas reflects on the question of whether and how China can be said to have become more responsible in international relations. In Chapter 6, Ann Kent discusses what China's participation in international organisations tells us about its learning about the responsibility of power. Stuart Harris, in Chapter 7, examines China's recent diplomacy in Northeast Asia. While in Chapter 8, He Baogang, addresses Beijing's policy toward Taiwan's bid for a UN seat, Gary Klintworth takes up in Chapter 9 controversial issues surrounding China and arms control.

### China and international organisations

Ann Kent introduces her article with some general propositions that seem in close agreement with those of other authors. The most important of these is that 'participation in international organisations both confirms sovereignty and constrains it'. She notes that the power conferred on states by such participation is 'balanced by the increased responsibility such participation entails'. On the strength of these propositions, Kent gives an overview of how China's participation in international organisations 'sheds light on its practical understanding of power and responsibility'.

Some authors in the volume take the view that China is not too different in its interest-based approach to responsibility from other powers, but Kent pays more explicit attention to this proposition and gives a good succinct statement of it. What does single China out, according to Kent, is that it has had a 'steep learning curve, mediated by its own ambitions, changing perceptions and unique perspectives'. In sketching these perceptively, Kent reminds us of China's 'self-constructed identity as a Club of One'; of China's special place as the one among the five Permanent Members of the Security Council which has to be courted more than the others, of China's tendency to free-ride on some big issues (thus evading responsibility), and of the pragmatic nature of Chinese foreign policy in spite of its articulation in highly principled and absolute terms. One of the most important observations in this section of Kent's chapter is that 'China's attitude to the international rule of law and its behaviour within international organisations is heavily influenced by its attitude to the domestic rule of law and its political culture'.

Kent concludes that China has both learned responsibility from its role in international organisations as well as learned the benefits of the appearance of being responsible. She notes that 'China's power has been enhanced by its willingness to negotiate its sovereignty'. At some domestic political cost, China continues to support international society and global norms because 'just as the world needs China, China needs the world'.

## Northeast Asia

Harris' analysis of China's diplomacy in Northeast Asia begins with some theoretical observations about the international system and norms that put him in close agreement with the general conclusions of Foot and Chan—there are some fairly basic standards which allow for some assessment of responsible behaviour, but these norms (such as peaceful resolution of disputes, respect for sovereignty, and appropriate engagement with international community regimes) can change in their subjective content over time. Harris therefore looks to China's Northeast Asia diplomacy for evidence of 'cooperative relationships in conformity with generally accepted international norms'.

Harris, echoing Chan's arguments, recognises that China's approach to international relations may not always be articulated in ways that conform to the concept of responsibility as it is understood in the West. He argues, however, that it is possible to track its behaviour against this benchmark, although it is difficult, he concedes, to ascribe motivations in all cases of China's foreign policy behaviour. Harris notes that realist-style interests of China are often visible and even prominent in China's foreign policymaking but also sees alongside these explicit foundations of China's behaviour a number of implicit ones, which he elaborates in his examination of China's recent diplomatic practice in Northeast Asia.

In a country-by-country review of China's diplomacy in Northeast Asia from an interests-based perspective, which is far too comprehensive to summarise easily here, Harris produces some important observations that reflect the views of some other authors within this volume to an extent. In discussing Chinese policy toward Xinjiang as an issue in Sino-Russian relations, Harris notes, as Foot did in general terms, that China's use of draconian internal repression measures in pursuit of what is definitely a legitimate security interest 'conflicts with what would be widely seen as the appropriate norms'. He notes that China, through the declarations of the Shanghai Five, is trying to reassert its view of the unacceptability of external interference in what it would still like to see as internal affairs.

In reviewing Sino-Japanese relations, Harris notes what appears to be a deeply ingrained Chinese instinct to avoid war with Japan, an instinct arising from the experience of war. On the US relationship, he notes the survival of some ideologically-based perspectives from an earlier era that give a competitive flavour to China's diplomacy. Harris notes that China sees and accepts considerable responsibilities toward regional stability in restraining North Korean missile developments. Harris' general concluding assessment is even more telling: the threats to Northeast Asian stability and peace are not likely to arise from any abrogation by China of its responsibilities, but from other causes.

## Taiwan

A fresh look at the China–Taiwan relationship from the perspective of China's responsibility in the international system is offered by He Baogang. He confirms Chan's intuition that for China, the greater its power, the greater the sense of responsibility it is likely to take or want in respect of the international system. Interestingly, He suggests that this is also the expectation of the international community—the more powerful a state, the greater its responsibility. He appears to reject instinctively a realist interpretation of international affairs, but contends that the proposition about the link between power and responsibility is 'not a moral issue' but a 'real political matter' (by which we infer '*realpolitik*'). A state like China, he says, has so many impacts on the world, especially its neighbours, that it must bear responsibility to them.

He's chapter is more specifically about China's approach to Taiwan's bid for a seat in the United Nations. Starting from the proposition that China's past position on Taiwan was a manifestation of the traditional concept of sovereignty, He argues that China can afford to exploit the flexibility of the sovereignty norm to take an interest-based approach to the Taiwan problem. He warns that, if China does not do this, the thorny question of Taiwan's representation in the United Nations will continue to raise its head throughout this century. The suggested innovation is to work for Taiwan's admission to the United Nations in a second China seat, rather than a separate Taiwan seat. Citing the precedents, He gives an exposition of how the change in China's position could be justified within the framework of its existing rhetoric on the Taiwan issue.

He's approach provides corroboration for some of the general conclusions presented in the chapters by Foot and Chan. There is room for a third-wave approach to sovereignty as something far from absolute. He goes further, saying that China's practice on sovereignty has already gone beyond strict adherence to its rhetoric on the sacredness of sovereignty. He cites the adjustments seen in China's Taiwan policy as evidence of its 'learning' about the possibilities of a flexible approach to the concept of sovereignty.

Returning to the interest-based analysis we have seen in other chapters, He concludes that the only question now is whether China's political leaders are prepared to bear the political costs associated with this innovative approach, an approach which would truly demonstrate that China had reached a very high level of maturity in its appreciation of the responsibility now falling on its shoulders as a rising Great Power.

## China and arms control

In his analysis of China's responsibility in acceding to, and then complying (or not complying) with, arms control regimes, Gary Klintworth is the only author in this volume to confront head-on the main source of the big questions about China's current position in the international community. There is no doubt that the question derives in large part from a 'black view of China' and that the currency and prominence given to the question is influenced largely by trends in US–China relations. Klintworth correctly observes that it is only the United States with its intelligence assets that is able to tick or cross the box on China's arms control compliance record. He does not offer a detailed analysis of the 'black view', preferring instead to cite one very good example of it. He contrasts this 'black view' with the US government's view during the second Clinton Presidency, which gave China a pretty good report card on compliance.

Klintworth's chapter, like others, is appropriately couched in terms of the theoretical debate about learning and motivations, though these aspects are not discussed at length. He canvasses two broad options for explaining China's unambiguous move to significant participation in a variety of arms control measures. The first is the basic instrumentalist one, that 'China's interest in arms control stems solely from concerns about *realpolitik*, defined in terms of a concern about China's global image and a desire to rein in the power' of the United States or Russia. The second flows from what Klintworth implies is a genuinely felt conviction in China, one of support for the 'same common security values as the United States'. He says that China wants to reduce global tensions where possible, especially in its relations with the United

States, in order to concentrate on economic development. At the same time, he is prepared to admit that in the longer term, this motivation may transform itself in a way which makes its current arms control commitments seem but an 'interim ploy pending China's attainment of superpower status'.

The Klintworth chapter provides one of the best catalogues of China's arms control record that is available in brief form. His article appropriately concludes with some observations about differences between the United States and China on national missile defence that go to the heart of a sophisticated understanding of the dual nature of responsibility—on the one hand, the Great Power's obligation to comply and behave, and on the other, an obligation for it to oppose (through peaceful dialogue) what it believes is unacceptable international behaviour.

## Contextualising China's understanding of power and responsibility

In a tantalising theoretical and historical essay on China's identity construction and the question of responsibility in international society, Yongjin Zhang in Chapter 10 addresses in a different fashion some of the issues flagged by Kent when she talked of China's steep learning curve mediated by its 'ambitions, changing perceptions and unique perspectives'. Zhang discusses China's 'self-constructed identity', but poses this in the context of mutually constructed identities. He asks: 'if identity construction is mutual, that is, it is constructed by distinguishing self against the Other, then how does perceiving China as the Other constitute part of China's identity formation?' Interestingly, he asks, 'why is there such a persistent dichotomy of China vis-à-vis the world (the West writ large)?'

The central analytical concern of Zhang's essay is to problematise China's security. Zhang begins with an important set of issues rarely addressed in commentary on China's security posture: 'How and why do the Chinese élites perceive what as the main problems for China's security?' Taking an inside-out perspective, Zhang looks at what he sees as the three most penetrating and transformational social experiences of China since 1949, namely, revolution, war and reform. He offers a series of interpretations, based on a sociological approach, as to how these three domestic social processes have significantly affected China's security conceptions and behaviour. He argues that it is these domestic social processes, interacting with the same social processes in international society, that have contributed significantly to China's identity construction of self vis-à-vis the Other. Such interactions have also made China a persistently insecure power and helped produce China's insecurity complex. For these reasons, Zhang suggests, revolution, war and reform as social processes in both China and international society and their interactions constitute an important social context within which proper understanding and judgment of China's attitudes towards power and responsibility can be evaluated.

The chapter by Zhang is in the tradition of historical sociology, tracing the direct impact of the broad social upheavals on perceptions of security. But it appears to have two other intertwined approaches. The first, an explicitly stated proposition, is that revolution, war and reform are not seen as purely domestic Chinese experiences, and for this reason the real sociological significance of these events can only be understood if the link between them and international society is fully appreciated. The second, more subtextual in nature, is that the issues of revolution, war and reform were so central in the formation of the Chinese élite and so traumatic that each of these as a process has had a deep impact on the cognitive processes of Chinese élites, an impact that extends beyond the conscious or unconscious memories of specific events.

We do not pretend that the essays in this book have provided answers to all the questions that were posed at the beginning of this introduction. This is not, after all, the purpose of this book. Our contributors perhaps differ as much as they agree on the question of subjectivity and perspectives in their evaluation of power and responsibility in Chinese foreign policy. We do hope that this collection suggests more lines of thought than it elaborates and opens up new areas of enquiry that go beyond the simple caricature of China as an erratic state and an irresponsible power.

## Notes

1 *International Security* has carried in the last few years a number of essays that engage in such debates. These include in particular, Avery Goldstein, 'Great expectations: interpreting China's arrival', *International Security*, 22, no.3 (Winter 1997–98), 36–73; David Shambaugh, 'Containment or engagement of China? Calculating Beijing's response', *International Security*, 21, no.2 (Fall 1996), 180–209; Gerald Segal 'East Asia and the 'Constrainment' of China', *International Security*, 20, no.4 (Spring 1996), 107–35; and Thomas J. Christensen, 'China, the US–Japan Alliance and the security dilemma in East Asia', *International Security*, 23, no.4 (Spring 1999), 49–80. The above essays are now published, with a few others, in a convenient collection by Michael Brown et al. (eds), *The Rise of China* (Cambridge, Massachusetts: MIT Press, 2000).

2 On the social balance of power, see John M. Hobson and Leonard Seabrooke, 'Reimagining Weber: constructing international society and the social balance of power', *European Journal of International Relations*, 7, no.2 (2001), 239–74.

3 For a brief summary of the national debate within the United States on this issue, see Michel Oksenberg and Elizabeth Economy, 'Introduction: China joins the world', in Elizabeth Economy and Michel Oksenberg (eds), *China Joins the World: progress and prospects* (New York: Council on Foreign Relations Press, 1999), in particular, pp. 7–15. Oksenberg and Economy have identified two groups which they call 'accommodationist' and 'confrontationist'. See also James Shinn (ed.), *Weaving the Net: conditional engagement of China* (New York: Council on Foreign Relations Press, 1996); and Ezra F. Vogel (ed.), *Living with China: U.S.–China relations in the twenty-first century* (New York: Norton, 1997).

4 See Richard Bernstein and Ross H. Munro, *The Coming Conflict with China* (New York: A.A. Knopf, 1997); and David Shambaugh, 'Sino-American strategic relations: from partners to competitors', *Survival*, 42, no.1 (Spring 2000), 97–115.

5 Such a containment strategy, in Sean Lynn-Jones' words, 'usually implied treating China as a potential military adversary, attempting to limit its economic growth, restricting its accesss to militarily significant technologies, punishing China for violating human rights, and strengthening US alliances and military capabilities that are at least potentially directed against China'. See Sean M. Lynn-Jones, 'Preface' in Michael E. Brown et al (eds.), *The Rise of China*, xii.

6 See in particular Paul Dibb, *Towards a New Balance of Power in East Asia: what are the risks as the Asian balance of power undergoes a fundamental change?* (Oxford: Oxford University Press, 1995); and Thomas J. Christensen, 'Chinese Realpolitik', *Foreign Affairs*, 75, no.5 (September 1996), 37–52.

7 For a caricature of different perceptions of China, see David Lampton, 'China', *Foreign Policy*, no.110 (Spring 1998), 13–27.

8 For the most recent debate, see Alberto R. Coll, 'Introduction: American power and responsibility in a new century', *Ethics and International Affairs*, 14, (2000), 3–10; and Tony Smith, 'Morality and the use of force in a unipolar world: the 'Wilsonian moment'?', *Ethics and International Affairs*, 14, (2000), 11–22.

9 See Hedley Bull, *The Anarchical Society: a study of order in world politics* (London: Macmillan, 1977), 200–29.

10 Ibid, 207.

11 For state responsibility in international law, see, among others, Ian Brownlie, *System of the Law of Nations: state responsibility* (Oxford: Clarendon Press, 1983).

12 Ian Harris, 'Order and Justice in 'The Anarchical Society', *International Affairs*, 69, no.4 (October 1993), 725–41.

13 In dismissing Revolutionary France and Hitler's Germany as Great Powers, Bull only stated that '[s]tates which, like Napoleonic France or Nazi Germany, are military powers of the first rank, but are not regarded by their own leaders or others as having these rights and responsibilities, are not properly speaking great powers'. Bull, *The Anarchical Society*, 202.

14 See for example, Daniel Warner, *An Ethic of Responsibility in International Relations* (Boulder, Colorado: Lynne Rienner, 1991); and Stanley Hoffmann, 'Political ethics of international relations', *Seventh Morgenthau Memorial Lecture on Ethics and Foreign Policy* (New York: Carnegie Council on Ethics and Foreign Affairs, 1988).

15 For a succinct and vigorous discussion of historical assumptions of power and responsibility in the Western political thought, see Leonard Krieger, 'Power and Responsibility: historical assumptions', in Leonard Krieger and Fritz Stern (eds), *The Responsibility of Power: historical essays* (London: Macmillan, 1967), 3–33.

16 See Yongjin Zhang, *China in International Society since 1949: alienation and beyond* (Basingstoke: Macmillan, 1998).

17 Oksenberg and Economy, *China Joins the World*, is the most recent example.

[18] This follows a similar line of arguments by Andrew Nathan and Strobe Talbott, among others. Andrew Nathan, for example, argues that China should 'behave in a way [in terms of human rights] that does not offend the conscience of that [international] community' in return for the benefits of full membership. Andrew Nathan, 'Influencing human rights in China', in James R. Lilley and W. L. Willkie (eds.), *Beyond MFN: trade with China and American interests*, 80. Strobe Talbott, Deputy Secretary of State of the first Clinton Administration was more explicit, stating, 'We believe China cannot be a full partner in the world community until it respects international obligations and agreements on human rights, free and fair trading practices, and strict controls on the export of destabilising weapons and military technology'. Strobe Talbott, 'US Deputy Secretary of State Strobe Talbott's speech to the Japan National Press Club on 25 January 1995' (Washington, DC: US Department of State, 1995). For theoretical arguments on human rights as legitimising norms, see Jack Donnelly, 'Human rights: the new standard of civilisation?', *International Affairs*, 74, no.1 (January 1998), 1–23.

[19] See K.J. Holsti, 'Dealing with dictators: Westphalian and American strategies', *International Relations of the Asia-Pacific*, 1 (2001), 51–65.

# 2
# Chinese power and the idea of a responsible state

**Rosemary Foot**

The interrelated themes of 'power and responsibility' are useful tools for understanding Chinese foreign policy during a troubled yet remarkable span of half a century of Communist Party rule. Evaluations of the behaviour of the People's Republic of China (PRC) over these five decades have often related directly to concerns about the use the PRC has made of its material and ideological resources. Has Beijing worked to support the dominant norms of the international order, or has it striven to overturn them? Has it ever deserved to be termed a 'responsible power', as the dominant states in the system have sought to define that term, or has it acted irresponsibly? To place this more explicitly within an international relations framework, has China shown itself since 1949, and more especially during the period of reform and opening since 1979, as capable of being socialised into supporting global norms, or have there been signs that its rising power over the past two decades—as realists would predict—has generated new tensions in the international system? Looking more to the future, what kind of challenge does its enhanced capabilities pose to the status quo?[1]

This chapter links the concept of power to the idea of a responsible state, or more exactly and in reference to an important body of writing in international relations, it links power and responsibility with those states that are judged to belong to international society. It tries to respond, therefore, to the question of whether China has had a responsible government over the past 50 years by connecting this assessment of its behaviour with the concept of international society. Writing in 1977, and building on the earlier work of Martin Wight and others, Hedley Bull argued that international society exists when a group of powerful states recognise that they share certain common interests from which limited rules of coexistence can be derived, and exhibit a willingness to share in the working of institutions that maintain those arrangements. Importantly, international society in this formulation acknowledges diversity in values but also a set of reciprocal interests.[2]

When the People's Republic of China was established in 1949, it undoubtedly posed a major challenge to those common interests and the rules that had been developed to underpin them, a challenge that lessened over time as China experimented with new forms of participation in the global system in the wake of its decision in the early 1970s to emerge from isolation and its later decision to embark on far-reaching reforms. At the time that China was beginning to move in this direction, however, those membership criteria were themselves undergoing change, embracing requirements beyond those that Bull had regarded as essential to include solidarist rather than pluralist conceptions of international society. Under these solidarist conceptions, common values and some notion of the common good, rather than the independent if common interests of sovereign and diverse states, were given priority.[3] Thus, Beijing found that it was lagging behind the dominant definitions of the responsible state soon after it had decided to become more fully integrated into international society. Moreover, the changes in definition posed particular dilemmas for a government keen to be recognised as a Great Power, yet vulnerable to certain of the criteria that more recently had become associated with the modern state in international society, especially those that shone the spotlight more directly on the domestic organisation of states.[4]

## The responsible state and international society

Great Powers in Hedley Bull's estimation derived that identity from characteristics that included but went beyond capacity, particularly military capacity. Such states also had to involve themselves in the provision of international order; indeed, they had special rights and duties when it came to maintaining order. This custodial role required agreement on a set of core and reciprocal interests, and then on the sets of institutions—such as war, diplomacy, international law, and the balance of power—that needed to be utilised in order to fulfil these requirements. Great Powers formed the core of international society not only because they shared an important set of interests and could generate a set of rules, but because they were capable of passing these rules on to others within the system. As Chinese leaders of the late nineteenth and early twentieth century discovered, the standard for their country to satisfy at a minimum involved the protection of the lives and property of foreign nationals, the conduct of diplomatic relations through the institutions of ambassadors and a foreign ministry, and an embrace of international law.[5] In this particular understanding of international society, sovereign status—that is, internal supremacy and external independence from outside interference—was seen as an essential starting point.

In more recent times, the UN Charter and the institution of the Security Council has been taken to reflect at least one important element of this Great Power management role. Article 2 of the Charter acknowledges the sovereign equality of states, and the norm of non-interference in domestic affairs. In addition, it emphasises the need for the pacific settlement of disputes and the non-use of force except for purposes of self-defence. In the first three post-war decades, states that generally supported these rules and that recognised the benefits that these norms of behaviour bestowed were designated responsible and capable of being embraced within the society of states. Those that rejected them were shunned, deemed irresponsible, and perceived as subversive of international order. Although other articles in the Charter limited the absolute rights of sovereignty and made reference to the need to promote human rights and fundamental freedoms for all, for most of the Cold War period, the Charter was interpreted in such a way as to keep the main focus on inter-state relations and to underpin the norm of non-intervention.

## Revolutionary China in the 1950s and 1960s

One such state that appeared to have rejected this status quo definition of international society was the People's Republic of China, established in October 1949. Its discourse, and much of its behaviour, suggested that it was not prepared to play entirely by the rules. The vigour with which it launched its challenge and its decision to make common cause with the Soviet Union gave meaning to the belief that not only had two power blocs come into being, but so had two ideological systems. In the early years of the PRC's existence, the new revolutionary state refused to take on automatically the diplomatic obligations that it had inherited from the Nationalist government, preferring as Mao described it, to 'open a new stove' and to 'sweep the house clean before entertaining new guests'. The arrest in Shenyang of the US Consul-General, Angus Ward, on 24 October 1949, on the spurious charge that Ward had 'seriously injured' a Chinese messenger at the Consulate, raised fears in the United States that diplomatic immunity would not be respected by the new Chinese government. China's primary goal in 1949, as the Foreign Minister Zhou Enlai put it, was to obtain swift recognition and establish 'brotherly friendship' with the Soviet Union and its socialist allies, while at the same time being 'hostile to the imperialists and to oppose them'.[6] Moreover, the Chinese leadership took more seriously than we once believed Stalin's invitation to Beijing to take responsibility for supporting revolutions in Asia, as its aid to Kim Il Sung's and Ho Chi Minh's plans for reunification and independent statehood demonstrated.[7] Beijing's decisions to assist with these struggles in Korea and Vietnam, assistance which has been described as crucial to the defeat of the French in Vietnam in 1954 and to

North Vietnam's ability to resist American might in the period 1965–68, stemmed in some considerable part from its ideas of socialist solidarity and commitment to world revolution. Its later material and verbal support for armed struggles in the Third World, together with its—albeit selective—support for Communist Parties in states ruled by the bourgeoisie also contributed to an image of a Chinese world order that saw virtue in contention and upheaval, not in order and stability.[8] Unsettled border claims and the continuation of the civil war struggle with the Nationalists on Taiwan regularly resulted in violence, representing—alongside its activities in support of the revolutionary struggles in Southeast Asia—direct challenges to the norms of non-interference and non-use of force.

What made these challenges particularly potent in the 1950s were that this apparent rejection of the dominant norms of international society coincided with a significant increase in China's power resources. During its first five year plan, finally begun in late 1952, growth rates were impressively high. US estimates put the annual increase in gross national product (GNP) at between seven and eight per cent in this period, with the expectation that, by the end of the decade, China would have 'tripled its electric power output, more than doubled its coal production, and increased the value of its machine industry some two and one-half times'.[9] This had been achieved on the basis of a political-economic model that represented a firm rejection of that offered by the liberal-capitalist states. These economic advances, coupled with China's holding the US armed forces—the most sophisticated military power in the global system—to a stalemate on the Korean battlefield, added to a picture in the 1950s of China as the 'wave of the future',[10] able in the near term to develop an alternative and potentially attractive vision of international society that would appeal particularly to the newly-decolonised states and would be based on its own distinctive membership criteria. As Zhou Enlai put it at the first conference of Afro-Asian countries held in Bandung in 1955, the various delegations should put aside differences and band together on the 'common ground' of overturning the 'sufferings and calamities of colonialism'.[11]

Further Chinese challenges to the established diplomatic order were to come in the 1960s, although these were clearly less positive in terms of the political and economic outcomes for Beijing than had been the case in the 1950s. During Zhou's visit to Somalia in February 1964, he proclaimed—much to the chagrin of a number of the vulnerable, newly-decolonised states—'revolutionary prospects are excellent throughout the African continent'. 1965 saw the publication of Lin Biao's *Long Live the Victory of People's War*. It divided the world into the countryside (Asia, Africa and Latin America) and the cities (Europe and North America) and argued that a united front among the poor and oppressed in the Third World would overwhelm the oppressors in the metropole. The behaviour of its diplomats in overseas postings during the Cultural Revolution resulted in over a dozen countries severing diplomatic relations with China. Cambodia's Prince Sihanouk, for example, in September 1967, charged Beijing with interference in his country's internal affairs in violation of the five principles of peaceful coexistence.[12] Beijing also decided to bring home all but one of its diplomatic personnel from abroad during this period in order that they could undergo intensive re-education in Maoist revolutionary precepts. The domestic chaos was permitted such free rein that the central authorities lost control of the Chinese foreign ministry for a time; and in Beijing the British mission was set on fire.

More broadly, China's contribution to global discourse on some of the core issues of the day connected with peace and security appeared particularly uncompromising. It depicted the arms control negotiations between the two superpowers as a sham and an attempt to impose hegemonic control, the Bretton Woods Institutions as leading predators in a capitalist economic order, and the United Nations in 1965 as a 'dirty international political stock exchange in the grip of a few big powers'. It charged that the Special Committee for Peacekeeping Operations was part of a plot to convert the United Nations into a 'US-controlled headquarters of international gendarmes to suppress and stamp out the revolutionary struggles of the world's people'.[13] China's determination to force a breach in relations with the Soviet Union in the early 1960s made more prominent still its role as outsider even within its nominal identity group, especially at a time when Moscow and Washington had embarked on negotiations that illustrated their Great Power management role and common purpose in the avoidance of nuclear war.[14] Beijing's promotion of a vision of a world in flux, one where hegemons had to be weakened and old political orders overthrown, rendered it a determined opponent of international society, not a potential new entrant into the club of responsible states.

## China as candidate Great Power and responsible state

Undoubtedly, China was always more complex as an international actor than the depiction presented so far. An identity as a radical socialist revolutionary state was clearly important to its leaders, but there was always another identity—that of a Great Power—that Beijing sought to acquire, together with the mutual acknowledgment if not respect of other powerful states in the system. The PRC, for example, wanted the seat on the UN Security Council that was held by the Guomindang (GMD); it delighted in its participation in Great Power deliberations at Geneva in 1954;[15] and it moved to develop and promote such norms of international conduct as the five principles of peaceful coexistence with its own stress on the value of state sovereignty, mutual interest, and non-interference. Like the other major states, it also began to embark on an overseas aid program even though its populace was poorer than many of its aid recipients.

Although China promoted the perception that it gave unqualified support to revolutionary movements wherever they might arise, in fact its level of support in the 1960s depended on the degree to which they, or the state of which they were a part, were willing to adopt policies acceptable to Beijing. It was 'not the objective class character of the society in question or the proclaimed ideology of the party in power'[16] that determined the attitudes of Chinese leaders. Moreover, for some of the weaker states in the global system, particularly those that had emerged from anti-colonial struggles, Chinese actions did not go beyond the bounds of appropriate behaviour. They were favourably disposed towards states such as China that had rendered them some assistance, even if that assistance had often only been verbal. Ambiguities in international law on the subject of the non-use of force in respect of national liberation movements[17] also undermined some of the claims that China was failing to uphold the principles of the UN Charter.

Yet, in the 1950s and 1960s, Chinese behaviour overall was overwhelmingly interpreted as reflecting a desire to articulate new conceptions of international society based on China's own historical and political-economic experiences, not as attempts to enter the existing club of Great Powers. Its more traditional diplomatic actions at the state-to-state level were insufficient to sway the dominant image of China as, quite probably, the most radical of the revolutionary states in the global system.

That depiction of China was to change, however, with China eventually seen more as a 'system maintainer', even 'system exploiter' than a 'system challenger' from the 1970s and early 1980s onwards.[18] During this period Beijing started to establish diplomatic relationships on a global basis, entered the United Nations (1971), and the Bretton Woods Institutions (1980) and, crucial to all these developments, improved and then normalised its relationship with the United States, even at the expense of its erstwhile socialist allies in Asia—North Korea and Vietnam. In the 1970s, despite greater international engagement, it still did not take on the responsibilities that came with its position as one of the Permanent 5 on the UN Security Council. It remained passive in the United Nations, failing to participate in many of the organisation's statutory subsidiary bodies, rarely sponsoring a draft resolution, or using its veto.[19] It continued to reject deep engagement in the global economy. Its decisions about trade reflected the principles of import substitution. It incurred neither foreign nor domestic debt, nor made use of foreign direct investment. Only gradually, especially after Mao's death and the introduction of Deng Xiaoping's reform agenda, during which

'Chinese themselves repudiated the 'Chinese model'',[20] did the Beijing leadership begin to act as though it wanted to fulfil the entry requirements of contemporary international society.

Those entry requirements still related to the idea of Great Power management of the system, but in the 1980s a responsible state had also come to be perceived as one that was in good standing in the international regimes that made up the substance of international life.[21] International regimes and organisations had rapidly advanced in number and issue area by this decade—to contribute to the central international society goal of international peace and security, expectations were that a state be involved with, among other matters, arms control arrangements, UN peacekeeping operations, the protection of the environment, and be supportive of the world trading order, all areas where China began to participate more fully.

This normative agenda, albeit demanding enough in its own terms, was to be further developed through the late 1980s and early 1990s. Connected strongly with the ending of the Cold War, but also representing a longer process of normative change, there was a third turn in meaning associated with the responsible state in international society. This involved new and broader understandings of the concept of security to embrace intra-state relations, and the idea of human security and human rights. The responsible state thus came to include one that was concerned less with the division between the domestic and international realms, but one that demonstrated a willingness to promote individual security within states and to foster legitimate forms of representation through adherence to democratic forms of government. An earlier conception of international society had rested on an understanding of sovereignty that emphasised non-intervention and non-interference and the freedom to act independently. Over the course of the post-war and especially post-Cold War eras, however, these normative foundations were to be weakened by the advent of global actors other than states, the embedding and development of different norms, and the creation of additional regimes designed to manage a more interdependent global system. Rather than building an international order of states that accepted differences in values but attempted to define a set of common interests, now there was a concern with world order, a desire to promote convergence towards certain core values, and a focus on the sovereignty of individuals rather than of states. The breakdown of the ideological Cold War divide provided new structural conditions that made it possible to promote ideas that affected directly the domestic organisation of states, and space to contemplate the methods necessary to bring about convergence towards a set of common values on which a solidarist global society could rest.

Much of the writing on state sovereignty in the 1990s, then, points to this third evolution in our understanding of what it means to be a sovereign state, ideas that are often subsumed under the term legitimate sovereignty. Legitimate sovereignty refers not just to an ability to control territory and peoples and to achieve recognition of that fact, or to be in good standing in international regimes, but now implies acceptance of certain rules that result in particular domestic structures. As Jack Donnelly has observed in reference to human rights, there has come into being a new standard of civilisation—states will only be entitled to full membership of international society to the extent that they meet the new criterion of observing international human rights standards. As he explains it, 'human rights represent a progressive late twentieth century expression of the important idea that international legitimacy and full membership in international society must rest in part on standards of just, humane or civilised behaviour'. He goes on, noting that 'despite the continuing split between national and international law embodied in dominant conceptions of sovereignty, the society of states has come to accept that our common humanity makes the way in which any state treats its citizens a legitimate concern of other states, foreign nationals and international society'.[22]

This, however, is not just the view of scholars working in this issue area. Many governments and their officials during this period demonstrated that they were already attuned to these requirements, some of whom resented these expectations as impositions by the strong, and others of whom either agreed with these broader goals or perceived them as an opportunity to indicate that their state had embarked on a new path. In the late 1980s, for example, the Soviet Foreign Minister, Eduard Shevardnadze, said to an audience of Soviet diplomats: 'The image of a state is its attitude towards its own citizens, respect for their rights and freedoms, and recognition of the sovereignty of the individual'. With the advent of political change within the former Soviet bloc, Hungary decided to signal aspects of its new identity when in 1988 it became the first East European state to ratify the Optional Protocol of the International Covenant of Civil and Political Rights—the right of petition for individuals who claim to be victims of a violation by a State Party.[23] Many states made similar moves, for example, Brazil and Indonesia, both of which set up National Human Rights Commissions as part of this desire to signal a change in domestic political behaviour.

Some of the major international institutions also came to be associated with the promotion of democratic politics and the humane treatment of one's citizens, often under the heading 'good governance'. While the World Bank has been constrained by its Articles of Agreement from advocating pluralist democracy, its definition of governance comprises such matters as improving accountability, transparency, the promotion of civil society and the rule of law.[24] Progress towards these goals and policies on military spending are taken into consideration when the World Bank makes lending decisions. The European Bank for Reconstruction and Development incorporated into its founding charter the requirement that aid recipients be 'committed to applying the principles of multi-party democracy, pluralism and market economies'. The Organization of American States (OAS) adopted a resolution in June 1991 that, in its preamble, required the 'political representation of [member] states to be based on effective exercise of representative democracy'. The resolution called for the organisation's Secretary-General to hold an immediate meeting of the OAS Permanent Council 'in the event of any occurrences giving rise to the sudden or irregular interruption of the democratic political institutional process or of the legitimate exercise of power by the democratically elected government in any of the Organization's member states'.[25] Although the supremacy of the norm of democratic entitlement may be honoured more in the breach than in the actual fulfilment, nevertheless by the mid 1990s some 130 governments had announced a legal commitment to holding open, multiparty elections based on a secret ballot and universal franchise. Moreover, many political actors had sought international validation of these electoral processes—that is, had decided to invite 'interference' in their own domestic affairs. International observers have been used not only to show to the world the country's commitment to democracy, but also to confirm the fairness of the result to domestic audiences, thereby undermining the basis for any internal challenge to the authority of the newly elected.[26]

Alongside the development of state-based international organisations, there has been a vast increase in the numbers and influence of non-governmental organisations (NGOs) in recent years. These too have created new norms and have played roles in shaping the determination of whether a government deserves the title responsible or not. NGOs, as new sites of authority,[27] can influence international perceptions of a particular state through the information they provide and their transnational networking capabilities. Their capacities can be considerable—between 1950 and 1993, the number of groups working primarily on human rights was estimated to have increased fivefold, doubling between 1983 and 1993.[28] One of the most prominent, Amnesty International, has built up a staff size and budget that compares favourably with the level of resources that the United Nations devotes to human rights issues as a whole.[29] NGOs have provided a vital input into such UN bodies as the UN Commission on Human Rights, the Human Rights Committee, the Committee against Torture, as well as working with individual governments and the world's media. These UN bodies are highly dependent on the information provided by the human rights NGOs, especially when attempts are made to move beyond the setting of standards into the monitoring of compliance. The pressure to conform to some notion of a common good now comes, therefore, from many different points of the system, rendering it difficult for any state to avoid some of the negative consequences of transgressing the dominant norms of the current global order.

## China's fulfilment of the new criteria

Neither political actors nor scholars are in agreement as to whether China seeks to fulfil over time all, some, or only a limited number of the current requirements for membership in the club of the responsible. Such an assessment is complicated because we have no clear signposts as to how much participation is enough to acquire the designation 'responsible', and because we have moved from what one scholar has labelled an international *gemeinschaft* community—a tighter more coherent community—to a *gesellschaft*—a looser more informal society.[30] A looser international society implies a larger range of views over what constitutes the dominant norms and a weakening of the basis of agreement over what best promotes international, or perhaps it would be more accurately described as global, order.

The developmentalist and cultural relativist rhetoric in the human rights area, for example, challenges the idea of the indivisibility and universality of human rights. Developmentalist arguments suggest that both domestic and international order is best maintained by states that are economically strong and advanced, and that the protection of civil and political rights has to give way when necessary to that larger goal of economic development. Moreover, this particular argument over human rights is difficult to interpret. It leaves observers unsure as to whether states such as China would otherwise seek to reach international standards as quickly as possible but for the constraint of their relatively low levels of economic development.

The assessment of compliance with the criteria for responsible statehood is made more problematic still because some major international regimes allow considerable room for manoeuvre, including the expectation of a period of delay when it comes to domestic implementation, a willingness often to accept procedural compliance without real fulfilment of regime norms, and a lack of action when states weaken treaties by filing reservations at the time of ratification.

The interpretation of behaviour in this looser international society is made even more difficult by the realisation that consensus, on which states exhibit responsible behaviour is, and has always been, a highly political act. The views of the most powerful states have always dominated, especially those of the United States since 1945. The hegemonic position of the United States, which derives from its all-round strength as a state and its influential role in many of the multilateral international organisations, has led it to take on what it and certain others perceive as a custodial role in the global system. Yet that same perceived role—what W. Michael Reisman describes as the 'actor of last resort in matters of fundamental importance to contemporary international politics'—has brought the United States to act unilaterally, and at times unlawfully, to preserve the ultimate goals of international society as it perceives them.[31] China and other states have justifiably cried hypocrisy and pointed to double standards when these instances of unlawful behaviour occur, but despite these criticisms, states have continued to invoke America's custodial role in moments of crisis. Nor have these criticisms made the United States refrain from labelling states 'rogue' or 'responsible', or as being in international society or outside of it.

On the eve of Premier Zhu Rongji's April 1999 visit to Washington, President Clinton on the whole described China's global and regional roles in positive terms, in marked opposition to the kinds of sentiments expressed in the US Congress and parts of the US media. China, he said, had helped convince North Korea to freeze the production of plutonium and refrain from further missile tests; it had helped avert nuclear confrontation in South Asia in 1998; in the 1990s it had joined the Non-Proliferation Treaty, the Chemical Weapons Convention, the Biological Weapons Convention and the Comprehensive Test Ban Treaty (CTBT), and accepted the safeguards, reporting requirements and inspection systems that went with them. It no longer provided assistance to Iran's nuclear program, had stopped selling Iran anti-ship cruise missiles, and had halted assistance to Pakistan's nuclear facilities. In the environmental arena, China and the United States were working together on developing cleaner technologies and cutting pollution. He hoped for and expected further progress on China's bid for membership in the World Trade Organization (WTO), with China finally agreeing to open its internal markets.[32] It was a remarkably positive picture that projected China as being in good standing in many of the core regimes of the global system, a country that over the course of the 1980s and 1990s had stepped inside the tent in many key areas of concern.

Academic analyses of security questions, economic integration, and the environment have also reached some reasonably positive conclusions about Chinese behaviour. In disarmament and arms control negotiations, Michael Swaine and Iain Johnston argue that the Chinese perspective has shifted over the last 10–15 years from viewing arms control as largely irrelevant to its concerns to a position that recognises that there are benefits to be had from participation. Whereas it had signed up to only 10–20 per cent of the arms control arrangements for which it was eligible in 1970, by 1996 this had reached 85–90 per cent. Much of this more positive behaviour, according to Swaine and Johnston, relates to China's wish to be viewed as responsible—in reference to Beijing's signature of the CTBT, they note that Chinese officials felt a pressure to join the process and move towards signature in tandem with other members of the UN Security Council and once clear support for the treaty emerged among the developing countries. China signed the CTBT even though this represented a considerable 'sacrifice' for China and a constraint on its power.[33] With respect to China's increased participation in UN peacekeeping operations, observers have noted that developing countries have pushed Beijing to become more actively involved in an activity that they saw as beneficial to domestic stability and regional peace,[34] similarly suggesting a Chinese concern with its international image.

Concerning the international trade regime, Margaret Pearson notes that China has made substantive concessions to gain entry to the WTO, has restructured its laws and regulations to attract foreign technology, investment and trade and has joined the global intellectual property rights regime. Further progress along these lines will be troublesome, but overall, Pearson concludes, it is 'difficult not to be impressed with the speed, magnitude, and depth of China's integration into the global economy during the post-Mao era'.[35] Many have commented on the social and economic costs that Chinese workers will initially bear as a result of membership of the WTO—especially those in much of the state-owned sector—but China has expressed its desire to take its place in this organisation both in order to reap economic advantages over the longer term, and out of a concern to establish its rightful place in the world's most important trading body. China's environmental policies have exhibited a similar blend of incremental progress, Lester Ross has argued. Beijing has become extensively involved in environmental treaties, provided these are not perceived to constrain its search for higher levels of economic development. Some of the domestic consequences of this involvement include the development of new institutions to help with the implementation of treaty requirements,[36] suggesting a sustained commitment to these decisions. It could be expected that China's new environmental bureaucracies would resist any attempts by Beijing to reverse course.

Obviously the nature of the international regime in question, especially its level of intrusiveness, the extent to which it might erode strategic independence, threaten political control or actually serve to enhance China's power have influenced Beijing's compliance and involvement, for reasons that have become familiar in studies of Chinese foreign policy behaviour. Clearly, China benefits materially from membership in multilateral organisations such as the World Bank, where it has long been the largest recipient of the Bank's development aid. Thus, instrumental interest may explain its cooperative and compliant behaviour in this instance, alongside the conditions for membership that each of the economic organisations imposes.

In other issue areas such instrumental reasoning is more difficult to advance. What becomes more salient is a Chinese concern for its international image and a desire to be regarded as a cooperative and responsible great power. Beijing constantly refers to its good record in adhering to the core regimes of international society, often contrasting its supposedly favourable record with that of the 'unilateralist', 'hegemonic' United States. In the area of arms control, China has acceded to treaties that have imposed some constraints on its military power since 1980, even though non-participation was unlikely to have incurred severe material costs.[37]

Although Beijing is extremely wary of Security Council authorisations under chapter VII provisions of the Charter (these relate to enforcement measures in reference to breaches of the peace) between 1990 and 1999 Beijing supported these 84 per cent of the time, abstaining on the rest.[38] Even in the problematic area of human rights, China has signed the two international covenants, and accepted some domestic scrutiny of its practices by the UN High Commissioner for Human Rights, a UN Working Group and one of the United Nation's special rapporteurs. This participation in the international human rights regime came partly in an attempt to undercut support for a draft resolution at the UN Commission on Human Rights that would condemn its human rights record. States have long since given up their attempts to impose economic and political sanctions (military sales remain the exception) against China as a result of its lapses in the human rights area, and the human rights regime itself does not contain material enforcement mechanisms. Nevertheless, even in the absence of such directly coercive means, China has been steadily drawn into procedural if not substantive support of a regime that in some senses represents a threat to Communist Party rule.[39] With the exception of some in the US Congress, certain members of the current Bush administration, and more widely the proponents of the 'China threat' school, many would accept on the basis of this record that in a number of areas China has become more responsible since the 1980s, especially in comparison with its behaviour in the first two decades of the PRC's existence.

Why China should be concerned about international image and an identity as a responsible state is not easy to explain, and the concern may arise for different reasons in diverse policy areas. Some leaders may also be more concerned about image—the foreign ministry, for example—than others. The explanation for its normative compliance in areas where instrumental reasons seem relatively weak appears to relate to a desire, particularly in multilateral venues, not to be singled out for disapprobation. Verbal sanctioning—potential or actual—argumentation and persuasion have had the effect of enhancing China's adherence to certain norms that are shared by many others—Beijing has seen the need to link itself to what is seen internationally as appropriate standards of behaviour, to "mirror' the practices of significant others over time'.[40] As Johnston and Evans report with respect to the arms control arena, 'in interview after interview of arms control specialists, [and in documents for internal circulation] a common response was that China had to join such and such a treaty or process because it was part of a world historical trend, because it was part of China's role as a responsible major power, because it would help improve China's image, and, more concretely, help China to break out of the post-June 4 attempts by some Western states to isolate China diplomatically'.[41]

## The new standard of civilisation: human rights and democratic governance

A number of governments and scholars are still reluctant to depict China as a responsible state because it is not yet clear how China will utilise the material power accumulated during economic reform over the longer term. To some extent, this relates to Beijing's stated willingness to use force, if necessary, to solve the Taiwan reunification issue and the suspicion that it might be willing to do the same in reference to outstanding claims in the South China Sea. China's domestic political arrangements have added to the uncertainty. President Clinton's positive appraisal of China, outlined above, inevitably contained less positive aspects, including calls for Beijing to 'respect the human rights of its people and to give them a chance to shape the political destiny of their country'. Many of the other democratic states would agree with this call and are motivated to pursue 'bilateral dialogues' with China in part to enhance the prospects for Beijing's adherence to international human rights standards. The Chinese government has been made aware that these matters of human rights and democratic governance have become the new standards of civilisation, the new set of criteria for membership in international society. This understanding helps explain why China decided in 1997 and 1998 to sign the two key covenants of the international human rights regime—first, the International Covenant on Economic,

Social and Cultural Rights on the eve of President Jiang Zemin's 1997 summit in Washington, and then, in October 1998, the International Covenant on Civil and Political Rights as the United Nations began celebrations for the fiftieth anniversary of the Universal Declaration of Human Rights (UDHR).[42] As of June 1997, it was joining 138 state parties to the Covenant on Civil and Political Rights, and 136 to the Covenant on Economic, Social and Cultural Rights, an act that signalled Chinese understanding of the new normative requirements and an unwillingness to remain an outsider in the UDHR's celebratory year.

Nevertheless, the human rights and democratic governance criteria for membership in international society are extraordinarily difficult for Beijing to satisfy because they threaten core values of the Party–State. The Chinese leadership witnessed the way in which political activists in the former Soviet Union and in Eastern Europe used those governments' signatures to the human rights provisions of the 1975 Helsinki Accords to publicise their demands and to exercise political leverage. Although Beijing has expounded the benefits of developing a rule of law[43] and has introduced much new legislation designed to improve human rights protections, proper adherence to international standards threatens Party rule and the leadership's view of how to secure domestic political and social stability. When Party leaders see what they regard as dangerous evidence of instability, they promote the so-called 'strike-hard' campaigns, which send signals to those in charge of law enforcement to cut corners to increase the numbers of arrests and convictions. Organised political activity not sanctioned by the Communist Party invites swift retribution and only cursory reference to the new criminal codes. Calls for the development of multi-party democracy elicited a statement by Li Peng—Chair of the National People's Congress—to a German newspaper that any independent group that tried to 'go for [a] multiparty system [or] to negate the leadership of the Communist Party [would] not be allowed to exist...China promotes democracy and practices the rule of law but our road is not patterned on the Western approach that features the separation of powers, a multiparty system and privatization'.[44]

Similarly alarming from Beijing's perspective has been the international debate over humanitarian intervention in response to evidence of gross violations of human rights, as articulated in a conspicuous form by the UN Secretary-General in September 1999. Kofi Annan's speech to the 54th session of the UN General Assembly averred that the global community had learned that it could not stand idly by watching gross and systematic violations of human rights, that state sovereignty was being redefined to encompass the idea of individual sovereignty, and that in our contemporary reading of the UN Charter we were 'more than ever conscious that its aim is to protect individual human beings, not to protect those who abuse them'.[45] The Chinese government, although it was by no means alone, took a particularly strong stand against these ideas, preferring instead to highlight the benefits of a more traditional definition of state sovereignty and non-interference. Beijing argued that these were the 'basic principles governing international relations', and that their absence would lead to new forms of 'gunboat diplomacy' that would 'wreak havoc'. More revealing still were alarmist Chinese statements in response to NATO's military intervention in Kosovo following the bypassing of China's and Russia's expected veto of any resolution tabled at the UN Security Council. In an authoritative article in *Renmin Ribao*, 'US-led NATO' was described as having 'cooked up' the 'absurd theory that 'human rights transcend sovereignty''. NATO's action demonstrated that

> once the United States believes that an incident of some kind has happened in one of these [developing and socialist] countries that does not fit US-style human rights or suit US interests, the United States can interfere in that country's internal affairs, violate its sovereignty, and even resort to the use of force, under the pretext that 'human rights transcend sovereignty'.[46]

As with the original European-based concept of international society, the Chinese government interprets the advancement of norms relating to humanitarian intervention, human rights and democratic governance as an imposition of the strong on the weak, based on a presumption of the superiority of values in one civilisation over those of another. For a time, other countries that had espoused cultural relativism or a commitment to Asian values had provided some protection and support for China and a period of respite, but this particular discourse faded in the wake of the Asian economic crisis. Nevertheless, many developing countries, along with China, do continue to see the concept of non-interference and sovereign equality as the final defence against the rules of a divided, unequal world. Beijing's interpretation of sovereignty highlights its identity as former semi-colony and Third World socialist state, not its position as Great Power with UN Security Council membership, nuclear weapons, and rising economic clout in the global economy. As such, its views can form the basis for a coalition among some of the weaker states in the global system, states that endorse China's arguments that the strong are not held to the same standards of accountability. Beijing is struggling to muster these forces in support of the more traditional definitions of state sovereignty against a normative order that has already shown clear signs of moving beyond this earlier and stricter interpretation. China is caught between the need, on the one side, to build coalitions with states that reinforce an identity that it has been trying to shed and, on the other, a desire to embrace the norms articulated by the most powerful states and influential international organisations in the global system.

Chinese leaders argue in response to criticism of China's domestic arrangements that they deserve praise and not blame for the developments that have occurred since 1949—that they have achieved enough domestically over the past five decades to satisfy the rules of international society. The Party has united the country, ended decades of civil war, sustained civilian rule, pacified the country's borders and most recently brought millions out of poverty. Despite these achievements, however, all of which have come at great cost to individuals, families, and communities, Beijing cannot escape the fact that the normative agenda of international society has expanded, as have the ambitions of China's domestic political reformers. Many of these reformers and political activists perceive in international human rights standards and in ideas of legitimate sovereignty the key to real political development in their country.[47] Undoubtedly, many outside and inside the country recognise that shifts from authoritarian rule to a more democratic form of governance are hazardous and pose enormous challenges to the maintenance of domestic order and thus to the stability of China's neighbours. Nevertheless, a continuing failure to address political reform in a serious way, on balance, risks more than trying to cling to the current political arrangements. If such change were seriously to be attempted, incrementally through constitutional and institutional reform, then this would clearly warrant China's depiction as a state responsible not only in the international but also in the domestic realm. In the absence of such shifts, China will, in important ways, remain outside global society.

## Acknowledgment

An earlier version of this paper was published in *The China Journal*, 45, January 2001:1–19. The author is grateful for all the comments received on earlier versions of the paper and also thanks *The China Journal* for permission to reprint the article in slightly updated form in this edited collection.

## Notes

1 Reading that is relevant to these polar positions includes Ross Munro and Richard Bernstein, 'China I: the coming conflict with America', *Foreign Affairs*, 76, no. 2 (March 1997):18–32; Robert S. Ross, 'Beijing as a conservative power', *Foreign Affairs*, 76, no. 2 (March 1997):33–44; David Shambaugh, 'Containment or engagement of China? Calculating Beijing's response' *International Security*, 21, no. 2 (Fall 1996):180–209; James Shinn (ed.), *Weaving the Net: conditional engagement with China* (New York: Council on Foreign Relations Press, 1996); Stuart Harris and Gary Klintworth (eds), *China as a Great Power: myths, realities and challenges in the Asia-Pacific region* (New York: St. Martin's Press, 1995). For one important reaction from the East Asian region see Jose T. Almonte, 'Ensuring security the ASEAN way', who has written: 'East Asia's greatest single problem is how to incorporate China into its regional arrangements—how to 'socialise' the country by reducing the

element of threat while accentuating the positive elements in China's regional relationships'. *Survival,* 39, no. 4 (Winter 1997–98):80–92.

2 Hedley Bull, *The Anarchical Society: a study of order in world politics* (London: Macmillan, 1977).

3 For a valuable discussion of Hedley Bull's work and his explanation of pluralist (accepting an ethic of difference) and solidarist (the idea of a global common good) conceptions of international society see Kai Alderson and Andrew Hurrell (eds), *Hedley Bull on International Society* (Basingstoke: Macmillan, 2000), especially chapter 1.

4 To name but three of these criteria, the concepts of good governance, humanitarian intervention and protection of human rights pose particular challenges.

5 See Gerrit W. Gong, *The Standard of 'Civilisation' in International Society* (Oxford: Clarendon Press, 1984); G.W. Gong, 'China's entry into international society' in Hedley Bull and Adam Watson (eds), *The Expansion of International Society* (Oxford: Clarendon Press, 1984):171–84; Yongjin Zhang, *China in the International System, 1918–20: the Middle Kingdom at the periphery* (Basingstoke: Macmillan, 1991).

6 Chen Jian, *China's Road to the Korean War: the making of the Sino-American confrontation* (New York: Columbia University Press, 1994):chapter 2 and p. 59.

7 Chen Jian, *China's Road*, especially p. 10 and pp. 73–75; Cold War International History Project, 'The Cold War in Asia', *Cold War International History Project Bulletin*, Issues 6–7, Winter 1995/96 (Washington DC: Wilson Center); Qiang Zhai, *China and the Vietnam Wars 1950–1975* (Chapel Hill: University of North Carolina Press, 2000); and more generally J. David Armstrong, *Revolution and World Order: the revolutionary state in international society* (Oxford: Clarendon Press, 1993).

8 Steve Chan, 'Chinese perspectives on world order', in T.V. Paul and John A. Hall (eds), *International Order and the Future of World Politics* (Cambridge: Cambridge University Press, 1999), 203.

9 Department of State 'National Intelligence Estimate (NIE): 'Chinese Communist capabilities and probable courses of action through 1960', *Foreign Relations of the United States, 1995–57* (Washington DC: Government Printing Office, 1986), 3:230–55; 'NIE: Communist China through 1961', *Foreign Relations 1955–57*, 3:497–510.

10 As a US National Security Council staff study of 6 November 1953 put it: 'The achievement of the Chinese Communist regime in Korea has been a military defeat of no mean proportions, and instructive as to the extent of Chinese Communist military capabilities. The Chinese Communists, with Russian assistance, were able to organise, train, equip, supply, and commit massive ground forces in the Korean peninsula. These forces fought with courage, aggressiveness, and with notably few desertions'. Department of State, *Foreign Relations 1952–54*, 14:289–90. The 'wave of the future' reference is taken from a private statement by the US Secretary of State, John Foster Dulles, to the press on 18 February 1957. See Department of State, *Foreign Relations 1955–57*, 3:482.

11 Quoted in Department of State, *Foreign Relations 1955–57*, 3:251.

12 See Peter Van Ness, *Revolution and Chinese Foreign Policy: Peking's support for wars of national liberation*, (Berkeley, California: University of California Press, 1970), 201.

13 Samuel S. Kim, 'Thinking globally in post-Mao China', *Journal of Peace Research*, 27, no. 2 (1990):193; *Beijing Review*, 10, no. 5 (March 1965.

14 China's direct and open criticism of the Soviet Union began after Moscow signed the Partial Test Ban Treaty in 1963.

15 As a *Renmin Ribao* editorial put it after China's participation at the Geneva Conference on Korea and Indo-China: 'For the first time as one of the Big Powers, the People's Republic of China joined the other major powers in negotiations on vital international problems and made a contribution of its own that won the acclaim of wide sections of world opinion. The international status of the People's Republic of China as one of the big powers has gained universal recognition'. Quoted in Michael B. Yahuda, *Towards the End of Isolationism: China's foreign policy after Mao* (London: Macmillan, 1983), 100.

16 Van Ness, *Revolution and Chinese Foreign Policy*, 189.

17 This ambiguity is discussed in Adam Roberts and Benedict Kingsbury (eds), *United Nations, Divided World: the UN's roles in international relations* (Oxford: Clarendon Press, 1993), 22–29.

18 These terms were first introduced by Samuel S. Kim. For one example of their use see his 'China's international organizational behaviour', in Thomas W. Robinson and David Shambaugh (eds), *Chinese Foreign Policy: theory and practice* (Oxford: Clarendon Press, 1994), 431.

19 Discussion of this passivity is in Samuel S. Kim, *China, the United Nations and World Order* (Princeton: Princeton University Press, 1979).

20 Gordon White, *Riding the Tiger: the politics of economic reform in post-Mao China* (London: Macmillan, 1993), 3.

21 Using Stephen Krasner's formulation, regimes are usually defined as the 'sets of implicit or explicit principles, norms, rules and decision-making procedures around which actors' expectations converge in a given area of international relations'. S.D. Krasner, (ed.), *International Regimes* (Ithaca, NY: Cornell University Press, 1983). For more on this idea of good standing See Abram Chayes and Antonia Chayes, *The New Sovereignty: compliance with international regulatory agreements* (Cambridge, Massachusetts: Harvard University Press, 1995), 27; and Thomas M. Franck, *The Power of Legitimacy Among Nations* (New York: Oxford University Press, 1990), 190.

22 Jack Donnelly, 'Human Rights: a new standard of civilization?', *International Affairs*, 74, no. 1 (January 1998):18, 21.

23 Shevardnadze quoted in Opening Speech by Lord Howe to Amnesty International London Seminar on Human Rights in China, 9 September 1996, 2. Information on Hungary from Dominic McGoldrick, *The Human Rights Committee: its role in the development of the International Covenant on Civil and Politics Rights* (Oxford: Clarendon Paperbacks, 1994), 17–18.

24 World Bank, *Governance: the World Bank's experience* (Washington DC: 1994).

25 Quoted in Thomas M. Franck, *Fairness in International Law and Institutions* (Oxford: Clarendon Press, 1995), 113.

26 Franck, *Fairness*, 117–18.

27 See Ann Marie Clark, 'Non-governmental organizations and their influence on international society', *Journal of International Affairs*, 48, no. 2 (Winter 1995):507–26.

28 Margaret E. Keck and Kathryn Sikkink, *Activists Beyond Borders: advocacy networks in international politics*, (Ithaca, NY: Cornell University Press, 1998), 10–11.

29 A.M. Clark, 'Strong principles, strengthening practices: Amnesty International and three cases of change in international human rights standards', (PhD dissertation, University of Minnesota, 1995), 8.

30 Barry Buzan, 'International society and international security', in Rick Fawn and Jeremy Larkins (eds), *International Society after the Cold War* (Basingstoke: Macmillan, 1996), 262.

31 W. Michael Reisman, 'The United States and international institutions', *Survival*, 41, no. 4 (Winter 1999–2000), 63. Reisman

also points to other factors that complicate the US role in multilateral institutions and contribute to its inconsistent behaviour: its 'prophetic and reformist role', its 'infra-organisational role', and its 'domestic-pressure reactive role'.

32 President Clinton's speech on US foreign policy, given at the Mayflower Hotel, Washington, under the auspices of the US Institute of Peace, 7 April 1999 (published as NAPSNET Special Report, 8 April 1999). Of course, President Clinton was making these remarks partly in the hope of generating a positive atmosphere within the United States and between himself and Prime Minister Zhu on the eve of the visit.

33 Michael D. Swaine and Alastair Iain Johnston, 'China and arms control institutions', in Elizabeth Economy and Michel Oksenberg (eds), *China Joins the World: progress and prospects* (New York: Council on Foreign Relations Press, 1999), 100–101, 108; Johnston and Paul Evans, 'China's engagement with multilateral security institutions', in Alastair Iain Johnston and Robert S. Ross (eds) *Engaging China: the management of an emerging power* (London: Routledge, 1999), 251.

34 Kim, 'China's international organizational behaviour', 421.

35 Margaret M. Pearson, 'China's integration into the international trade and investment regime', in Economy and Oksenberg, (eds) *China Joins the World*, 191.

36 Lester Ross, 'China and environmental protection', in Economy and Oksenberg (eds), *China Joins the World.*

37 Johnston and Evans, 'China's engagement', 247–51.

38 It voted for 91.5 per cent of all the 625 resolutions passed in this period. For details see Sally Morphet, 'China as a Permanent Member of the Security Council, October 1971–December 1999', *Security Dialogue*, 31, no. 2 (2000), Table 2, 154, 160. This compares with a 42 per cent level between November 1971 and December 1981; 66.7 per cent 1982–86; and 86 per cent 1986 and July 1990. With reference to chapter VII resolutions, it is worth noting that the period 1990–99 included the Gulf War, the wars in the former Yugoslavia, Somalia, Liberia, Rwanda, East Timor, and so on (some 174 chapter VII resolutions in all).

39 For a fuller exposition of this argument see Rosemary Foot, *Rights Beyond Borders: the global community and the struggle over human rights in China* (Oxford: Oxford University Press, 2000).

40 The influence of norms in socialising states and in inducing compliance with international regimes is discussed in such works

as Chayes and Chayes, *The New Sovereignty;* Martha Finnemore, 'Constructing norms of humanitarian intervention', in Peter Katzenstein (ed.), *The Culture of National Security: norms and identity in world politics* (New York: Columbia University Press, 1996); Franck, *The Power of Legitimacy;* Audie Klotz, *Norms in International Relations: the struggle against Apartheid* (Ithaca, NY: Cornell University Press, 1995); and Harold Hongju Koh, 'Why do nations obey international law?', *Yale Law Journal,* 106, no.8 (1997). The idea of 'mirroring' others' behaviour as a result of social interaction is discussed in Alexander Wendt, 'Anarchy is what states make of it: the social construction of power politics', *International Organization,* 48, no. 2 (Spring 1992), 397.

41 Johnston and Evans, 'China and multilateral security institutions', 253.

42 China has now ratified the Covenant on Economic, Social and Cultural Rights but, as of writing (August 2001), not the Covenant on Civil and Political Rights.

43 In March 1999, the Chinese Constitution had been revised to read: 'The People's Republic of China shall be governed according to law and shall be built into a socialist country based on the rule of law.' See BBC Monitoring Reports, *Summary of World Broadcasts, (SWB),* Asia-Pacific, FE/3486 G/9-10, 18 March 1999.

44 'Li Peng on press freedom, legislation and political parties', *Beijing Review,* 4–10 January 1999, 35–42.

45 United Nations, 'General Debate', UN document A/54/PV.8, General Assembly (Washington DC: United Nations, 22 September 1999).

46 Chinese reactions can be found in *Renmin Ribao,* 14 May 1999, excerpted in *Summary of World Broadcasts,* FE/3535, G7-8, 15 May 1999; FE/3512, G/6, 19 April 1999; FE/3525, G/1, 4 May 1999; and *International Herald Tribune,* 24 September 1999.

47 As the tenth anniversary of the Tiananmen bloodshed drew near, Bao Tong, former aide to the deposed Zhao Ziyang claimed his constitutional right to free speech and the positive benefits that had come from earlier challenges to political orthodoxy: 'Who says divergent views are of no avail? Every bit of progress China has made since the 5th April Tiananmen Movement in 1976 and the third plenary session of the 11th Party Central Committee in 1978...are all attributed to the Chinese common people's efforts to rectify and overcome the mistakes made by Mao Zedong'. *Summary of World Broadcasts, B* FE/3525, G/6-7, 4 May 1999.

# 3
# Power and responsibility in China's international relations

**Gerald Chan**

Sharing the same bed while dreaming different dreams.
**Chinese saying**

This chapter focuses on two aspects of China's international relations—power and responsibility. As the concept of power in international politics is well known, the chapter will pay more attention to the concept of responsibility.

Is China a responsible state in international society? This question is becoming increasingly interesting as China grows strong and comes to play a greater role in world affairs. To answer the question, one has to consider the following subsidiary questions.

- What is meant by responsibility?
- How can the responsibility of a state be assessed?
- What is China's responsibility?
- To whom is China responsible?
- What international society are we talking about?
- Why raise the issue of China's responsibility now?

Before I attempt to answer these questions, I have been agonising for quite a while over whether I should use the phrase 'China's international relations' or 'Chinese international relations' in the title of this chapter. 'China's international relations' gives the impression that China is a single political entity—the Chinese state in this case—whereas the use of the word 'Chinese' in 'Chinese international relations' opens up a much wider scope to include not only the People's Republic of China (PRC) as a single political entity, but also Chinese thinking, Chinese style, Chinese political philosophy, and much more, apart from other political actors in China. In the following analysis, the word 'China' sometimes carries the wider connotation of including things 'Chinese'.

This chapter is basically a concept paper.[1] It aims to make a survey of the area covered by the questions presented above from a macro-perspective. It does not attempt to define rigorously what is meant by power or what is meant by responsibility because, in so doing, it would be all too easy to become mired in disputes over details concerning definitions. Fortunately, many scholars have done excellent research in defining the concept of power, if not the concept of responsibility. I will only touch on some working definitions for the purpose of facilitating an analysis of more substantive issues.

## What is meant by responsibility?

According to *The Concise Oxford Dictionary*, the word 'responsible' can mean

> 'liable to be called to account (to a person or for a thing)...morally accountable for one's actions; capable of rational conduct; and...of good credit, position, or repute; respectable; evidently trustworthy'.

Seemingly the word 'responsible' or 'responsibility' carries some legal, moral, as well as social, connotations. As legal, moral, and social standards vary, to a greater or lesser extent, from one culture to another, the concept of responsibility is therefore laden with value-judgments—responsibility refers to something ethical or desirable. In comparison, the concept of power is more concrete and real; it refers to something feasible or practical.[2]

The word 'responsibility' in Chinese is *zeren*. The first character, *ze*, carries the idea of duty, and the second character, *ren*, carries that of burden. In traditional China, duties and burdens are handed down or assigned by superiors and elders to their juniors and the young in a hierarchically structured society. Duties and burdens also come with certain social and occupational positions within a family or in the wider society. There are certain duties that one is expected to perform and burdens that one has to shoulder. In other words, there are things that one, as a member of a family or society, *ought* to do. This word *ought* carries a moral rather than a legal obligation.

Indeed morality plays a significant part in Chinese foreign-policy behaviour, depending on the time and circumstances in which events take place. As Shih Chih-yu has skillfully argued, Chinese leaders often 'present themselves as the supreme moral rectifiers of the world order'.[3] He gives the following examples to support his argument,

- China's policy towards the Soviet Union was aimed primarily at shaming the Soviets for their betrayal of socialism
- China's policy towards the United States demonstrates China's anti-imperialist integrity
- China's Japan policy blames the Japanese for a failed Asiatic brotherhood
- China's Third World policy is intended to be a model for emulation.[4]

To the traditional Chinese mind, responsibility flows from something that one owes to another. Chinese leaders today probably feel they owe little or nothing to the outside world or, for that matter, countries in the West. Rather, it is the West that owes them a 'debt', because Western imperialists exploited China and humiliated their people for over 100 years before 1949. Why then should China be responsible to the outside world, or to the West, since it does not owe them anything? On the contrary, the West should according to this thinking be held responsible to China for what it had done to the country in the past. As a first step, Western countries should refrain from interfering in China's internal affairs.

Some Western analysts have pointed out that Chinese leaders are using this kind of 'victimhood' to drum up domestic support for their policies and to shore up their bargaining position with Western powers by shaming them.[5] Some even suggest that the 'culture of shame and humiliation' is a 'nationalist myth'.[6] To the many Chinese who have suffered enormously, either physically or mentally, directly or indirectly, however, it was and is still very real. The fact that the story of Western exploitation of China and the lessons to be learnt have been passed on from one generation to another as a painful reminder does suggest that it is a factor to be taken into account when dealing with China and in assessing its responsibility.[7]

## How can the responsibility of a state be assessed?

A common way to judge the credibility of a state is by judging what it does rather than what it says. In other words, a state could be judged by its deeds, its actions. But who is in a position to pass judgment? Is the UN Security Council, or its General Assembly, or its International Court of Justice capable of doing so? Is it countries in the West or in the East? Those in the North or in the South? Some powerful states? Or some form of international regimes or norms? How valid are their judgments if they do pass them? We know that there is no complete consensus on this amongst states, sometimes not even amongst a group of like-minded states. There are few generally accepted principles of international common law, except perhaps the UN Charter. But even some of the fundamental principles of the UN Charter are under dispute. For example, member states of the United Nations are divided as to whether humanitarian intervention should take precedence over national sovereignty.[8] Some states choose to obey some laws while breaking others, whether they relate to human rights, trade, or political sovereignty. What is responsible to some may appear irresponsible to others. International responsibility is by and large a product of international civic awareness, but is very much grounded in, and defined by, local cultures and ideologies and is therefore severely contested at times.[9]

If absolute or complete consensus is difficult to achieve, then relative or near consensus may be possible. Very often, a group of like-minded states take collective action to tackle world problems on the basis of some sort of relative or near consensus.

To the Chinese mind, the linkage between power and responsibility depends on one's position in the scheme of things. It is of utmost importance to position oneself properly—only when one's position is properly established and 'named' can one behave in a 'correct' way.[10] The idea of *dingwei* or positioning therefore becomes significant in determining one's behaviour. Apart from positioning, the term *dingwei* can mean the search for a place, the seeking of a proper role, or the undertaking of a process of negotiation to firm up one's position, thereby enabling one to avoid potential conflicts in the future. Because of the Chinese sense of history and collective memory, it is not inconceivable to assume that the idea of *dingwei* can be extended from China's domestic situation to its view of the world.

The Chinese sense of responsibility is very much tied to one's position of power, as indicated by the saying *quanli yu yiwu jundeng*, which can be roughly translated as, and represented by, the following approximation

$$\text{duty} + \text{burden} \approx \text{power} + \text{benefits}$$

where *yiwu* should be understood as 'appropriate' work (duty + burden) in the traditional meaning of the term, rather than 'voluntary' work.

It is useful to make a distinction between two forms of power—power as of right, which is derived from one's proper position; and power as of might, which is an empirical substance. The wielding of power can therefore be righteous when exercised from a proper position, but can be hegemonic and imperialistic and therefore morally corrupt when exercised for the purpose of selfish gain without rightful entitlement according to some set of moral principles. The conflict between China and the West, therefore, may not be purely over material interests or relative power gains, but may also be over ideological and moral principles, more so than most people would readily admit.

China's international position will therefore affect how it is going to behave, exercise its power, and fulfil its 'responsibilities'. To Chinese thinking, China's position in the world is buttressed by its power relative to others, and hence there is a need to understand

and determine accurately its comprehensive national power and that of other countries so that China can know where it stands in relation to others and how it should relate to or behave towards them.[11]

Although the concept of comprehensive national power and its measurement lack precision,[12] its utility, to some Chinese analysts at least, lies in its ability to serve as a rough guide to assessing one's position in the world. One of the reasons why this concept has become so popular amongst Chinese analysts these days is that, since China is becoming strong, there is a need to take stock of its powers and its power base. Here of course we are dealing with something fuzzy rather than something precise, as the power of a state is difficult to measure and the situation of the world is ever changing. Hard power, such as military hardware, is relatively more static and is easier to measure, while soft power, such as culture or morality, is more fluid and hence more difficult to measure.

## What is China's responsibility?

If we follow the Chinese line of thinking about *dingwei di wenti* (the issue of positioning), then we need, first of all, to ask what China's global position is before we attempt to make an assessment of its global responsibility. China conjures different images for different people. Some of the salient features of China's position may include the fact that China

- has a huge population
- is a nuclear power
- is a permanent member of the Security Council of the United Nations
- is a member of many important international organisations
- is a contributor as well as a recipient of aid.

Any assessment of China itself, let alone its responsibilities, must start with an understanding of China in the recent past, a China that had suffered for some 100 years under Western imperialism,[13] experienced periods of internal strife, civil wars, and Japanese invasion, and then 30 years of excesses under revolutionary, communist rule. It has only begun to open up to the outside world, more 'voluntarily' than before, since the late 1970s, and has by now attained some sort of normality and stability. China, however, is facing many difficulties in its development path—apart from its huge population, it is still a relatively backward developing country in the midst of drastic and fundamental socioeconomic change.[14] It is still suffering from domestic political insecurity arising from crises of identity and legitimacy.[15] What can one expect of China in its international behaviour?

**A huge population.** The task of feeding and sheltering 1.3 billion people has not been easy for China. The government is determined to eradicate poverty and raise the living standard of its people to the extent that it argues that the right to subsistence is more important than individual freedoms. Deng Xiaoping once reminded us that, if the Chinese were starving and forced to flee their home country in search for food elsewhere, would it not cause problems for the neighbouring region and the world at large? The world therefore has an interest to see that China can bring its people out of abject poverty and that the country can remain stable. In a speech made at Cambridge University in October 1999, President Jiang Zemin said that 'to ensure [the rights to subsistence and development] for our people is in itself a major contribution to the progress of the world's human rights cause'.[16] To achieve the goals of modernisation and to raise the living standard of its people, China has been opening its doors and adopting new economic measures since the late 1970s, including the establishment of Special Economic Zones and the opening up of coastal and regional cities to foreign trade and investment.

**A nuclear power.** The successful testing of China's first atomic bomb in 1964 came as a morale boost to a people who had suffered and sacrificed so much. The depth of pride felt by Chinese, including those overseas, that China could join the rank of nuclear powers was almost boundless. China is proud not only because it is a nuclear power, but also because it is a signatory to the Comprehensive Test Ban Treaty, which it signed in September 1996.[17] In the wake of the Pakistani and Indian missile and nuclear tests in April and May 1998, there were rumours that China might reconsider its treaty obligations and resume nuclear testing. On 3

June 1998, President Jiang Zemin pledged, in his first public reaction to nuclear tests in South Asia, that 'China has no intention of restarting its nuclear tests'.[18] Either as a strategic move or as a gesture to maintain world peace, China has also pledged not to use nuclear weapons first and has asked other nuclear powers to do likewise. So far it has not stationed a single soldier or held military exercises outside its claimed territorial boundaries.

As a regional power, China has joined the Four-Party talks to find ways to end the conflict in the Korean Peninsula. It has joined and actively participated in regional security dialogues, such as the ASEAN Regional Forum and the Council for Security Cooperation in the Asia Pacific, and in regional economic groupings, such as the Asia Pacific Economic Cooperation forum and the Pacific Economic Cooperation Council. In the recent East Asian economic crisis, it resisted temptations to devalue its currency because a devaluation would have triggered another round of crisis. Consequently, China has had to endure a fall in economic competitiveness and consequent decline in exports. It has also made financial contributions to help some neighbouring countries affected by the crisis.[19]

**A permanent member of the UN Security Council.** As one of the five permanent members of the UN Security Council with veto power, China can influence world events in a significant way and can bargain with other powers from a position of some strength. It speaks out on principles of non-interference, thereby helping the world's poor to resist the world's rich because in most cases of foreign intervention in domestic affairs it is the rich that intervene in the affairs of the poor rather than the other way round. China's burgeoning involvements in UN peacekeeping activities in Cambodia in 1992 and operations in Kuwait, Palestine, Liberia and the Western Sahara have enhanced its image as 'a good international citizen'.[20] Its most recent response, in which it chose not to exercise its veto after Jakarta agreed to the UN intervention in the East Timor crisis, is seen as 'responsible'.[21]

**A member of key international organisations.** Even by Asian standards, China is a latecomer to the world of international organisations, when compared with countries like Japan and India.

China only started joining inter-governmental organisations (IGOs) when it gained its seat in the United Nations in 1971 and international non-government organisations after it adopted its open-door policy in the late 1970s. China is now a member of some 282 IGOs and 2,311 INGOs,[22] including the United Nations, the World Bank and the International Monetary Fund, and other major organisations such as the International Red Cross and the International Olympic Committee. The reasons for joining these organisations are many, and include China's concerted effort to establish and consolidate its international legitimacy in competition with Taiwan, the transfer of technology, investment attractions, and so on. China's involvement in international organisations is very much a process of mutual legitimisation and mutual learning. It offers China an opportunity to learn about international norms, practices, and expectations.[23] China's participation in and contributions to international organisations, though increasing steadily, are still limited and hindered by a number of factors. These include

- tradition and ideology—the global structure of international organisations is very much a product ofWestern experience and most Chinese find participation in a social setting on an equal, individual footing, as exemplified by China's participation in international organisations, more alien than other cultures
- power dominance—the goals and agenda of international organisations are dictated by Western interests
- China's own lack of civic awareness and international understanding
- the paucity of its financial resources for participation in international organisations
- the use of English as the medium of communication in most international organisations.

Despite these limitations, China has intensified its participation in international organisations since the 1970s, and joined the World Trade Organization in 2001, having reached an agreement with the United States in November 1999 on the terms of entry, which included the freeing up of China's telecommunication and banking industries.[24]

**The giving and receiving of aid.** China gave the largest amount of aid when it was relatively poor. This was largely directed to African countries such as Tanzania and Zambia in the 1950s and 1960s, for reasons that have been seen as ideological and strategic in nature. Now that China is getting relatively richer, it still sporadically gives aid—usually on very generous terms—to countries in Africa and elsewhere in order to compete with Taiwan for diplomatic recognition. More interestingly, it is not shy of asking for and receiving international aid when it suffers from natural disasters or giving aid, increasingly through the International Red Cross, to others to alleviate their sufferings when approached.[25] Apparently, the philosophy of aid-giving in China has changed from purely strategic considerations to a combination of strategic and humanitarian objectives. The fact that it is willing to accept humanitarian aid from a wide variety of outside agencies and countries demonstrates that China has become more 'normal'—receiving aid from the outside is not regarded as a national shame.

Apart from the above points, China has more generally cooperated with other countries in certain areas of global concern, such as human rights, environmental protection, and arms control. It has signed or ratified some 220 multilateral conventions,[26] and is currently involved in the codification and development of international law, serving as members of Chinese nationality in the International Law Commission of the United Nations, the International Court of Justice, and the International Tribunal for the Former Yugoslavia War Criminals.[27] China has been seen as doing its part in maintaining the smooth transition to Chinese sovereignty of Hong Kong in 1997 and Macao in 1999. It has also curbed excessive outbreaks of anti-US feelings as a result of the US bombing of its embassy in Belgrade in May 1999 and the US spy plane incident at Hainan Island in April 2001. In an effort to make its government policies more transparent to its own people as well as to outsiders, the Information Office of the State Council of the PRC started to publish White Papers in 1990.[28] So far, 26 White Papers have been published on policy issues ranging from human rights, defence, to those relating to Taiwan and Tibet.[29] China's human rights record leaves a lot to be desired, but the country has signed the two international covenants on human rights—the International Covenant on Economic, Social and Cultural Rights and the International Covenant on Civil and Political Rights—and has engaged in human rights dialogues with other countries and groups.[30]

This is not to suggest any direct causal relationship between China's sense of responsibility and its foreign-policy behaviour, but rather to indicate that China might be seen as behaving more responsibly these days.

## Responsible to whom?

Aside China's responsibility to its own people (an interesting subject of investigation in itself given the fact that China is slowly evolving into a slightly less authoritarian system), to whom is it responsible outside its borders? If we accept the Chinese thinking that it owes little to the outside world, then this will be a moot point. Also, little room may be left for growth of a spirit of voluntarism and adventure, and a greater sense of responsibility towards the outside world given centuries of inward-looking development. A number of Chinese scholars have, however, just begun to debate China's responsibility to the outside world, especially to the Asia Pacific region.[31]

## What international society? Is China in or out?[32]

The international society as we understand it today is, like it or not, dominated by the West, particularly the United States. The existing set of international laws, rules, and norms are very much the product of Western experiences. Tying China to international society therefore basically means making China agree to the rules of the games played by Western powers. To what extent should China be involved in such a system? Should it instead make an effort to change or redefine the system? These are some of the issues that China has been struggling with since it came into substantive contact with the outside world. The process of interdependence and multilateralism is not new; rather the actors involved in the international system are changing, as is the power distribution amongst them, their relationships, and the issues involved in such relationships.

Underlying the idea and practice of bringing China to international society[33] is the assumption that China is not in—it is out; it is the Other. This is basically a Western perspective. From China's point of view, it has long been part of international society, but has not been a hegemonic power in the global sense of reaching out and setting rules for others to follow; rather it has been an underdog of the system. China has been struggling through this system, trying to change the rules but without much success, mainly because it was weak. Now that it has become stronger and more confident, it wants to integrate more with the outside world, demanding international respect and the place that it thinks it deserves and establishing a presence that the West cannot ignore.

US policy towards China has been one of 'congagement'[34]—a combination of containment and engagement. During the Cold War, containment predominated, but in the post-Cold War era engagement has come to the fore. The United States is sometimes unsure whether it should engage or contain China because it is not certain whether China is in or out of international society. If China is in, then one set of rules will apply. If it is not, then another set of rules applies.[35]

Engaging China means socialising China into the existing system so that it can become one of Us—a responsible member, abiding by its rules and norms. As pointed out by Wang Hongying,[36] however, socialising China has its limits. First, while China can learn to be more cooperative through participation in multilateral activities, it can also come to realise and reassure itself of the effectiveness of the use of force in world affairs. In other words, China can become more liberal as well as more realist (in the *realpolitik* sense). China suffered tremendously under the West's so-called 'gunboat' diplomacy in the past and has recently witnessed the use of force by the United States in the Gulf War and in Yugoslavia. Chinese leaders were shocked when they saw on television the pin-point accuracy and firing power of high-tech weapons and the scale of destruction caused. They realised how far behind their weapons system was and decided that their military modernisation had to be accelerated.

Second, the process of multilateralism only affects a very small number of Chinese officials who are dealing with foreign affairs and trade. Their preference for multilateralism faces strong domestic opposition from the military as well as from the state industrial sector.[37] The effects of these officials' individual learning are yet to be established empirically, not to mention the generally assumed spill-over effects from the individual level to the state level.[38]

Third, the traditional world view based on Sinocentrism and on a hierarchically structured world order presents obstacles to embracing multilateralism. The Chinese realist school of thought tends to favour bilateral dealings over multilateral cooperation.[39] China's policy towards resolving disputes over the Spratly Islands in the South China Sea is a case in point.

Socialising is a slow and tortuous process, especially for an old and established civilisation like China. For most Western observers and decisionmakers, who expect quick results, socialising China can be a frustrating exercise because China sometimes appears to be responsible, sometimes not.

## Why raise the issue of responsibility now?

The reason for raising the issue of responsibility seems obvious—China is becoming strong, or has the potential to become very strong. In parallel with its growing strength, China is increasingly involved in world affairs. When China was weak and isolated, responsibility did not seem to figure much as an issue, especially when viewed from a Western perspective. At that time it was, for the West, a matter of trying to contain China, confront it, stop it from spreading its form of communism and revolution, and use it as a lever to balance the power of other countries such as the former Soviet Union. The assumption here is that a rising China should assume greater responsibilities in world affairs.

However, responsibility to international society is not the language used by decisionmakers in China.[40] Nevertheless, the meaning of responsibility has changed over time—in the revolutionary days, it meant responsibility to support and promote international struggles. Mao Zedong was of the opinion that it was responsible behaviour to help the proletariat of the world revolt and overthrow the decadent, imperialist regimes and the 'old world order'.[41] Now the term means Great Power responsibilities. As pointed out by Jia Qingguo, a professor of international politics at Peking University, China opposed military intervention in Yugoslavia, partly to fulfil its responsibility of upholding international law.[42] More generally, China pledges never to become a hegemon (meaning a bully) even if it becomes rich. This, to Chinese leaders, is responsible behaviour towards achieving world peace.

The term responsibility is not used by Chinese academics in their writings. A comprehensive and up-to-date Chinese encyclopaedia of international politics makes no reference whatsoever to the term 'responsibility'.[43] On the contrary and as should be expected, the ideas of power and power politics are covered extensively; so are related topics such as national interest and national sovereignty.[44] By and large, Chinese international relations literature dwells mainly on policy analysis at the state-to-state level.[45] When China exercised its veto against the deployment of UN peacekeeping troops in certain countries that had diplomatic relations with Taiwan such as Haiti and Guatemala,[46] it was obviously trying to balance its national interests with its international obligations as a permanent member of the UN Security Council. When China negotiated its terms of entry to the World Trade Organization, it was again trying to balance its national interests with its international obligations to adhere to the rules and regulations of the international (read Western) trading regime. The contradiction between realist and idealist aspirations,[47] though not clearly spelt out in the current academic literature, does seem to enter into the calculus of decisionmakers in China nowadays.

## Conclusion

Let me sound a note of warning here. Since there is no concrete evidence to show that Chinese leaders take their global responsibility into account when they make foreign-policy decisions, there is a danger that we may be setting up a straw man only to destroy it—an academic exercise in futility.

Having said that, we may still ask: is China then a responsible state? The answer to this question is elusive. Unless we have a commonly accepted set of standards to help us to make an assessment, we can hardly say for sure that one country is more responsible than another. Also, unless we make an international comparison across countries, we can hardly say conclusively that country A is more responsible than country B.

If we compare China's situation now with its situation say some twenty years ago, then, by using the correlation between position and behaviour as a yardstick, we may reasonably conclude that China has become more responsible. If Chinese leaders, by dint of their positions of power in the country, do feel some strong sense of responsibility, then it is most likely to be a sense of responsibility towards their own families and eventually their nation and civilisation, rather than towards the outside world. After all, the 'outer' world was, at least in the pre-modern days, unimportant to most Chinese, élites and commoners alike.[48] Things have changed, of course, especially as a result of globalisation of various kinds, but tradition and culture still persist.[49]

## Notes

1 For a more quantitative analysis on a similar topic, see Gerald Chan, 'Is China a 'responsible' state? Assessing its multilateral engagements', Paper presented at the International Studies Association convention held in Hong Kong, 26–28 July 2001.

2 E-mail communication with Professor K.K. Leung of the Department of Applied Social Studies, City University of Hong Kong, November 1999.

3 Shih Chih-yu, *China's just world: the morality of Chinese foreign policy* (Boulder, CO: Lynne Rienner Publishers, 1993), 243.

4 Ibid.

5 Steven Goldstein, quoted in CNN news at http://cnn.com/SPECIALS/1999/china.50/asian.superpower/neighbors.

6 Michael Yahuda, 'China's foreign relations: the Long March, future uncertain,' *The China Quarterly*, Vol. 159 (September 1999):652. Ishihara Shintaro, a former right-wing LDP member of Parliament and currently the Governor of Tokyo, once rejected outright the existence of the Nanjing Incident in 1937 as a fabrication. Ishihara is but one among many extreme right-wing nationalists in Japan.

7 Chen Jie, 'China's Spratly policy,' *Asian Survey*, Vol. 34, no. 10 (October 1994):894.

8 Frank Ching, 'UN: sovereignty or rights?' *Far Eastern Economic Review*, 21 October 1999, 40.

9 Personal communication with Dr Ray Goldstein, School of Political Science and International Relations, Victoria University of Wellington, New Zealand, 8 October 1999.

10 A traditional Confucian thought, deriving from the popular saying that *mingzheng, yanshun*, meaning roughly that 'if one's name is properly given, then one's words can become righteous'.

11 Apart from Confucian influence, this line of Chinese thinking can also be attributed to the teachings of the famous Chinese strategist Sun Tzu, author of *The Art of War*, who wrote 'know one's situation and the situation of others, fight a hundred battles and be able to win them all'.

12 See Gerald Chan, *Chinese Perspectives on International Relations: a framework for analysis* (Basingstoke: Macmillan, 1999), 30–33.

13 Michael Yahuda, 'China's search for a global role,' *Current History*, Vol. 98, no. 629 (September 1999):266.

14 Jia Qingguo, 'Economic development, political stability and international respect,' *Journal of International Affairs*, Vol. 49, no. 2 (Winter 1996):573–76.

15 Wang Fei-ling, 'Self-image and strategic intentions: national confidence and political insecurity,' in Deng Yong and Wang Fei-ling (eds), *In the Eyes of the Dragon: China views the world* (Lanham: Rowman & Littlefield Publishers, 1999), chapter 2.

16 *Evening Post*, Wellington, 23 October 1999, 8.

17 China has yet to ratify it. The Treaty needs to be ratified by the 44 nuclear-capable states. Twenty-six have ratified, 15 have signed but not ratified, including the United States, and three (India, North Korea, and Pakistan) have not even signed. See *Time*, 25 October

1999, 20. The treaty was under review by China's People's National Congress as of mid 2000. See *www.fmprc.gov.cn/eng/5196.html*, accessed on 3 August 2001.

18 *South China Morning Post*, 4 June 1998. Earlier, an anonymous senior Foreign Ministry official in Beijing was quoted as saying that China would consider resuming tests if the nuclear arms tension between India and Pakistan worsened (*Ibid.*, 2 June 1998).

19 For example, China contributed US$1 billion as part of an IMF effort to bail out Thailand during its financial crisis.

20 J. Mohan Malik in *International Herald Tribune*, 8 October 1999, electronic edition.

21 Ibid.

22 Union of International Associations, *Yearbook of International Organizations 2000/2001* (Munich: K.G. Saur, 1999), 1488. The figures do not include those for Hong Kong.

23 For an incisive analysis of China's learning process in nuclear non-proliferation issues, see Hu Weixing, 'Nuclear nonproliferation', in Deng and Wang (eds), *In the Eyes of the Dragon*, chapter 6. David M. Lampton discusses the issue of learning in in his book *The Making of Chinese Foreign and Security Policy in the Era of Reform* (Stanford: Stanford University Press, 2001).

24 *Asiaweek*, 26 November 1999, 50–53.

25 For some discussions on the origins of China's shift from its strict observance of self-reliance to its acceptance of international aid, see Gerald Chan, *China and International Organisations* (Hong Kong: Oxford University Press, 1989), 75–80.

26 www.fmprc.gov.cn/premade/8275/duobian.htm, accessed on 26 June 2000.

27 E-mail communication with Dr Zou Keyuan, Research Fellow, East Asian Institute, National University of Singapore, October 1999. For China's approach to, and compliance with, international law, see Zou Keyuan, 'Chinese approach to international law', in Hu Weixing, Gerald Chan and Zha Daojiong (eds), *China's International Relations in the 21st Century* (Lanham: University Press of America, 2000), 171–93.

28 These White Papers are the products of the Bureau of Overseas Propaganda of the Chinese Communist Party's Central Propaganda Department. The Information Office of the State Council is under the dual leadership of the State Council and the Central Propaganda Department. See Wan Ming, 'Human rights and democracy,' in Deng and Wang (eds), *In the Eyes of the Dragon*, 102 (and note 9).

29 www.china.org.cn/e-white/index, accessed on 4 July 2001. These twenty-six papers are

- Progress in China's Human Rights Cause in 2000
- China's Population and Development in the 21st Century
- China's Space Activities
- China's National Defence in 2000
- Narcotics Control in China
- The Development of Tibetan Culture
- Fifty Years of Progress in China's Human Rights
- National Minorities Policy and Its Practice in China
- China's National Defence
- The Development of China's Marine Programs
- Human Rights in China
- Criminal Reform in China
- Tibet—Its Ownership and Human Rights Situation
- The Taiwan Question and Reunification of China
- The Situation of Chinese Women
- Intellectual Property Protection in China
- Family Planning in China
- China: arms control and disarmament
- The Progress of Human Rights in China
- The Situation of Children in China
- Environmental Protection in China
- The Grain Issue in China
- On Sino-US Trade Balance
- Progress in China's Human Rights Cause in 1996
- Freedom of Religious Belief in China
- New Progress in Human Rights in the Tibet Autonomous Region

30 On 28 February 2001, the Standing Committee of the National People's Congress of the PRC ratified the International Covenant on Economic, Social and Cultural Rights, with some reservations on issues relating to labour rights. A spokesman of the Standing Committee said that it took China three years and four months to ratify the Covenant, compared with Britain's 8 years, Italy's 11 years and Belgium's 15 years. 'The United States, however, has not yet ratified the covenant, though it signed it 24 years ago'. The spokesman also said that Taiwan's signing of those Covenants in the name of China in 1966 was 'illegal'. See *Xinhua News* in www.china.org.cn, (accessed 4 July 2001). Ratification of the Covenant on Civil and Political Rights is still pending, as of mid 2001.

31 See Ye Zicheng, 'Zhongguo shixing deguo waijiao zhanlue shizai bixing [Strategy of Great Power diplomacy is imperative for China—some problems on China's diplomatic]', *Shijie jingji yu zhengzhi* [World Economics and Politics], no.1 (2000), 10; Pang Zhongying, 'Zai bianhua de shijieshang zhuiqiu Zhongguo de diwei [To establish China's status in a changing world]', *World Economics and Politics*, no. 1 (2000), 38; and Chen Quansheng and Liu Jinghua, 'Quanqiu zhong de Zhongguo yu shijie [China and the world under globalisation]', *Zhongguo waijiao* [Chinese Diplomacy], no. 3 (2000), 4.

32 For some analyses in this area, see Alastair Iain Johnston, 'Engaging myths: misconceptions about China and its global role', *Harvard Asia Pacific Review*, Vol. 2, no. 1 (Winter 1997–98), 9–12; and Samuel Kim, 'China in and out of the changing world order', *Occasional Paper 21*, World Order Studies Program, Center of International Studies, Princeton University, 1991.

33 See, for example, 'The World of China, or China of the World', *China Today*, December (2000):10–13.

34 The word 'congagement'—a combination of containment and engagement—comes from the research of a team of scholars at Rand. See Zalmay M. Khalizad et al., *The United States and a Rising China: strategic and military implications* (Santa Monica, California: Rand Corporation, 1999), 72–75. Gerald Segal, in his article 'Tying China into the international system', *Survival*, 37, no.2 (Summer 1995), suggests also that the West should contain China on one hand, but tie China into the world economic market at the same time. The rationale is that the more China is connected with the world the less likely it will use force to settle disputes (thanks to Dr Huang Xiaoming and Christina Chan of the School of Political Science and International Relations, Victoria University of Wellington, for their advice and help in tracing the sources).

35 For an interesting short essay on the myths surrounding US engagement policy towards China, see Johnston, 'Engaging myths: misconceptions about China and its global role'. For a book-length treatment on engagement policy from the perspectives of some Asia Pacific countries, see Alastair Iain Johnston and Robert Ross (eds), *Engaging China: the management of an emerging power* (London: Routledge, 1999). In the latter part of the Clinton administration, the United States regarded China as a 'strategic partner'. In his presidential election campaign, George W. Bush said that China was a 'strategic competitor'. After his visit to Beijing in July 2001,

Secretary of State Colin Powell used the term 'constructive cooperation' to describe the current state of US–China relations. Despite the change of rhetoric, the term 'congagement' seems to sum up well in a single word the US policy towards China in the past three decades or so.

36 Wang Hongying, 'Multilateralism in Chinese foreign policy', in Weixing Hu, Gerald Chan and Daojiong Zha (eds), *China's International Relations in the 21st Century: dynamics of paradigm shifts: dynamics of paradigm shifts* (Lanham: University Press of America, 2000).

37 Thomas J. Christensen arrives at a similar point. See his 'Pride, pressure, and politics: the roots of China's worldview,' in Deng and Wang (eds), *In the Eyes of the Dragon*, 246. He recalls from his research in China that 'the foreign ministry (*Waijiaobu*) is so reviled in other sections of the government that it is now often referred to as the *Maiguobu* (translated as Ministry of Compradors or, perhaps, Ministry of Traitors), 255 (note 15).

38 For an up-to-date and detailed analysis of related issues across a number of functional areas such as trade, defence, human rights, the environment, and others, see David M. Lampton (ed.), *The Making of Chinese Foreign and Security Policy in the Era of Reform* (Stanford: Stanford University Press, 2001).

39 A recently published book in China casts serious doubts about the benefits of the process of globalisation to China and sparks off heated debates amongst academics about the merits of China's active interactions with the outside world. The book, entitled *China's Road: under the shadow of globalisation*, was co-authored by Wang Xiaodong and Fang Ning and published by the Chinese Academy of Social Sciences Press. It has become a best-seller in the country. See *Far Eastern Economic Review*, 13 January 2000, 16–18.

40 Personal communication with Dr Huang Xiaoming, 13 October 1999.

41 E-mail communication with Professor Ting Wai of the Department of Government and International Studies, Hong Kong Baptist University, 26 November 1999.

42 E-mail communication with Professor Jia Qingguo, Associate Dean of the School of International Studies, Peking University, October 1999.

43 Liu Jinji, Liang Shoude, Yang Huaisheng, et al. (eds), *Guoji zhengzhi dacidian* [A dictionary of international politics] (Beijing: Chinese Academy of Social Sciences Press, 1994).

[44] See, for example, Yan Xuetong, *Zhongguo guojia liyi fenxi* [Analysis of China's national interest] (Tianjin: Tianjin People's Press, 1996).

[45] Gerald Chan, 'A comment on an international relations theory with Chinese characteristics', *Asian Review*, 8 (Autumn and Winter, 1998): 176–84 (in Chinese).

[46] See Wang Jianwei, 'Managing conflict: Chinese perspectives on multilateral diplomacy and collective security', in Deng and Wang (eds), *In the Eyes of the Dragon*, 80–81.

[47] Personal communication with Dr Huang.

[48] Richard J. Smith, *Chinese Maps: images of 'All Under Heaven'* (New York: Oxford University Press, 1996), 78.

[49] This is attested by the 'anti-globalisation' book in China. See note 39 above.

# 4
# China's power: searching for stable domestic foundations

**Greg Austin**

China is fighting to contain the dynamism of its society as numerous forces compete for the spoils of power and wealth in a rapidly evolving political, legal and social milieu. This struggle was unleashed by the Chinese government itself when it decided to move away from doctrinaire policies of a command economy and total control of ideology, a process which began very slowly and cautiously in 1978, but one which has been gathering pace and momentum ever since. So, at the same time as managing the liberalisation of the economy and society, the government of China is struggling to institutionalise a new social and political contract to set the rules by which the new competition for wealth and power will be governed.

But the circumstances are not easy. To adapt an observation made by the *Economist* magazine, if Japan is a country in trouble, China would probably like to swap its troubles for Japan's.[1] Even when China's GDP matches that of Japan, the per capita levels will be one-tenth those in Japan. That means one-tenth of the money to spend on schools, health, and housing. In circumstances of growing public demand for even a modest share of China's new prosperity, the low per capita GDP available for social goods increases pressure on the government to be frugal in allocating money to military forces. President Jiang Zemin reportedly observed to former Japanese Prime Minister Takeshita that his biggest task since taking office had been to feed and clothe the 1.2

billion Chinese.[2] Former Vice-President Rong Yiren has said that it will be at least fifty years before China becomes a middle-income country.[3] But when President Jiang Zemin sketches what he calls 'grim challenges', he also notes that China has 'unprecedented favourable conditions' to meet them.[4] This is the reality of China as perceived by its government.

This chapter reviews the domestic political foundations of China's power as it passed the 50 year anniversary and in the year or so since. The chapter is an attempt to describe leadership perceptions of the government's power against the observable reality of the dynamically evolving society that it faces. The chapter assesses China's power by the relatively simple yardstick of how governmental and national capacities, along with the government's record of achievement, have responded to the dynamic evolution.

## The political effects of the whirlwind of economic reform in a weak state

The 22 year history of the boom in China's national economic performance, beginning with strategic decisions on opening up and reform under the leadership of Deng Xiaoping in 1978, is well known. Between 1978 and 2000, the Chinese economy enjoyed dramatic annual growth rates which, according to official Chinese statistics, averaged about 10 per cent per year. In gross GDP, China was set to overtake Japan within several years and the United States in several decades. Deng's decision to reform grew in part from the problems of governance facing China as a result of the Cultural Revolution and the excesses of communist dictatorship even before that.

There is no doubt, however, that the reform policies, equivalent not only to radical structural adjustment in the national economy but also to redefinition of political power, national identity and purpose in the political sphere, brought their own share of even more serious governance problems and large-scale turmoil. In large part, the student 'rebellion' in Tiananmen Square in 1989 was just one manifestation of this massive change. In the decade since, the scale of the governance problem facing the Chinese leadership has become a common theme among scholars writing about China's economic future, even scholars with an optimistic outlook on China's future. Problems of income distribution, jobs, and sustainable development posed major challenges to policy. One assessment from the early 1990s noted that a 'scenario of leadership factionalism, provincial indiscipline, popular political antipathy, government financial squeeze and bureaucratic foot-dragging' could not be dismissed.[5] The consequences of such an eventuality, the author noted, would be a rapid decline in economic performance and a rapid rise in political confrontation. Such assessments could also be found amongst Chinese commentaries, many of which acknowledge that the Communist Party needed to reform itself, particularly to deal with the debilitating effects of corruption on social order.[6]

But through the early 1990s, the implications of the revolution in China's economy for the continued political order of the country became more severe.[7] A growing consensus developed among the leadership, all with fresh memories of the Tiananmen incident in 1989, that without more political stability the whole edifice of the state (the Chinese Communist Party (CCP)) might collapse, leading to their own loss of power, or even worse, their prosecution and possible execution for crimes. At the 1997 session of the National People's Congress (NPC), the government introduced a new defence law which highlighted the continuing priority for the People's Liberation Army (PLA) in preventing 'domestic armed rebellions or armed riots aimed at subverting state power, and overthrowing the socialist system', to quote the Defence Minister, Chi Haotian.[8] Chi said that such rebellions and riots remained a serious threat in China.[9] Thus, while impressive growth rates and increasing national self-confidence became a defining feature of the Chinese economy in the 1990s, so too did a growing sense of vulnerability and urgency begin to seize Chinese leaders about their capacity to maintain economic and social stability.

The dynamism of China's society is more than matched by the dynamism of some of China's leaders and their policy settings to address the country's problems in recent years. In March 1998, a blueprint for the most radical shake-up of China's government since 1978 was revealed. The essence of the new policies was to make China 'rich, strong, democratic and civilised'.[10] The country's leaders decreed a historic metamorphosis of the purpose of the central government in China from control of the economy to supervision of it. There were four planks to the radical shake-up—strong economic leadership to sweep away the last vestiges of socialism, including universal welfare supports, radical reform of the armed forces and defence industry, strong legal leadership to build durable foundations for a stable free market society, and the expansion of participatory democracy. These four planks corresponded in the Chinese leaders' eyes to the four goals—rich, strong, democratic and civilised. This new spirit was to be China's way of burying the ghost of the Tiananmen Square repressions and reincarnating the spirit of Chinese *glasnost* and Chinese *perestroika* that existed between 1985 and 1989, but which since then had in some important respects been suppressed by the government itself.

The future directions of Chinese domestic policy were sketched by the Chairman of the State Council, Zhu Rongji, in a press conference in March 1998 immediately after taking up his appointment.[11] They included

- transformation by the end of 1998 of both the purpose and structure of the national administration by cutting 44 ministries, commissions or other agencies to 29, of which a number had been, or were to be, corporatised[12]
- stabilising some 450 medium and large state-owned enterprises as fully corporatised entities by the year 2000
- completion of a regulatory framework for the banking sector premised on prudential supervision and depoliticisation of their operations by the year 2000
- rationalisation of the domestic grain market to ensure political stability and allow eventual removal of subsidies[13]
- transformation of the domestic investment and capital market system to bring it fully into line with internationally accepted market practices
- the total commercialisation of all residential properties to change housing from a welfare offering of the state into a market commodity

- introduction of a new national medical health scheme removing free universal medical care
- reform of the tax system.

In contrast to these medium-term goals, which must have been endorsed by other senior leaders, Zhu also announced that the most urgent policy priority would be substantial increases in domestic investment to maintain economic growth and provide insurance against flow-on effects from the economic crises in South Korea, Indonesia and Thailand.

Two years later, in March 2000, Zhu was able to report that the government had had considerable success in implementing these reforms and that the country had weathered the changes quite well. He said the country faced more opportunities than challenges. In particular, he claimed early success in turning around the state-owned enterprises in the textile industry one year ahead of schedule (he did not mention though that this sector is uncharacteristic in that it enjoys a high level of foreign investment, has therefore enjoyed high levels of technological renovation, and has high levels of export earnings to hard-currency destinations).[14] He also claimed significant progress in the old industrial bases of China, especially the Northeast, where low productivity, high unemployment and bankruptcy had become common characteristics of state-owned enterprises. Reasonable progress was made in the other areas of policy, according to Zhu, especially in social welfare reforms, such as unemployment compensation. In December 2000, Zhu reported that the state-owned enterprises had 'basically' achieved the goals set for them in the three year period.[15] But there were still serious problems, Zhu said. One of these he noted on the same occasion was that 'the incomes of peasants in some principal food producing areas had declined'. He predicted that, if these and other problems were not addressed immediately, there would be a major negative effect on stability in rural areas.

Without reference to stability in the 'rural areas' of China, it is impossible to appreciate fully the gravity of the situation facing China's leaders as they see it. The 'rural areas' of China represent 900 million of the country's 1.3 billion people. Stability of the rural areas is quite simply the stability of the country as a whole. Zhu Rongji has described a problem of public order at the grass roots level,[16] a problem he characterised on another occasion as urgent.[17] The Chairman of the Standing Committee of China's National People's Congress, Li Peng, admitted in March 2001 that 'not enough has been done to find out about the real state of law enforcement at the grass roots'.[18] In February 2001, the government issued a White Paper on 'improving agricultural work' which reasserted the primacy of the rural areas of China in the country's overall national economy and its social stability.[19] It called for lifting unnecessary burdens off the peasants' backs and a better response from officials to otherwise unexplained 'mass incidents'. Through the 1990s, there have been a number of large-scale violent incidents in China's countryside that have largely gone unreported in the West but which underpin the new-found determination of the leaders through the 1990s to lift burdens off the peasants' backs.[20]

The prospect of new social unrest in the cities is also something the Chinese leadership is actively contemplating as part of the necessary structural adjustments associated with greater internationalisation of the economy. A number of public commentaries have warned of the inevitable impact on the country's economic security (and by implication on its social order) of the structural adjustment that will be necessary as a consequence of China's accession to the WTO.[21]

There are a number of other sources of the public order crisis in China and, as much as China would like to deny the possibility, these sources do include the classic problems of cross-border ethnic loyalties. This is really only significant in western China, where members of the Uighur community and some other Turkic ethnic groups have been waging a terrorist campaign against the Chinese government in support of claims for independence from China. According to sources in Beijing, the Chinese government now feels it is losing the fight against the Muslim separatists. The reasons cited for this by Beijing sources are as follows.[22] There is now a net outflow of Han Chinese from Xinjiang. This has come about because the policy of migration of Han Chinese to Xinjiang was a policy of forced migration, when jobs were assigned by the Party and people had little choice but to go where they were sent. Now that China effectively has a free labour market and controls on residency have largely evaporated, many of the forced migrants to the west are returning to their original homes (for family reasons) or to other places in the richer provinces for economic reasons. Even a number of Han Chinese born in the west find it more attractive for economic reasons to migrate eastwards. This net outward migration is a long-term problem for the Chinese leadership and, though it can be corrected over time with special incentives, the issue bears heavily on leadership calculations of the nature of the problem.

The rebellion in western China weighs even more heavily on Chinese leadership perceptions of internal security because official sources in Beijing believe that China has lost control of infiltration across the borders with Tajikistan and Kyrgyzstan, two tiny countries of Central Asia facing immense problems of governance and armed incursions of their own. China has significantly increased its military relations with Kyrgyzstan at least and is providing support to the development of its border surveillance programs. But these programs are at a low level and the flow of weapons, money and drugs to support the operations of the rebels in Xinjiang has increased in recent years.

But even if this sort of cross-border ethnic strife is in China confined largely to the western border, the 'separatism' that it represents is demonstrated profoundly and gravely by two other cases—those of Taiwan and Tibet. And these, as is well known in the West, evoke particularly neuralgic responses from senior Chinese officials. Beijing's long-term assessment of both of these problems individually is not good.[23] This is the reason in the case of Taiwan for Beijing's new threat in the White Paper on Taiwan in 2000 that Taiwan should not indefinitely delay reunification and that doing so would be tantamount to a declaration of independence. The planned visit to Taiwan in 2001 of the Dalai Lama represents Beijing's worst nightmare in terms of the two territories and the independence goals of their leaders.

In the midst of such concerns, the rise of a politically robust movement such as Falun Gong, claiming millions of adherents throughout society, but especially in the Communist Party, the armed forces, and the security services, saw anxiety levels in the Chinese leadership over internal security reach a level in 2001 not seen since the height of the Cultural Revolution or the first years after the 1949 victory. The level of their concern can be judged by many manifestations—the ferocity of the crackdown on Falun Gong, the emphasis on internal security in the current missions of the PLA, increases in pay for the PLA, the creation of new government mechanisms to coordinate internal security policy, and repeated leadership statements about the urgency of solving the public order crisis in all fields from gun smuggling to border security.

## China: a weak state?

The issue identified in Chinese official sources as a crisis of public order should more correctly be seen as a crisis of political legitimacy. Chinese leaders appreciate this better than most outside observers. The impressive gains of the 1980s and 1990s brought some new legitimacy to the Communist Party, which had squandered most of its popular support before 1978 through repeated political campaigns or repression, and through several sharp economic reversals that remained bitter memories despite impressive economic and social gains in some years. But a continuing crisis of legitimacy arises from the government's inability to find quickly enough politically acceptable solutions to a number of serious problems, some firmly rooted in China's demographic pressures and resource foundations (and therefore largely beyond short-term solutions over which Beijing has control), and others more of a systemic or political character (equally hard to change in the short term with radical readjustments in political order).

### Demographic pressures and resource foundations

China is a resource rich country, both in natural and human terms. The large population size suggests massive potential economic advance because it presents a large pool of skilled workers and a large internal market to boost domestic demand, and therefore domestic production. China does have a huge imbalance between arable land and population—7 per cent and 25 per cent of world totals respectively. But China now has little difficulty producing enough food for most people in the country. Per capita consumption levels of meat, fruit, eggs, aquatic products and vegetables are all higher than world averages. China will face little difficulty feeding itself as long as weather conditions, market conditions and distribution systems remain at least as they were through most of the 1990s. Advances in technology, especially genetic engineering, take-up of reserved wasteland which is currently not used, and institution of a number of financial instruments to insure against losses due to natural disasters will contribute to a general improvement in China's food supply situation.

Yet China does face huge resource constraints for an economically developing country and these constraints do shape leadership perceptions of China's power position in the world. China's dependence on the outside world for critical resources, critical technologies and critical investment funds dictate not only friendly policies toward the providers of those, but also a domestic economy responsive to their continued provision. An absolute precondition of this responsiveness is an economy that is open to investment and innovation, and from the point of view of internal stability this means continual adjustment to the global market through domestic structural reform. Chinese officials are acutely aware that China has no 'birthright' to foreign investment in a global order where many other developing countries are even more attractive as investment destinations, and they are aware of the downturn in new foreign investment into China in the last two years.

While on current indications China can easily feed itself well into the next century, it is highly unlikely that China will be able to fuel itself for decades to come. Even before China became a net importer of oil in 1993, it needed to import oil to obtain certain types of product or to supply certain localities. Between 1990 and 1993, crude oil imports jumped from 2.9 million tons to 15.6 million tons. Imports of petroleum products more than doubled in 1993 compared with the previous year (from 7.68 million tons to 17.4 million tons).[24] In 1996, oil imports were 37.5 per cent higher than the 1995 level, and 700 per cent higher than the 1990 level. Import requirements in 1997 were projected to hit 25 per cent of total Chinese consumption.[25] The market impact of China's purchase of oil on the international market, and the level of its consumption of domestically produced oil, will be such as to increase the dependence of major oil consumers, including China and Japan, on Middle East oil.[26] The pace of development of Chinese offshore oil and gas resources has picked up considerably in recent years but offshore fields are unlikely to redress a situation of Chinese dependence on substantial imports of energy. The offshore fields will produce only a fraction of total Chinese energy requirements.[27]

A similar picture is presented by industries dependent on oil extraction, such as petrochemicals. China is now self-sufficient in many petrochemical products but does import significant amounts of selected products, in some years importing more than 50 per cent of consumption.[28] By 2005, according to one estimate, China will import over 40 per cent of its naphtha consumption, over 50 per cent of its gas oil, and over 30 per cent of its gasoline consumption.[29] Its dependence on imports will extend to almost all intermediate petrochemical products, with actual import quantities dependent on pricing policy and technology shifts in domestic production. According to industry specialists, this increasing dependence will not be significantly altered by the availability of projected new sources of offshore crude oil in disputed areas and China will probably be forced to abandon its preference for self-sufficiency in petrochemicals.[30]

The only solution for China in the medium term will be to import substantial amounts of oil and petrochemicals, and to develop simultaneously new nuclear and hydropower sources. In 1993, China decided to increase investment in expansion of the power industry by 25 per cent of its current share of GDP. Foreign investment in domestic power production was also to play an important part in easing power shortages, but even with these expansion plans, the prognosis was still bleak—energy shortages across the country would basically only ease.[31] Some reliance on other forms of energy production, such as solar, wind, tidal and waste cycle, can be expected but there is little sign of the massive government investment in these sectors that would be needed for them to make more than a tiny contribution to the energy mix. To continue to import oil and other industrial inputs in increasing volumes, China needs to maintain high levels of foreign exchange reserves and/or high export volumes. It is the judgment of China's economic decisionmakers that both depend on increasing the openness of China's economy.

China is also technologically dependent on the outside world. As one commentator put it in the *People's Daily* in February 2001, 'the pressure [on China] caused by the leading edge of economically, scientifically and technologically advanced countries...will exist permanently'.[32] When China began its economic reforms in 1978, the rapid development of the technology base was one of the leader's dreams. It had been hoped that, if China could quadruple its GDP by the year 2000, then advance in technology would come almost by itself as part of the economic advance.[33] The decision to allow foreign investment had been justified within the leadership of the Communist Party in large part on the grounds that such investment would bring the high technologies that would enable China to become even more self-reliant and more powerful. The flows of high technology did not happen, partly because of the sharp interruption to China's international economic links after the Tiananmen Square repressions, but mainly because China simply was not attractive as an investment site for high technologies. One of the biggest obstacles to this was the failure for many years of China to join international regimes for protecting intellectual property rights, and even after it did join, to enforce them. In addition, incentive regimes for import of technology were often frustrated by other control mechanisms.[34]

By 2001, the technological part of the open door policy had not been fulfilled and the leadership began to fear that China was falling even further behind. Chinese productivity levels remain very poor. The need to advance the country's science and technology base was put up as the long-term unifying strategy or rationale for all government policy. The belief, as expressed by President Jiang Zemin at the 15th Party Congress and echoed by his new Prime Minister in 1998, was that advanced technology, understood in its broadest sense, was the key not only to national strength in conventional military terms but also in terms of economic competitiveness, resilience and adaptability. Repair of China's flawed record on intellectual property rights, which has even resulted in executions for crimes relating to intellectual property rights, has to be a central part of this strategy.

China's perceived vulnerabilities in relation to rapid technological advance in the United States helped galvanise political opinion in the leadership in 1997 and 1998 for the massive governmental changes, including reorganisation of ministries, announced in March 1998. These moves included reorganising the State Science and Technology Commission into a Ministry, having pointedly dismissed its head some several months earlier, and reorganising the Commission for Science, Technology and Industry for National Defence (COSTIND) by increasing its powers, bringing under its wing powerful research and development capacities, and appointing a civilian head to direct it.

China remains a developing country in many respects, and its leaders think of it in this way as often as they see its more positive features, such as rapid economic growth, substantial international trade, and very high levels of gold and foreign exchange reserves. The population of China has reached 1.3 billion, of which one billion live outside the major cities. As suggested above, even with purchasing power parity estimates of Chinese gross national product (GNP) which put it just behind Japan, Chinese per capita GNP would be one-tenth that in Japan, a relativity which has enormous consequences in a range of areas from living standards to infrastructure spending. Things have been so bad in China in this respect that in 1994 the government had to establish an international poverty alleviation fund to help it support the 130 million citizens then living below China's poverty line.[35] In 1998, the number of poor people in rural areas alone was 50 million in spite of four years of relatively successful work in poverty alleviation.[36] And unemployment pressures continue to mount because of structural adjustment in the economy. In 1998, the relevant Chinese minister announced that each year for the following several years, six million new job-seekers would be looking to enter the workforce, and four million former workers would be retrenched from state-owned enterprises and government jobs. This would represent an addition to a floating labour force estimated to be in the tens of millions that is highly dependent on the construction industry and other sources of temporary manual labour. According to Chinese government statistics, about seven million new jobs were created in 1997. Without rapid expansion of the employment market, China could accumulate ten million additional unemployed people in three years. If these are concentrated in older industrial cities in the northeast which are in fairly rapid decay, the social and political consequences would be serious.

China's government has settled on a course of internationalisation of its economy in three dimensions—trade, inward investment, and outward investment. As a signatory to the Bogor Declaration on reduction of tariffs and non-tariff barriers and as a member of the WTO, China is committed to open and free trade to the same extent as other members of the world community. On some estimates, China is one of the most trade dependent economies in the world—some 30 per cent of GDP in 1996, and more than 40 per cent for the several years before that.[37] China's receptivity to foreign investment in recent years is well known, but has developed only gradually beginning in 1978 with moves in the offshore oil sector, and extending eventually to almost all sectors of economic activity, including by 1995 to some of the most sensitive strategic minerals and military industry sectors. According to a Chinese official, the country was the second biggest recipient of new foreign investment for each of the five years to 1997.[38] Joint ventures using foreign investment accounted for 37 per cent of China's total trade in 1994.[39] By the late 1990s, the third leg of China's internationalisation strategy—outward investment, such as the buying of foreign companies or funding of foreign enterprises—was still embryonic, but as in the case of Japan, one of the most important aspects of China's impact on global economic relations will be its capacity to accumulate external assets.

Since China had in relative terms both a closed economy and a closed society in the 1960s and 1970s, the rapid pace of the internationalisation process by 1998 guaranteed that China's entry into the global economy would be a very bumpy ride, bringing with it a variety of conflicts with trading partners, foreign investors and international organisations. The ability of the Chinese government to resolve these economic conflicts easily in the twenty years after 1978 was seriously impeded by the slow pace of development of its domestic legal institutions and its bureaucracy. Not only were these hobbled by the political chaos of the Cultural Revolution, even after 1978 they were hobbled by continuing serious divisions in the leadership of the Communist Party about the virtue of opening up to the outside world and about how that was incompatible with Communist ideology. Even in 1997, after the collapse of the currencies in South Korea, Indonesia and Thailand, there were strong voices in the higher levels of the Communist Party arguing that China had allowed itself to be too exposed to the global economy. The correct policy for China, according to this view, was self-reliance, and this terminology still figures prominently in the rhetoric of China's leaders. Jiang Zemin reportedly told top leaders that no other country would help China if it were faced with a similar crisis.[40]

## Political fragility

The above factors which might more or less be regarded as long-term or relatively persistent 'environmental' conditions can be contrasted with what could usefully be called politically contingent factors. China can change these comparatively quickly, though not without cost, if it wants. While communist ideology has all but disappeared in practice in China, important remnants of the totalitarian regime of governance that accompanied the ideology remain in place. But, without a coherent ideology, the political system has no social glue that gives the government legitimacy in the eyes of most of the people. The struggle to find a new ideology and to establish a new social contract with a very distrusting population is a defining feature of Chinese politics today. How that struggle resolves itself in terms of the institutions of politics will determine the future directions of Chinese foreign policy and will therefore determine ultimately China's real international power.

Political power in China remains diffused through an immensely powerful informal network surrounding several formal organs of the Communist Party and there are no publicly-visible political conventions or rules on how to replace the top leaders. Each succession is a contest of political wills that involves mobilisation of key constituencies throughout the informal networks. The leaders of the coercive instruments of the state (the armed forces and security services) remain central to all major transitions of power. In such a system, a change of leadership represents a greater risk of political instability than in a system where the leadership jockeying is confined to leading groups in a political party.

The government structure of China exists in name and practice under a state constitution promulgated in 1982 (the fourth in 33 years), but the highest level leadership of this formal structure is subordinate to control by senior leaders of the CCP. Thus a Minister, or the State Council (of Ministers), carries out the orders of small group of senior CCP members who may or may not hold the leading positions in the CCP. Thus, when Jiang Zemin steps down from the post of President of China, and possibly from the post of Secretary-General of the CCP, he will probably remain the most powerful politician in China and retain his post as Chairman of the Central Military Commission as a manifestation of this.

Under the Constitution of the CCP, its leading bodies are nominally subject to control from the Central Committee of the CCP, whose authority is exercised between meetings of its Politburo. The authority of the Politburo is exercised between its meetings by a Standing Committee. In practice, the real lines of authority have operated downwards from the Standing Committee, with the Central Committee subject to its direction, and the

Politburo itself occupying some sort of middle ground. Cross-cutting these official structures are powerful informal networks (that could loosely be termed 'factions')[41] typical of any political leadership system.

The Standing Committee of the Politburo of the Central Committee of the CCP is in some respects the most powerful formal organ across the full range of policy, but at different times it has been rivalled by the Party's Central Military Commission (CMC) in respect of security policy, by its Political and Legal Commission (PLC) in respect of internal security and law and order, and by its Secretariat in respect of ideology.[42] Decisions of the Standing Committee are subject to direction and influence from other sources. The most important are informal networks under the influence of retired or serving leaders of the CCP whose authority does not depend on a formal appointment in the government or in the CCP. The role of Deng Xiaoping in directing major decisions by China's government after his retirement from all formal positions was a good illustration of this. But other informal networks and channels of political authority exist. Deng was only the foremost of a group of veteran leaders, such as former President Yang Shangkun, former Defence Minister Zhang Aiping, and former Politburo members, Wan Li and Bo Yibo. This system is quite distinct from a parliamentary system in a liberal democracy where informal power exists but is largely subordinate to more transparent processes of administration on the floor of the national parliament and in the offices of the leaders of the executive branch of government subject to parliamentary control, supervision or appointment.

The power of the informal networks has been enhanced by several structural or contingent features of the political system. China is governed from Beijing as a self-styled dictatorship centred on the core organs of the CCP. Its constitutional and legal system emerged from a revolution which comprehensively replaced the existing political structures of the Chinese state. Though a very large country, China's administrative controls were so weak and its national wealth so dissipated that it was ravaged by a long civil war, foreign invasion and the depredations of colonial interference for the first half of this century, China presented to the CCP a very weak foundation on which to build any legal and constitutional system. Even after 1949, the foundations of domestic order did not fare well. CCP leaders have acknowledged they were their own worst enemies. Political and legal authority was consistently subject to severe strains from successive power struggles within the leadership or sharp disagreements on policy (often the one inflamed, or was used for, the other). For most of the history of China, the country has not had a stable political system which might have eventually matured into one which could deliver constitutional legitimacy to the rulers or methods they used to rule. The continuing house arrest of the former Secretary-General of the Communist Party, Zhao Ziyang, who was purged prior to the Tiananmen Square repression on 4 June, is an example of the lack of order in the political system. Another example of the latent instability of China's political system is the introduction into the National People's Congress (NPC) in March 1997 of a law which, *inter alia*, explicitly provided for control of the armed forces by the CCP rather than by the government of the state (State Council) as provided for in the state constitution of 1982.[43]

The standing threat to regularisation of the system first emerged in 1957, peaked in the so-called Cultural Revolution, and, although much reduced by 1998, has not altogether subsided in spite of considerable progress toward the rule of law through a process of national legislation, judicial renovation, and an easing of many aspects of the totalitarian system. New forces and contingencies have emerged to threaten the steady progress toward rule of law promised both by Deng's 1982 state constitution and by a blossoming of political reform between 1985 and 1989. While the massive economic progress registered by China in the last decade gives the CCP leaders new opportunities for control, the wealth has created new centres of power (wealthy entrepreneurs or provincial authorities) and new processes of power (corruption for personal wealth). Both of these factors act against regularisation of any formalised constitutional processes. Thus, the decisionmaking environment is conducive to the continued role, and perhaps even enhancement, of the informal networks, including through the traditional mechanism of enlarged meetings. The power of the person, and the informal political levers he or she is able to control, remain more of a consideration than authority deriving from formal occupancy of leadership positions. Even when these most respected veterans of the pre 1949 years have died, other second-generation veterans will still seek to interfere. For example, the former Politburo member, Qiao Shi, who retired from his leadership posts in 1997 and 1998, will continue to be an important second level force in Chinese politics through the network of patronage by appointment that he established through his decades of work at the highest levels of the country's legal system and intelligence services.

The most serious contingent element of the leadership policy environment in the 1990s was the transition associated with the death of Deng Xiaoping who, though his power was far from absolute, was the single most powerful ruler of China after 1978. This contingency has been complicated by the death of other leading revolutionaries who ruled China after 1949 and who relied on that historical role for political authority. It was these other senior leaders, such as Peng Zhen and Chen Yun, with whom Deng shared power in his position as 'first among equals'. The transition from strong, personalised leadership to leadership by consensus of a larger group without clear commanding authority, creates the danger of prolonged and more severe bureaucratic disputes' and weak policy decisions.[44]

The uncertainty generated in the early 1990s by the imminent death of Deng had all but dissipated by the time of his eventual passing in February 1997. Chinese policymaking had settled into a fairly routinised process within the upper circles of the CCP albeit through informal as well as formal mechanisms. Yet one fundamental characteristic of political leadership in China remains its lack of constitutional stability and the resulting inability to command a functional level of responsiveness in many circumstances. Reliable evidence for this exists at middle levels of government (since no studies are available of the highest level of policymaking) but it seems more than reasonable to assume that the lack of institutional regularity at lower levels, which seriously impedes policy implementation,[45] is also present at the highest level. The prognosis must be that unless there is a sustained abatement of political competition in the leadership, and some consolidation of process and norms, then political direction in China will continue to be contested and followed only fitfully.[46]

In this situation, where the top leadership must obtain the consensus of a larger number of constituencies at the centre, and where there has been a relative decline of centralised economic power in favour of provincial authorities, policy decisions which favour one group at the centre at the expense of many others will not be politically viable.[47] This factor appeared to be in play in the deliberations for leadership changes in the lead-up to the 15th Party Congress where, according to independent sources, the various contesting parties could not agree on a resolution without direct intervention of one or more of the veteran leaders. The retention of former Prime Minister, Li Peng, as second highest in Party protocol standing even after he resigned the job of Chairman of the State Council was almost certainly at the urging of Party elders. Such incidents would confirm the observation that the structure of 'court politics' in China still 'calls forth a supreme leader', a 'final arbiter', to save the court from institutional deadlock or unresolved personal rivalries.[48]

China thus remains an authoritarian state without a core ideology other than that of the corporatist state. Even though the 1997 Party Constitution allows for complete intra-Party democracy (Article 11), including the election of Party officials at all levels, the Party did not allow nomination of alternate candidates for senior Party posts at the 15th Congress at which the new Constitution was adopted. The new Constitution forbids public dissent by members from Party decisions and prohibits circulation of internal party deliberations without approval (Article 15). Until 1999, the focus of state coercion against 'dissidents' was limited largely to those advocating the end of Communist party rule, the creation of free trade unions, or the secession of any part of the country, or those making public personal attacks on particular leaders. As in many other states, China continued to protect through coercion what it regarded as 'state secrets' and 'public morals'. China's legal system remained draconian when engaged against any of its citizens, not just political dissidents.

By 2001, the brutal crackdown on the Falun Gong movement had achieved an intensity not seen since the repression in 1989 of student and democracy movements, but the Falun Gong repressions took on a far greater scale given the reported size of the movement, its penetration of party and military organisations, and its geographic spread throughout China (not to mention Hong Kong, the United States and elsewhere outside China). The re-emergence of the Political and Legal Commission within the Communist Party at the end of the 1990s in an era of sustained internal unrest and an intensifying crackdown on Falun Gong has reopened a new point of institutional contest in a leadership system that was only just beginning to settle into some order. The head of the Commission, Luo Gan, who supervises all civilian internal security operations is simultaneously a Party Secretary, Politburo and State Council member, making him one of the most powerful men in the leadership. Luo shares responsibility for the People's Armed Police with the Central Military Commission and the General Staff Headquarters.

China's leaders also sense the fragility of their political system and the weakness of their state in terms of centre–region relations. According to Hu Angang, one of China's leading experts on relations between the central government and the provinces, 'China's economic miracle has taken place at the expense of the central government'.[49] Writing in 1993, Hu and a colleague, Wang Shaoguang, reported that the central government's income and expenditure as shares of GDP in 1989 were the second lowest in the world after Yugoslavia, and that China would pay the same price in political terms if it did not remedy this defect.[50] The Chinese government responded by instituting the first national taxation system in the history of the country in 1994, but by mid 1995 Hu saw the national income as a share of GDP still dropping—to 9.1 per cent as opposed to 14.2 per cent in 1992.[51] These problems are compounded by disagreements between regions on internal trade, where some provinces or localities actually create their own barriers to movement of goods. One writer has predicted that a 'fragile equilibrium' between the central government and the regional administrations will continue 'until a general crisis unfolds or until the time is ripe for constitutional reform'.[52] An Australian government report in 1997 observed that, without radical tax reform, Chinese policies aimed at bringing to the poorer parts of China the economic advances some of the coastal provinces have enjoyed would not suceed.[53]

The problems of governance have been increased as a result of pressures for a new relationship between the central government of China and regional authorities. On the one hand, the central government has favoured a multitude of forms of government and these forms increased in the period of reform. While provinces, municipalities and autonomous regions existed under Mao, Deng added new types of regional status—special economic zones (1979), open port cities (1984) and coastal economic areas (1985). By 1988, Hainan Island was declared a new province and became a special economic zone. In 1996, the city of Chongqing was declared a municipality. The motive for re-crafting administrative relations between the centre and regions in the above cases was largely economic, but the central government has also been responsive to more sensitive political issues of regionalism. This is unambiguously the case in respect of the Special Administrative Region (SAR) established for Hong Kong under the 'one country, two systems' concept. The Chinese government holds out the hope of applying a similar system to Taiwan, with the island retaining its own armed forces. The leaders have also been sensitive to the need to combat separatist sentiment in Xinjiang and Tibet with concessions on regional autonomy (combined with more traditional iron fist methods). With the status of Taiwan as part of China increasingly under threat—since most people in Taiwan do not want to be a part of China—there is even greater pressure on the government of China to maintain its nascent federalism—'one country, many systems'—and to develop it exclusively in peaceful directions.

Genuine federalism would be a complete innovation in China's political history. The communists have in political terms rejected federalism as being synonymous with warlordism, as a 'recipe for feudalism and national disintegration'.[54] Yet, as prominent Chinese scholars have pointed out, the historical patterns of centre–region relations cannot be sustained. The only practicable solution would be to improve the tax base of the central government while giving the regions 'by means of constitutional procedures, far reaching legislative autonomy'.[55]

## Persistent weakness

As night follows day, the radical policies announced in March 1998 were certain to provoke strong opposition from organised political forces, from newly organising political forces, and from the natural conservative tendencies in society. In the fiftieth anniversary year, the reform wing of the Communist Party was clearly ascendant within the Party itself, and was sufficiently entrenched to weather challenges from conservatives within its ranks for some time in the absence of a major social, political or economic upheaval. Moreover, the reform wing has sufficient disposition to the use of coercion to repress competing political forces outside the Party, such as the free trade-union movement, that there is little sign of an alternate government. There is a broad awareness in China that politics can undo economic gain if it becomes uncontrolled. Memories of the Cultural Revolution between 1966 and 1976 and of the economic and social backwardness of China in 1978 are fresh enough to convince many people to let politics take care of itself.

By 2001, the reform wing of the party was still clearly ascendant, as discussion below of changes in ideology suggests, but there appeared to be a resurgence of sorts by more doctrinaire elements and of the coercive arms of state power, such as the PLC of the Party. It is more than likely that the issue of how to balance the quest for new popular legitimacy and the leadership consensus on a need to crack down hard was a central battleground of leadership politics.

By 2001, with the adoption of the Tenth Five Year Plan, the government was advocating even faster reform as the only means of addressing the country's balance sheet of problems. Zhu identified faster economic liberalisation as the only way of easing unemployment pressures.[56] But the main lines of the government response have not been in economic policy, but in reform of the basic approach to governing the country. The government is looking for a new social contract based on greater democratisation, with Chinese characteristics, while strengthening the coercive position of the state to limit and channel that democratisation.

## Coping with systemic fragility

This systemic fragility will not be too difficult for Chinese leaders to cope with as long as no organised opposition group mounts a frontal assault to take power from the CCP. A continuation of gradual evolution to more participatory politics in circumstances of rising living standards will help prevent a strong opposition group from emerging in the population at large, but, as discussed above in connection with internal security, there are serious doubts within the CCP leadership about its ability to satisfy public demand for perpetuation of the state welfare system. The only way China can now avoid a major political upheaval in the country is to speed up the pace of democratisation so that the blame for decisions that undermine the welfare and rights of significant sections of the population can be shared. This conclusion has been reached by the CCP leadership, who believe that use of force against demonstrators on a large scale such as in 1989, would only bring down their system more rapidly, not sustain it.

Most of China's leaders have not yet resolved the contradictions in their own vision between economic and social advance on the one hand and political reform on the other. In 1998, in the face of a newly prominent and illegal movement advocating free trade-unions, the leaders have resorted to traditional forms of repression. Without some resolution at the highest levels of the leadership of how to make the transition to a more pluralist society in which power is genuinely shared with non-Party groups on a formalised basis, then the prospect must be for greater social unrest, not less. The following sections sketch some elements of the leadership's response to its crisis of legitimacy.

## The dynamics of power without ideology: defining a new social contract

The significance of the changes to the Constitution of the Chinese Communist Party (CCP) approved at its 15th Congress in 1997[57] was unambiguous. Communism is not officially dead in China, but it might as well be. The new Party Constitution contained new theses about Communism. It saw the time-scale in which communism could be achieved as so distant that for all practical purposes it was admitting that communism was simply not achievable. The document said that it might even take 100 years to see socialism, which would be an early transition stage to communism, in China.[58] The leadership has justified its shake-up of the government structure not by reference to ideology so much as by reference to pragmatism and the spirit of the times. They said the former government administration system was simply no longer appropriate, having been developed under a command economy and under an incomplete legal system. It was also simply so big that it cost far more than it was worth to maintain.[59] Communist ideology was, in essence, buried and, according to the new Party Constitution, the three criteria by which any policy should be judged had now become its contribution to increasing the country's productive forces, increasing national strength, and satisfying the material and cultural needs of the citizenry.

By the end of the 1990s, China's system of government and ideology was more liberal than those of predecessor 'authoritarian statists', such as Benito Mussolini and the Italian fascists. Italian fascist theorists saw the state as supreme, as the director and controller of all things.[60] The state had a heroic and historic mission, and democracy of any sort was rejected. Italian fascism also rejected the concept of individual material benefit independent of the state interest. The trend in Chinese politics since 1980, however fitful and in spite of leadership discomfort, has been to the reduction of the power of the state in favour of a pluralistic vision, both in economic management and social policy. Pluralism in politics has not been as strongly supported in the leadership of the Communist Party, but it did emerge between 1985 and 1989 and, despite sustained repressive measures from the government, had by the mid 1990s resurfaced unmistakably, slowly gathering strength by 1999. The government continued to arrest dissidents but the level of Party tolerance of political dissent was much higher than in most of the 1990s. Within the constraints outlined in the previous paragraph, in almost all domains of policy, even military policy, authors could discuss almost any idea in public media without fear of state retribution. Party members were generally free to raise orally within closed party meetings any idea, as long as it was not disseminated further without Party approval.

In the years since the Party Congress in 1997, even more ambitious plans for economic and social reform had emerged, to the accompaniment of yet further redefinitions of the essence of communism—or what was more commonly called socialism with Chinese characteristics. The essence of communism and the CCP was redefined to mean protecting the cause of China's 'advanced social productive forces', preserving 'China's advanced culture and 'representing the fundamental interests of the greatest majority of the Chinese people'. This formula, attributed to Jiang Zemin, is called the 'the three represents'.[61] The enhancement of the people's living standards is the 'fundamental point of departure' for the 10$^{th}$ Five Year Plan, and the goal of increasing incomes for the peasants is included in this. These strategies have been identified in public by Chinese leaders as the way of ensuring continued power for the CCP. Another new thread of CCP ideology to emerge firmly by the turn of the century was the idea of 'ruling the country with virtue'.[62] This slogan formed part of the CCP's urgent crackdown on corruption, also identified by the leadership as essential if the Party was not to be overthrown. Zhu Rongji has echoed these lines of policy in less doctrinaire terms. He has identified the need to 'take into full consideration the general public's capacity to tolerate the changes and not shift costs formerly borne by the government onto the general public'.[63] He talked of the need to avoid 'coercion and commands' when pursuing the restructuring of agriculture. He said that there was a need to continue guarantees of financial assistance to laid-off workers in the cities.

## The state structure: reorganised for new coercion

After the sudden emergence of Falun Gong as a politically active force in 1998, a very important new exception to tolerated activities became participation in, or support for, such religious or quasi-religious groups. But two observations might be made about the crackdown on Falun Gong. First, the crackdown is a sign of the CCP's insecurity in the face of all of the threats to internal order mentioned above. Second, and as a consequence, the severity of the crackdown can be attributed to a perceived need to root out any form of opposition lest it be seen as a spur or example of success to others making a fundamental challenge to CCP authority, such as those in Taiwan, Tibet, Xinjiang, the China Democracy Party, the embryonic free trade-union movement, or illegal religious groups (Catholics and Muslims). There appears to be a broad consensus in the leadership on the need for the crackdown. Even Zhu Rongji seems at one with the coercive strategies of the state being used hand in glove with the new approach of emphasising popular support.[64] He has warned of acts of sabotage inside China by hostile forces from outside the country. He said that the problem of strengthening social stability, national unity and border defence was urgent.

The re-emergence of the PLC mentioned above, even when a new supervisory and Policy mechanism called the Commission for the Comprehensive Management of Public Order (CCMPO) had been created in the early 1990s, is a very strong sign of just how seriously the CCP leaders view the internal security threats. In February 2001, a new cross-ministry and cross-commission permanent body responsible to the Politburo was created specifically to supervise an intensification of the crackdown on Falun Gong.[65] The CCMPO and the PLC now hold joint meetings under the direction of Luo Gan. Luo has complained publicly about the low allocations of funds for the operation of subsidiary PLC's throughout the country and called for constant increases.[66] The priority tasks for the PLA were identified in March 2001 by Jiang Zemin with strong reference to the internal security mission as 'safeguarding state security, promoting the unity of the motherland and maintaining social stability'.[67] An increase of pay for PLA members (including the People's Armed Police) of 30 per cent in 2000 (supposedly to keep pace with civil servants' pay increases) may be another reflection of concern about internal security.[68]

## Democratisation, Chinese style

But the CCP leadership has learnt, as the new trends in ideological formulation indicate, that carrying a big stick is by itself a self-defeating strategy. Even in calling for a harsh crack-down, Luo Gan calls for improvements in the fair administration of justice in order to keep the people's trust. The CCP has returned to the principle of expanding the democratisation of the country, albeit conceived in terms of dictatorship of the centre. This centralist democracy has two elements—the first, village elections, has been around now for a number of years; the second, also in an embryonic form has been visible for many years, but has gained a new prominence in ideology. This is the principle of 'popular supervision', not only through more vigorous investigations by local and regional people's congresses, but through a move that looks remarkably like the first steps of *glasnost* by Gorbachev—that of 'opening government affairs to the public'.[69]

A move toward grass-roots democratisation, involving contested popular elections of township (or village) heads and direct election to township and county level people's congresses, launched in 1988, survived the anti-democratic mood in the leadership after 1989.[70] The legislation was amended in 1995, and, by 1998, some 600,000 representatives in county level congresses across the country were chosen by secret ballot with universal adult suffrage in contests with more than one candidate per post, and in which any ten or more voters are able to nominate a candidate. The main non-democratic feature of the process has been the intervention of candidate selection committees to reduce the number of candidates from all of those nominated to a select few.

Higher level people's congresses, including the NPC, are still elected by indirect methods, and the CCP's tolerance of non-communist membership of the congresses decreases the higher the level. In county congresses, many representatives are not Communist Party members, and party discipline is not an issue because local issues, on which more often than not there is no central Party line, dominate the agenda. At the NPC, nothing remotely like an opposition has been allowed to form, but there is considerable freedom of speech on most matters, except for those that go to the heart of Communist Party rule. This freedom of speech is heavily constrained though by a highly formalised and ritualistic schedule of speeches which allows little time for comment from the floor by members who do not get offered a speaking part by the Party leadership. No nomination for a state leadership post put forward by the Communist Party had been rejected by the NPC though there have been important protest votes. For example, in March 1998, ten per cent of deputies voted against the appointment of Li Peng, former Prime Minister, as chairman of the NPC Standing Committee, and the Executive Vice Chairman, Tian Jiyun, received fewer votes than any of the other Vice Chairmen. The main place where freedom of speech has significant impact is in the work of the committees of the NPC, where government ministers are often called to account and where some fairly vigorous inquiries and investigations have been conducted.[71]

## Conclusions

Communism may be dead, but free-market capitalism and liberal democracy do not yet have firm roots in China. Since becoming Prime Minister, Zhu Rongji has led the battle to make the free market secure in China. He will leave the politically risky task of making a transition to liberal democracy to people like Tian Jiyun in the National People's Congress, to the leaders of a number of low-profile central organisations, like the Institute of Political Science,[72] and to intellectuals working vigorously and with great subtlety throughout the country toward that end. The new leaders of China want liberal democracy in China, but they understand this more as an economic event that liberates market forces and allows some sharing of the burden and blame of economic decisionmaking, rather than as one of philosophical disposition or democratic consent for 'responsible government'. Thus the very foundations of domestic governance, and therefore of China's international position, remain fragile.

This judgment is reinforced when one considers the lack of arrangements for transition away from one-party rule to genuine pluralism. The Communist Party has withered on the vine, having effectively lost control of most of the lower level cells nationwide. While these still function as Party cells, they might as well be completely independent of the Party because they do nothing to propagate the Party line. They exist primarily as debating clubs, control over which brings with it the traditional perks of Party status. The leaders acknowledge this problem in private but they know that they have written the script for the collapse of ideology as a glue that binds the Party, and therefore the Party-state. Efforts to find a substitute for Communist ideology have been made, and public commentary within China on neo-authoritarianism or nationalism derive mainly from a need perceived in the Party to find a substitute. But the depth of these sentiments is hard to judge. Much of the discussion is from Communist Party members responding to what they see as signals from above. On this reading, the battle for the future of Chinese politics will be fought between more radical, more liberal minded reformers and less radical, less liberal reformers in the Communist Party and by their supporters in the armed forces and security services (such as the Ministries of State Security and Public Security).

Yet the scale of disadvantage and disaffection in China is so great and growing so rapidly that major social and political turmoil seems inevitable. One new mass movement across China—Falun Gong—has already arisen, and others are likely to emerge. It will be in the response to such outbreaks of disorder that the future of the Party-state and its policies will lie. If the more liberal reformist elements of the Party come to dominate these decisions, coercion will be avoided in favour of spreading democracy (and the blame) and by patching up regional welfare problems on an ad hoc basis. If the less liberal though still reformist elements in the leadership dominate decisions, sustained resort to coercion and a deterioration of the social contract are inevitable.

China is in the grip of a political revolution that was put on hold in 1989 and is now being pursued by more surreptitious methods, and which is being fuelled on a daily basis by rising discontent among the 'losers' and by the increasingly radical measures of the 'winners' seeking to defuse the growing discontent. The leadership of the Communist Party might well be able to keep 'riding the tiger' but the new business interests of key officials and the traditional Chinese social characteristic of 'law blindness'[73] suggest that this battle will be won or lost according to the ability of the government or the society to placate the newly discontented constituencies, not in the niceties of political ideology. If this cannot be achieved more quickly and more effectively than it has been so far, the almost inevitable outcome will be resort to force and the fragmentation of society.

## Acknowledgments

The author would like to thank Professor Stuart Harris and Dr Jonathan Unger for comments on earlier versions of this chapter.

## Notes

1 *The Economist*, 21 March 1998, 13.
2 *Kyodo*, 22 August 1994, FBIS-CHI-94-163, 23 August 1994, 3.
3 Jiji Press Newswire, 31 October 1994 (Reuters), 1 November 1994.
4 'China: Jiang Zemin Congress Report', *Xinhua*, 21 September 1997, carried in FBIS-CHI-97-266, 23 September 1997: .
5 William H. Overholt, *China: the next economic superpower*, (London: Weidenfeld and Nicolson, 1993), 67, 68.
6 Ma Zhongshi, 'China dream in the global 1990s and beyond', *Strategic Digest*, 24, no. 1 (January 1994), 71, 77, reprinted from the Beijing-based journal *Contemporary International Relations*, 3, no. 7 (July 1992). This line is common amongst the privileged members of Chinese society and Party members.
7 See Greg Austin, 'The strategic implications of China's public order crisis', *Survival*, 37, no.2 (Winter 1995), 7–23.

8 'Draft law on national defense submitted to NPC', *Xinhua,* 6 March 1997, carried in FBIS-CHI-97-064, 6 March 1997.

9 For an elaboration of this issue, see Austin, 'The strategic implications of China's public order crisis'. In terms of Chinese military posture, the new sense of vulnerability provoked by the public order crisis has important effects. More allocations are almost certainly being made to internal security and border defence, which are predominantly army and police responsibilities. Such expenditures will have penalties for investment in high technology weaponry and power projection capability (predominantly navy and air force). The relative share of defence spending going to the ground forces may well have increased in the past two to three years—but it is almost impossible to know.

10 The phrase was used in a speech by Tian Jiyun, Executive Vice Chairman of the Standing Committee of the National People's Congress, and Politburo member from 1987 to 1993, who took that position at the height of the reform era. For text, see 'China: Tian Jiyun on NPC Standing Committee work', *Beijing Xinhua*, 10 March 1998, carried in FBIS-CHI-98-074, 15 March 1998.

11 For a translated text of the press conference carried on Beijing Central television, 19 March 1998, see 'China: Zhu Rongji's news conference' FBIS-CHI-98-078, 20 March 1998.

12 Former Premier Li Peng acknowledged the historic significance of the changes on 5 March 1998: 'China will focus on reorganising or abolishing departments directly in charge of economic management and reinforcing departments handling macroeconomic controls, and those supervising law enforcement'. See 'China: Li Peng unveils ministry restructuring plan in NPC report', *Xinhua*, 5 March 1998, carried in FBIS-CHI-98-063, 4 March 1998.

13 This is a complex and circular problem. High domestic surpluses in some regions have lowered income for farmers, forcing the central government to raise subsidies. Rationalisation of the grain market will initially bring about some regional drops in farm incomes but the government expects that nationwide liberalisation of the market will simultaneously get more grain to poorer areas and eventually lead to sustained higher market prices for farmers based on this increased demand. The central government has been trying to break the control of regional grain bureaux for a number of years but has so far not been able to do so. Zhu did not say that the proposed system would bring about a shift from free universal health care to one involving a substantial element of patient fees and medical

insurance, but this has been made clear in other statements and in the trend of health services in China.

14 'Zhu Rongji's Work Report to the NPC', *Xinhua*, 16 March 2000.

15 'Zhu Rongji inspects Jiangsu, Zhejiang 7–13 December; comments on economic, other issues', *Xinhua*, 13 December 2000, FBIS-CHI-2000-1213.

16 'Zhu Rongji's Work Report'.

17 'Zhu Rongji inspects Jiangsu'.

18 'Chairman Li Peng reports on work of standing committees', *Xinhua*, 19 March 2001, FBIS-CHI-2001-0319.

19 'PRC issues opinion on improving agricultural, rural work', *Xinhua*, 12 February 2001, FBIS-CHI-2001-0212.

20 See Austin, 'The strategic implications of China's public order crisis'.

21 See, for example, 'CPPCC members discuss impact of globalization on PRC', *Xinhua*, 11 March 2001, FBIS-CHI-2001-0311.

22 Interviews with the author, October 2000.

23 Interviews with the author, October 2000.

24 Sun Hong, 'Oil-products imports to increase', *China Daily*, 28 May–3 June 1995, 1, carried in 'Petroleum imports to increase this year', FBIS-CHI-95-103, 30 May 1995, 67–68.

25 Xu Dashan, 'Robust economy fuels oil imports', *Business Weekly (China Daily)*, 12–18 January 1997, carried in 'China: strong economic growth boosts oil imports', FBIS-CHI-97-008.

26 That region's share of global production has been estimated to rise from 20 per cent in 1990 to 38 per cent in 2005. Hisahiro Kanayama, 'The future impact of energy problems in China', *Policy Paper 124E*, International Institute for Peace Studies, Tokyo, June 1994, 4.

27 Shen Qinyu and Wu Lei, 'Focus on Gulf Region in developing oil industry', *Guoji maoyi wenti*, 6 February 1995, 9–12, translated in 'Article views oil shortages, foreign sources', FBIS-CHI-95-102, 26 May 1995, 57. See also Kanayama, op. cit., 2.

28 See Table B33, in Paul W. Fields and Richard G. Stellman, *Petrochemicals in China* (Houston: Pace Consultants Inc., 1994), 15.

29 See Alan Troner and Sarah J. Milner, *Energy and the New China: target of opportunity* (New York: Petroleum Intelligence Weekly Publications, 1995), 70.

30 Ibid., 30.

31 Qin Jingwu, 'China's rapidly developing oil industry', *People's Daily* (Overseas edn), 29 December 1993, 1, translated in 'Yearender reviews energy industry growth', FBIS-CHI-094-002, 4 January 1994, 48.

32 *People's Daily*, 16 February 2001, 1, carried in '4th RMRB commentator on realizing socialist modernization', FBIS-CHI-2001-0220.

33 China undertook a number of initiatives or campaigns to boost science and technology performance, and the overall goal of tying technology to market forces was enhanced through some liberalisation and commercialisation of state sector research centres. For a brief account, see C. Harvie and T. Turpin, 'China's market reforms and its new forms of scientific and business alliances', in J. Chai and C. Tisdell (eds), *China's Economic Growth and Transition*, 488–89.

34 Pitman B. Potter, 'Law reform and China's emerging market economy', in Joint Economic Committee of the United States Congress, *China's Economic Future: challenges to US policy* (Armonk, New York: M.E. Sharpe, 1997), 240.

35 China's official poverty line stood at 550 yuan (US$66) a year in 1997.

36 'China: Li Peng on impoverished people in NPC work report', *Xinhua*, 5 March 98 (GMT), carried in FBIS-CHI-98-063, 4 March 98.

37 Li Yang, 'CASS's financial research center chairman: 'seeking to reconcile quantity and quality—China's foreign reserve situation and developmental trend', *Guoji maoyi*, 20 September 1997, 4–7, carried in 'China: size, makeup of foreign exchange reserve analyzed', FBIS-CHI-97-339, 5 December 1997.

38 'China: foreign investment in China expected to grow in 1998', *Xinhua*, 7 December 1997, carried in FBIS-CHI-97-340, 6 December 1997.

39 Mark O'Neill, *Reuters*, 20 January 1995, citing *China Daily*.

40 Jen Hui-wen, 'Jiang Zemin, Zhu Rongji on taking precautions against financial risks', *Hsin Pao*, 5 December 1997, 16, carried in FBIS-CHI-97-342, 8 December 1997.

41 The term factions is a little strong, but there are clear divisions within the leadership around particular groupings of powerful families.

42 The Secretariat was only re-instituted in 1980, as part of a program of political reform. The Political and Legal Commission (PLC) was reinstated at the same time. According to some sources, the PLC was abolished in 1988 and replaced by an informal leadership group directing policy in this field. See Carol Lee Hamrin, 'The Party leadership system', in Kenneth G. Lieberthal and David M. Lampton (eds), *Bureaucracy, Politics, and Decision Making in Post-Mao China* (Berkeley, California: University of California Press, 1992),

119. By 2000, the PLC had re-emerged more formally, probably in response to the country's public order crisis, especially the crackdown on Falun Gong.

43 'Draft law on national defence submitted to Chinese', *Xinhua*, 6 March 1997, carried in FBIS-CHI-97-064, 5 March 1997.

44 Michael D. Swaine, *The Role of the Chinese Military in National Security Policymaking*, (Santa Monica, California: National Defense Research Institute, Rand, 1996), xii.

45 This is the conclusion of a number of studies. See Kenneth G. Lieberthal, 'Introduction: the 'fragmented authoritarianism' model and its limitations', in Lieberthal and Lampton (eds), *Bureaucracy, Politics, and Decision Making in Post-Mao China*, 15–19. Lieberthal makes the assumption that these patterns probably hold true, and will continue to do so, for the highest level of leadership.

46 Ibid., 27. As Lieberthal assessed such circumstances: 'policy decisions will lack the clarity, consistency, and detail that are necessary to bring a high probability of lower-level compliance, there is apt to be widespread sabotage of national directives by officials at each subnational level'.

47 Susan L. Shirk, *The Political Logic of Economic Reform in China* (Berkeley CA: University of California Press, 1993), 246. This judgement is particularly germane to understanding the priority given by the leadership to the armed forces in China, either as an adviser on strategic policy, or as a recipient of budget allocations. Both aspects are addressed later in this chapter.

48 Andrew J. Nathan and Robert S. Ross, *The Great Wall and the Empty Fortress: China's search for security* (New York: W.W. Norton & Company, 1997), 125.

49 Cited in Willem Van Kamenade, *China, Hong Kong, Taiwan Inc.* (New York: Vintage, 1998), 257.

50 Wang Shaoguang and Hu Angang, *Guoqing baogao: Jiaqiang zhongyang zhengfu zai shiqiang jingli zhuanxingzhongde zhudao zuoyong; guanyu zhongguo guojia nengli de yanjiu baogao* [Report on the State of the Nation: strengthening the leading role of the central government during the transition to the market economy; Research report concerning the extractive capacity of the state] (Beijing/New Haven, Connecticutt, 1993), 21–25, cited in Van Kamenade, *China, Hong Kong, Taiwan Inc*, 267–68.

51 Van Kamenade, *China, Hong Kong, Taiwan Inc*, 269.

52 Ibid., 277.

53 East Asia Analytical Unit, *China Embraces the Market* (Canberra: Department of Foreign Affairs and Trade, 1997), 287.

54 Van Kamenade, *China, Hong Kong, Taiwan Inc*, 276.

55 Ibid., citing Hu Angang, author of several controversial articles on centre–region relations.

56 'Zhu Rongji inspects Jiangsu, Zhejiang 7–13 December; comments on economic, other issues', *Xinhua*, 13 December 2000, carried in FBIS-CHI-2000-1213.

57 For text, see 'China: text of CPC constitution', *Xinhua*, 22 September 1997, carried in FBIS-CHI-97-226, 23 September 1997.

58 References to socialism or to other time-honoured Communist slogans in the Constitution as in other official statements serve two purposes—first, to provide an organisational glue for the Party, which is seen by the leadership as the only vehicle which can deliver political stability; second, to serve as a rhetorical device to buy off the political opposition within the Party who still believe in communism or doctrinaire variants of socialism.

59 Speech by State Councillor, Luo Gan to the Ninth National People's Congress, 6 March 1998, 'China: Luo Gan explains restructuring plan', *Ta kung pao*, 7 March 1998, B1-B2, carried in FBIS-CHI-98-068, 9 March 1998.

60 See Benito Mussolini, 'The doctrine of Fascism', in Adrian Lyttleton (ed.), *Italian Fascisms: from Pareto to Gentile* (London: Jonathon Cape, 1973), 44–49.

61 For one elaboration of this, see 'Xinhua's notes on drafting 10th Five Year Plan', *Xinhua*, 16 March 2001, carried in FBIS-CHI-2001-0316.

62 See, for example, statements attributed to Jiang and Li Peng in 'Central CPC propaganda dept holds forum on running the country with virtue', *Xinhua*, 21 February 2001, carried in FBIS-CHI-2001-0221.

63 'Zhu Rongji Work Report'.

64 'Zhu Rongji Work Report'.

65 'Li Lanqing heads CPC's new office in charge of cracking down on Falun Gong', *Ming pao*, 12 February 2001, carried in FBIS-CHI-2001-0212.

66 'Luo Gan on maintaining social stability', *Xinhua*, 21 December 1998, carried in FBIS-CHI-98-364.

67 'China's direction of army administration through 10th Five Year Plan', *Wen wei po*, 15 March 2001, 1, carried in FBIS-CHI-2001-0315.

68 An account of the reasons for the 17.7 per cent increase in China's military spending in 2000 is given in 'Wen Wei Po signed article

explains China's military spending increase', *Wen wei po*, 12 March 2001, 3, carried in FBIS-CHI-2001-0312.

[69] For an elaborate account of this, see 'PRC circular on opening government affairs to the public', *Xinhua*, 25 December 2000, carried in FBIS-CHI-2001-0105.

[70] China has five levels of government—township, county, city, provincial and national. There have been laws in China since the 1950s providing for direct election to some of the lower levels but these elections were controlled by the Communist Party for most of the time since then. It was only in 1988 that the first moves to direct election in contested ballots involving non-communist members freely nominated from the community was introduced for the heads of village committees.

[71] The eventual arrest on corruption charges of the Mayor of Beijing, Chen Xitong, who also was a member of the Communist Party Politburo, stemmed from loud complaints in the NPC about several decisions he had taken on building sites.

[72] This institute was established by the Chinese Communist Party in the Academy of Social Sciences in 1989 after the violent end to the demonstrations in Tiananmen Square on 4 June. The purpose was to propagate a Chinese version of democracy to counter domestic and international visions of liberal democracy. By 1992, when the leadership was no longer pre-occupied with this goal, the institute turned to a research agenda more in line with the aspirations of the demonstrators than with traditional Chinese communist concepts of 'democracy'. By 1998, they had been regular advisers to the Ministry of Civil Affairs in the conduct of the nation-wide direct electoral processes for the lower levels of government.

[73] In *China, Hong Kong, Taiwan Inc*, 18–19, van Kamenade raises this point and analyses it in terms of China's 'moralistic culture lacking a strong legalist tradition'. Most Chinese, he said, live according to the dictates of how to secure a better life and that these dictates are followed even when the law might suggest otherwise. Whether this trait is exclusively Chinese is not questioned, but it has certainly been one of the dominant features of social and political interaction in China in the 1980s and 1990s. van Kamenade cites the dismissal in 1993 of 60 per cent of the people working in law enforcement in the city of Jiamusi for their connections with organised crime. The heavy implication of law enforcement officials and party officials in crime and in covering up crime is still a recurrent theme in official statements on the public order crisis in China.

# 5
# The PLA, the CCP and the formulation of Chinese defence and foreign policy

You Ji

In 1997, the People's Liberation Army (PLA) celebrated its 70th birthday. Without the PLA, the People's Republic of China (PRC), which just marked its fiftieth anniversary, would not exist. Looking back, a lot of changes have taken place in both the PLA and the PRC. How can we summarise these changes in the PLA and its relations with the Chinese Communist Party (CCP), and its child, the PRC? This chapter describes this evolutionary process in the following characterisation: from protecting revolution to serving national interests. In a way, this 50-year process of evolution has seen a profound transition in the PLA. In its relations with the Party, the PLA has slowly moved beyond symbiosis. In its modernisation, the PLA has changed from being a semi-revolutionary, semi-professional army into a true professional military. In terms of its overriding functions, it is gradually shifting its emphasis from domestic politics to external missions. This has inevitably re-shaped its behaviour in the foreign policy arena, and these changes will accelerate and become more visible as China moves into the post-Jiang era.

## A new balance of power between civilian and military leaders

In modern societies there are two types of civil/military relations. In democracies, the military is under objective control based on the foundation of two pillars. First, objective control promotes professionalism as a distinct value judgment in the military. Professionalism regulates soldiers' political ambitions and purifies their behaviour. Second, objective control promotes an institutionalised process to restrict the actions of generals to within a legitimate range. Under objective control, the armed forces have a simple function—guarding the nation against external threat.[1] This liberal model makes the military more a client of the state than a tool of a political party or leader.

In contrast, armed forces in authoritarian countries have a much wider range of missions. There, the emergence of independent nationhood parallels the rise of military power. The soldiers are motivated by revolutionary ambitions which are fuelled by ideological ferment and nationalist frenzy brought about by colonial suppression. This fosters a strong tendency for military intervention in domestic politics, because the military tries to ensure the nation is following the appropriate political course. Often the generals are under a different kind of civilian control—the subjective control under which the military displays its loyalty to one particular political leader. Revolutionary goals, political/ideological preferences and national interests become blurred in the minds of generals who see their duties as ranging from domestic politics to international pursuits.[2]

China's civil/military relations fall largely in the second category, largely because of historical factors. The Party founded the army and established effective control mechanisms within it to ensure that soldiers stayed loyal to the CCP and the revolution. The PLA has not disappointed the Party in this regard. During the 28 years of armed struggle for survival and national power, the CCP and PLA fought side by side, forging a symbiotic relationship—the demise of one would signal the demise of the other.[3] The PLA has come to the rescue of the Party several times since the founding of the PRC, the latest occasion being the clampdown of the Tiananmen rebellion in 1989, which drew a sharp contrast with the Red Army in the USSR in 1991.

On the other hand, there have been clear signs that this symbiotic relationship is losing its power on both sides. After all, survival was no longer a pressing issue once the PRC came into being. As the new state consolidated and adapted to a peaceful environment, the soldiers' revolutionary zeal was gradually replaced by professional concerns. The civil–military relations characterised as war-time symbiosis underwent qualitative change and are now centred around shared interests. In peacetime, the closeness of CCP–PLA relations is based on a common interest in preserving their privileged position in the nation's politics. This may provide the basis for long-standing partnership. Eventually, however, the military may decide that protecting a deeply corrupt political party is a liability in protecting its own interests and adopt a more independent position. This process of divorce between the civilian and military authorities happened in almost all Chinese dynasties in their last days. It has also happened in most transforming communist societies. The likely outcome of this development would see the military surviving the decay of the Party and remaining the most important institution of power in the new political system. Taiwan's recent experience has demonstrated the possibility of this development on the mainland. In Taiwan, the Nationalist military (Guojun) continues to serve the new government as a key political player while its founder has lost power.[4]

Yet the PLA is no longer the only key interest group in the political system, even though it remains the most powerful one. Other power groups have emerged and become entrenched. For instance, the state bureaucracy now wields enormous power in state affairs. Under this new power structure, the PLA's corporate identity is highlighted rather than reduced. With irreplaceable functions to perform in society, the space for the PLA to improve its professionalism is constantly growing. Today, modernisation and regularisation have become the primary concern of the officers and soldiers, although this is still decorated in the rhetoric of revolution. The PLA has never before been driven so strongly by the same forces as Western militaries—the ideal of professionalism, defined by 'expertise, responsibility and corporateness'. What exactly has actually happened in CCP–PLA relations during the fifty year life of the PRC? Comparison of different eras is the best indicator.

## Transition from strongman control to institutionalised leadership

One clear indication of the PLA's deepening professionalisation has been the disappearance of personal control by the strongmen. The historical legacy of the CCP and the PLA meant that the military came under personal control in the Mao and Deng eras. The object of loyalty of the armed forces was not the nation, the state or even the Party, but one particular individual. Personal control is a particular type of civil–military relations in which one political leader is able to impose his own preferences on the military without consultation with the high command. In China, this resulted in the bitter lessons of the Cultural Revolution when Mao forced factional politics into the PLA.[5] Indeed, when politics enters the military, the military becomes politicised and fragmented, which gravely undermines national security.

Deng Xiaoping believed that personal control may be a necessary evil when an overriding authority is needed to push through controversial reforms. This can best be seen from his incitement to Yang Baibing in 1992 to raise a slogan of 'baojia huhang' (meaning that the PLA had a mission to protect Deng's reforms), in order to intimidate the first line party leaders who were thought to deviate from Deng's political line. This was the most serious military interference in Chinese domestic politics in the reform era, and in a way was not that different to when Mao drew the PLA into party factional infighting in 1966.[6]

Deng, however, also realised the danger of this personal control to the nation's political stability and the PLA's professionalisation. He was keenly aware that he was the only person left in the Party capable of exercising personal control over the PLA. He realised that there would be a vacuum of civilian control over the military after his death unless measures were taken while he was still alive. He saw personal control as an unhealthy form of civil–military relations that had to be eliminated. Consciously or unconsciously, he actually campaigned for a kind of objective control in his last years and tried to establish institutionalised civilian authority over the PLA. To this end, Deng dismissed the Yang brothers, despite the fact they were his closest personal friends, largely because they represented a group of politically ambitious officers that could potentially form a second power centre *vis-à-vis* Jiang Zemin, chairman of the CMC (the Central Military Commission). In this way, Deng placed national interests above his personal feelings—a great historical service to long-term stability in the PRC. More importantly, he tried to enhance the institutional authority of the CMC chair in the hands of a civilian leader. First, he retained for his successor all the institutional powers he held. Among these is the power of final veto over personnel appointments and ultimate control of the nuclear button. Second, he promoted a number of professionally-minded generals to key posts in the military. These generals had no political ambition and were not interested in ideological dispute. Third, Deng endorsed the CMC's new idea of shifting the PLA's national defence strategy from his own notion of 'fighting a people's war under modern conditions' to 'fighting a regional war under high-tech conditions', a move which helped unify the strategic thinking of the whole PLA.[7]

In the meantime, Jiang, with Deng's backing, strengthened the management process over the PLA. The most important measure in this regard was to establish clearer lines of power and responsibility with the chair of the CMC as commander-in-chief. The decisions that the chair can make personally and what he has to discuss in the meetings of the CMC and in the meetings of the Politburo Standing Committee are now defined clearly. Meetings of this standing committee are important in that the guiding principle of decisionmaking there is collective leadership. This institutionalises civilian authority over the generals and prevents another strongman emerging to take over the military. Clear provisions are now in place which establish how policy powers are divided between the military and civilian leaderships.[8]

Progress in institutionalising civil–military relations in the post-Deng era can be attributed to the efforts of both Party and PLA leaders to establish regulations governing the bilateral interactions. First, regulations have been introduced to prevent civilian and military leaders from involving themselves in areas outside their responsibilities—a phenomenon which, in the past, has been the catalyst for the formation of party factions and political–military alliances. In the last decade, there have been no signs of party leaders trying to infiltrate and influence the military with their own power manoeuvring, and vice-versa. As the military is effectively insulated from civilian politics, the PLA high command is able to maintain a high level of autonomy. As a result, unity in the military leadership has reached a level unseen since the late 1950s.

Second, both Party and military leaders cooperate to prevent general intra-party policy debate escalating into factional strife. A series of codes of conduct have been implemented for consensus building, including extensive consultation, debate in Party/PLA fora and decisionmaking that takes all affected interests into consideration. Efforts are made to limit the scope for disputes between civilian and military leaders to intensify and get out of control. Specifically, there is stricter division of power in relation to policy formulation regarding civil and military matters. Basically, PLA leaders distance themselves from interfering with non-military decisions and civilian leaders are forbidden from interfering in military administration. On issues of national security, the Politburo, with the participation of top PLA commanders, is the locus of decisionmaking power. In addition, stronger channels of communication have been developed between relevant government departments in the fields of foreign affairs and defence. Various inter-departmental leadership groups composed of both civilian and military leaders have been set up to coordinate China's international pursuits.[9]

## The changing role of the military in Chinese politics

As pointed out by Harry Harding, the military's role in national politics has been characterised by an intriguing paradox. On the one hand, the PLA possesses an impressive array of resources with which to influence national policy. On the other hand, the PLA has never seriously challenged the civilian leadership on any major policies, even on those related to national defence.[10] On the contrary, it has been ordered to do things which are in direct conflict with its own interests. One typical example was the Party's deliberate policy to reduce the military budget throughout the 1980s. Deng asked the military to exercise patience with, and tolerance to, this policy even though it gravely undermined the PLA's modernisation efforts.[11] Similarly, the PLA was ordered to give up the bulk of its industrial and commercial interests in 1998. This eliminated a substantial proportion of the PLA's extra-budgetary income, adversely affecting the living standards of a large number of service men and women. Generally speaking, the civilian authorities have maintained an impressive balance between providing the PLA a privileged position in the country's governing process and placing constraints on the PLA's exercise of political influence.

Three factors may offer an explanation of this paradox. The first is historical, but may no longer be valid.[12] For a long time the PLA was fragmented because it was made up of a number of relatively independent field armies. This prevented it from developing a complete corporate identity. Civilian leaders also often adopted a divide and rule strategy, pitting one group of senior officers against another in Party politics. Therefore, individual generals from different service origins were constantly involved in the Party power struggles.[13] Without a concerted voice in talking to civilian leaders, the potential influence of the PLA was greatly curtailed

The second factor limiting the PLA's political influence is institutional. The ultimate sign of the Party's effective control over the military is the appointment of a civilian as commander-in-chief.

The military may have some influence over the choice of candidate but does not have veto power over this vital issue. From the outset, the Party established a complete set of controlling institutions within the military—the network of party committees and political departments which are charged with missions of personnel management, discipline reinforcement, ideological indoctrination, internal security, welfare and recreational activities. Party functionaries are active officers with military rank equal to the commanders. This is the foundation of the 'double commander-in-chief system' (shuangzhangzhi) in the PLA. This web of institutional controls has been quite effective, providing a means for Party leaders to interfere in PLA affairs.

The third factor is cultural. Throughout Chinese history, civilian control over the military has been the rule, while military intervention has always been strongly denounced. Although military involvement in politics has occurred from time to time, this was mostly when the central government was on the verge of collapse or when no effective civilian government existed at all. Since ancient times, the military has always been subject to a powerful cultural pressure to obey orders from the civilian leadership, particularly the emperors.[14] In the nineteenth century, the army took advantage of national chaos to become the most powerful institution in China. As peace and stability gradually returned and China embarked on a path of deradicalisation in the late 1970s, this cultural tradition of civilian supremacy over soldiers was restored. This is one of the reasons why Jiang Zemin, a civilian with no military experience whatsoever, has been able to command the PLA with relative ease.

Despite all these constraints, the PLA is still the dominant political institution in the PRC. And it pursues its political and corporate interest powerfully. It draws its strength and influence from many sources. First, it is a large and disciplined organisation that controls lethal weapons. Its internal structure is far more cohesive than that of any other political and social organisation in the country. As in other countries, the numerical, organisational, economic, and coercive weight of the military easily makes it a force nobody can safely ignore.[15]

The second source of PLA power is its legitimacy among the majority of the population. The PLA was long viewed by the population as the best army China had ever seen. It helped restore order in the country after over a century of chaos. It lifted China's international status as a great power by fighting to a stalemate with the United States in Korea. It actively participated in the domestic economic construction and has contributed to natural disaster relief at a scale no other social organisation could hope to match. Mao's call to 'learn from the PLA' was genuinely answered by the people in the 1960s.

The Cultural Revolution gravely tarnished the PLA's image, when it was involved in Party factional infighting and was used as an instrument of class struggle. The PLA worked hard to repair the damage during the Deng era but suffered another major setback in 1989. For a while, the notion that the PLA was a people's army seemed far from reality.

After more than a decade, however, the PLA's public image and standing has reached a new high. During the 1990s, the PLA was involved in numerous disaster relief efforts. Its fight against the massive flooding across the country in 1998 moved many TV viewers, as they saw over one hundred PLA generals and more than 500,000 soldiers working on the river banks day and night to save the lives of a large number of ordinary people. Certainly the population resent the level of corruption amongst PLA personnel and the privileges attached to the organisation. On balance, the PLA is still respected, especially in rural areas. It is regarded as indispensable for maintaining social order. This public support gives the PLA an advantage in its interactions with other political institutions in China.

The third source of PLA power is institutional and rests on the politically independent status of the CMC. The CMC wields power with a high level of autonomy. Officially, it occupies the same level in the Party hierarchy as the State Council and the Standing Committee of the National People's Congress. Theoretically, it is under the Politburo in the hierarchy, but in reality it largely operates outside the Politburo's reach. This is because Mao deliberately separated the government and military systems under the formula of '*zhengzhijiu yi zheng, junwei yi jun*'—the Politburo's realm is state affairs and the CMC's is military affairs. Deng inherited this tradition. The CMC reported its affairs only to him throughout the 1980s. Following his two predecessors, Jiang has made efforts to prevent his Politburo colleagues from becoming involved in CMC affairs. The CMC has created its own autonomous power centre and enjoys the final say on many things ranging from personnel to legal, commercial and cultural matters. Reflecting the notion that political power comes from the barrel of a gun, whoever controls the CMC becomes the ultimate ruler of the nation. Jiang's rise in the Party is due largely to the fact that he has been accepted by the PLA as undisputed chair of the CMC. As a result, the Party and the PLA are jointly coordinated under Jiang as party boss and commander-in-chief.

These changes show the PLA transforming gradually from a revolutionary army driven by ideological ferment to a professional, increasingly depoliticised military, conscious more of the national security issues and inclined less to get involved in intra-party factional activities. The PLA has acquired a cohesive corporate identity. Its corporate interest is best protected when there are no destructive outside intrusions. As the symbiotic relationship weakens, the PLA's new identity will affect its relations with the Party. This can be further seen from an analysis of the PLA's efforts at professionalisation.

## Rising professionalism and corporate identity

The PLA has been a professional military all along, even though it has taken many other missions regarded as non-military by Western standards. It is unlikely that a non-professional military could fight to a stalemate with the powerful US army as the PLA did in the Korean War. The PLA has long been called a revolutionary professional army, similar to the nature of the Israeli armed forces. In the last two decades, however, the Chinese military has lost its revolutionary nature but is increasingly showing signs of becoming a fully professional organisation.

## The changing ideological foundation of civil–military relations

One major aspect of CCP–PLA relations before the Dengist reforms was the strong ideological current in the armed forces. Ideological control was an integral part of Party control over the PLA. Therefore, the PLA became class-based and an ideological model for the rest of society. Since the 1980s, the ideological foundation of the PRC has gradually shifted towards nationalism.[16] This has had a profound impact on civil–military relations. First, ideology is seen as being too abstract to serve as a basis for the modernisation efforts of the PLA—an ideologically inclined military would reject professionalism as a primary goal of the armed forces. Second, it is easier for the Party and the PLA to find common ground in nationalism, specifically defined as national sovereignty, national reunification, territorial integrity, vital economic interests and national prestige in world affairs. As the PLA is no longer required to serve the narrow purposes of the working class, it is able to embrace a wider definition of national interests, and is thus more readily accepted by the population, which has been growing increasingly cynical about communist ideology. Third, as Party–military relations are guided by common national goals rather than ideological correctness, there is less need for the Party to indoctrinate the soldiers forcefully—soldiers pick up patriotism themselves. Bilateral relations consequently become easier to maintain.

## Setting up new strategic national defence guidelines

One key measure of a professional military is its defence strategy. Since 1949, the PLA has altered its defence strategy several times, shifting from following Mao's people's war doctrine to adoption of Revolution in Military Affairs (RMA) as the guide for modernisation. With this evolutionary process the PLA has gradually shifted from being a tool of revolution required by the people's war principle to the guardian of national security with an emphasis on external missions. Indeed, the RMA type of war cannot be targeted against domestic enemies. The PLA's adoption of RMA has provided a timely guideline for improvements in its national defence strategy, both in theory and in practice. PLA generals are now trying to translate the RMA concepts into their professional war preparation—they are now more convinced than ever that winning a hi-tech war requires hardware superiority, sound tactics, and a suitable force structure. In 1993, the CMC put forward a new national defence strategy as a guide for modernisation of the PLA. The current campaign of disseminating RMA ideas within the Chinese military will further improve this strategy and address its doctrinal defects.[17] First, the new strategy stresses the necessity of forward defence, recognising that in a high-tech war the enemy can launch precision strikes from long distance.[18] While expanding defence depth may not stop long-range attacks, if the enemy can be effectively engaged in the outer defence line, the PLA may at least inflict greater human losses on the enemy and secure precious early warning for further defensive mobilisation.

Second, the high-tech strategy is largely an offensive oriented strategy, reflecting the shift in emphasis from the 'defensive' towards the 'active' side of war preparation. Following the Gulf War, the PLA quickly realised that high-tech wars will not be fought along fixed defence lines. Trench warfare will rarely occur. Accordingly, China's military approach has changed from *yifang weizhu fangfan jiehe*, or 'defence as overall posture, offence as the supplement', to *linghuo fanying gong fang jiehe*, or 'adroit response based on a combination of offensive and defensive capabilities'. Technological innovation has increasingly blurred the boundaries between offensive and defensive weaponry. Digital battlefield, electronic soft kill, and pinpoint elimination of the enemy's key targets all indicate that it is the offensive side that can seize the first initiative of the war and has the best chance of success. The offensive posture and pre-emptive strike are especially crucial for a weak military at the beginning of a high-tech war.[19]

Third, the strategy is forward-leaning. Its high-tech focus aims mainly at defence against strategic concerns, namely the major military powers. At the same time, the strategy is flexible in principle, catering to different scenarios, from major wars to small-scale border conflicts. This is the PLA's response to China's changing security environment in the post Cold War era. The new strategy is also forward-looking, geared to preparation for action in the new century. It prescribes concrete measures for weapons programs, force organisation, campaign tactics, and research priorities, which are not aimed at equipping the PLA in the next few years but at the frontiers of hi-tech breakthroughs some decades from now.[20]

What is the significance of this new military thinking to the professionalisation of the PLA? Simply put, it has set a proper direction for development. Without a sound strategic theoretical framework, even if the PLA acquired sophisticated weaponry in the new century, this weaponry could not be used to its full potential.[21] Proper guidelines, high-tech weaponry, and a foresighted vision for development form the basis of a much more open and pragmatic PLA.

## Creating an élite officer corps

No more than ten people remain in the military leadership who joined the Party before the founding of the PRC. And they will all depart the scene in less than three years. Soon the revolutionary tradition will disappear from the PLA. This will certainly facilitate professionalisation. Already the majority of top office holders are highly-educated technocrats without personal experience in revolution. They are imbued with common sense and scientific knowledge, but they lack the spirit of radicalism that characterised earlier military leaders in China. The result is that they are less likely to form factions among themselves along political and ideological lines. This new tendency can be seen more clearly at the lower levels in the PLA. Now 600,000 officers (90 per cent of the whole officer corps) have higher education qualifications, 20,000 officers have a Masters degree and over 4,000 officers have doctoral degrees. This new organisational make-up marks a clear break from the PLA's earlier tendencies.[22] Sooner rather than later the PLA will become further depoliticised and de-ideologised.

The fundamental change has gone much deeper than the organisational make-up of the officer corps. There are many other signs of professionalisation resulting from the change of guard. The PLA high command has substantially reformed military training and education. Officers have to go through an extended period of re-learning to meet the new requirements of fighting wars in the new era. Now, all military officers have to study new technologies, handle computers and get familiar with the targeted enemy forces. Promotion is closely tied to their study efforts. One of the assessment criteria is the extent and quality of their published material in both academic journals and internal policy debate. For instance, to be promoted into senior posts each officer must undertake a period of intensive study in the 'advanced class of generals' in the PLA National Defence University.[23] It is said that the CMC chairman and vice-chairmen all read the students' graduation theses. In this way they are able to identify talented successors from this class.

Wang Zhuxun's promotion serves as a telling example of the emerging élite nature of the PLA officers corps. He was commander-in-chief of the 14th Group Army when he joined the class for generals in the early 1990s. He wrote a graduation thesis entitled *The Strategic Path of Yunnan*, which argued that if there were a war on China's coast, China's strategic path through the Pacific would be blocked. This would seriously affect China's economy because more than two-thirds of China's exports and imports follow this route. Then he suggested that China should prepare an alternative strategic path that would, according to his opinion, run from Yunnan through Burma to the Indian Ocean. His thesis caught the attention of General Zhan Zhen, the third most senior military leader in China, who passed it onto Jiang Zemin. Jiang also praised the thesis highly, claiming that Wang Zhuxun was exactly the kind of person needed for the military modernisation, a person who had broad strategic vision. Wang was later promoted to the post of commander-in-chief of military region. More generally, almost all the current top office holders have an impressive list of publications. This has lifted the PLA's level of professionalism.

## Wars and responsibilities

How does China's international behaviour fulfil its responsibilities as a major world power? This is a tricky question. People can hold different interpretations of what is responsible. One nation can perceive its behaviour on the world stage to be quite reasonable but other states may think just the opposite. Despite the increased strength of liberalism and the democratic peace thesis in the post Cold War era, the world is in reality still dominated by nation-states pursuing national interest above everything else. The best example of this is the US efforts to build NMD regardless of the opinions of the world community, including western countries.

## Serving national interests as the top mission

In the history of the PRC, the PLA has been involved in nine wars and armed conflicts. These can be roughly divided into two groups—wars fought for ideological reasons and wars fought for the protection of national sovereignty and territorial integrity. The first group includes the Korean War with the United States in the 1950s, the Vietnam War in the 1960s, the Sino-Soviet border conflict in 1969, the Sino-Vietnamese War in 1979 and the Sino-Vietnamese border clash in the first half of the 1980s. The second group is comprised of the Sino-Indian Border War in 1962, extension of the civil war with the Guomindang (GMD) in the 1950s and 1960s, the suppression of the Tibetan Revolt in 1959, the recovery of Xisha Island in 1974, and the maritime clash with Vietnam in 1988. Some cases in the second category were not without ideological motivation.

The number of wars that China initiated or was forced to launch has been declining. Most of the actions were taken in the 1950s and 1960s, and no war involving China took place in the 1990s. This downward trend has underscored two important facts. First, after China gave up treating other nations with any ideological prejudice, the reason for war was significantly reduced. Second, even though China has always adopted a non-negotiable approach towards sovereignty and territorial issues, it realised in the 1980s that as a responsible international player it should always place peaceful settlement of disputes above military threat.[24] Professor

Iain Johnston of Harvard University found that China's involvement in militarised disputes diminished over the period 1949–92 and found that this correlated with a reduction in border controversies and an increased sense of status internationally. And this was correlated with China's greater economic interdependence with the world economic system.[25]

This fundamental change has been behind the abandonment of Mao's slogan of 'liberating' Taiwan in 1979. Deng's proposal to settle Hong Kong and Taiwan problems with a formula of 'one country, two systems' was the best offer China could make for a matter concerning national sovereignty. At the same time, China also proposed to other countries that territorial disputes should be resolved through dialogue and mutually acceptable terms. Under this guideline, China has successfully reached border agreements with Russia, Mongolia, Central Asian countries, Burma, Pakistan and Vietnam. Its land border negotiation with India is progressing well at this moment. All this has shown that China sincerely holds the principle of peaceful reunification of the lost territories. Indeed, China has made more concessions than its counterparts in all these negotiations. Contrary to the claim that China has an expansionist agenda, we can see that the Chinese map is smaller now than at any time in the last century. And its presence in the South China Sea is the smallest among all the claimants.[26]

Removing the ideological basis for war and emphasising peaceful settlement of territorial disputes represented major progress toward China becoming a responsible member of the international community. This is derived from China's overriding national goal of economic development. Objectively speaking, the PLA has never been opposed to dropping military threat as the foundation of foreign and defence policy. It was the primary victim in various wars fought along these lines. It paid a heavy price in achieving a stalemate with the United States in the Korean War and it almost suffered a nuclear surgical strike from the USSR in the 1969. China's peace-centred foreign initiative in the post-Mao era has given the PLA an opportunity to tackle its major problem—backward equipment. As a professional army and a key component of the Party–state, however, the PLA has never wavered in carrying out orders of war from the civilian leadership. As a tool of revolution in the past it viewed the United States as an imperialist power and the USSR as a revisionist enemy. In settling territorial disputes, it crossed the border to attack several of its neighbours. In the absence of revolutionary zeal, the PLA will have to forge a new identity and a new mission. If this new role is to serve as guardian of national interests, to what extent will this affect its external behaviour? Does this role promote modernisation efforts? These are crucial questions that may cause disagreement between the civilian and military leaders. So far there has not been any major conflict but tension is always beneath the surface, since an economics-in-command political line may delay many key arms upgrading programs, owing to the relatively low priority allocated to developing the military.

It is necessary to define how PLA generals see the concept of national interests. First, the PLA's role in the national interest is to secure the PRC from the external threat. Second, national interests entail efforts to guarantee the integrity of national territories, including efforts to recover territories lost due to China's historical weakness. Although it is very unlikely that China will be invaded, it suffers constant intimidation from Western powers—the 1989 sanctions, the forced inspection of the Yin He shipment, the de facto containment and the continuing Cold War mentality of 'peaceful evolution'. The interventionist tendency in international relations worries the PLA and this has made its responsibility to recover lost territories an even heavier burden to shoulder. China does have human rights problems and ethnic conflicts at home—separatist movements are active in Tibet and Xinjiang and receive international support. Taiwan's ongoing drift away from the mainland poses an immediate challenge to the PLA. All this has convinced the PLA that it is living in a hostile world,[27] and the cruel truth is that it is far from being ready to face the challenge.

## The war or peace discourse

The reduced involvement of the PLA in the country's domestic politics has, as mentioned earlier, reduced the scope for disagreements between the civilian and military leaders over internal policy. This is especially true in the economic field. The PLA does not have any serious disagreement with the market-oriented reforms, although it believes that they have created new challenges to the maintenance of its corporate cohesion.[28] In terms of politics, the PLA probably supported Jiang's surprisingly hardline response to Falun Gong in 1999—another example of Party and military sharing vital interests in the monopoly of power. In terms of military policies, the PLA has had a high level of autonomy in military administration and Party interference has been minimal since the early 1990s. The Party sometimes denies specific military demands for weapons development, such as when it vetoed the PLA's request to build an aircraft carrier. On the whole, however, the CCP tries to meet the military's hardware upgrading needs. It does this partly because it recognises that continued relations are founded on give and take, but also because a powerful army helps the Party consolidate its power.

In the area of foreign and defence policy, however, discord is discernible between the two, mostly related to how to respond to events in Sino-US and cross-Strait relations. The mainstream civilian leadership is now composed of Jiang Zemin and Zhu Rongji, both of whom are more pro-West than their predecessors and possibly even their successors. They were trained in the Western-style universities in the 1940s. Although strong nationalism propelled them to join the revolution then, they all had an unfulfilled dream of studying in the United States. And their world outlook is wider than those who will form the core of the fourth generation leadership which received communist education in the 1950s and 1960s. They know that China now has its best chance in many centuries to become economically rich and militarily powerful. The military threat to China is minimal, except for foreign involvement in the Taiwan Strait. The world situation is mostly peaceful and will remain so for a long time. The domestic situation is fairly stable, thanks to both political restrictions and economic growth. So China's security should be enhanced through promoting world peace.[29] The only thing that could hinder the rise of China is war with Taiwan.

This is the reason why the civilian leaders have decided that China's foreign policy in the post-Cold War era should be non-confrontational towards the West. The bottom line of this policy guideline is to handle the Western challenge cleverly in order to create a stable international environment for China's economic take-off. This is the key principle Deng laid down for his successors.[30] Following this principle, Jiang always takes a long-term perspective in handling acute conflicts with the West. Even if the quarrels involve matters of Chinese sovereignty—for example, US arms sales to Taiwan—Jiang tries to leave room for compromise later for the sake of maintaining at least a workable economic relationship. The exception to this was China's policy towards NATO's Kosovo war.[31]

At times this may present a problem for the military. But the PLA has so far not challenged Jiang's soft foreign policy tone. As mentioned earlier, the PLA has become increasingly externally-oriented and non-interventionist towards intra-party politics. This makes the job of the civilian control over the armed forces a lot easier for the post-Deng leaders, quite contrary to many analysts' predictions. No one dismisses the fact that the PLA still wields enormous political influence, especially at times of succession. Yet the PLA chooses to use that influence prudently and selectively. On the whole, its weight has been most clearly felt in areas of foreign and defence policies. This is a key political role played by the PLA, but it does not fall outside range of activities considered legitimate by western countries.

The PLA has for some time been prevented from taking tough attitudes towards international politics. It tolerated the suppression of its budget increase for a decade in the 1980s. Reacting to the civilian request, the military pledged not to use force to resolve the South China Sea dispute in 1993 when other claimants continued to occupy islets in dispute. It voiced its support for Jiang's peace initiative towards Taiwan, embodied in his pronouncement that 'Chinese do not fight Chinese' in 1995, despite its full awareness that the move would not work. When its program of upgrading land and sea-based long-range nuclear missiles was at a crucial stage of development, the PLA accepted the civilian leaders' 1997 decision that China should stop nuclear tests. Moreover, it let go of its vast economic and commercial machine in 1998 at the order of the Party. Of course all this was not done without a level of disgruntlement on the part of the PLA. Yet, the fact that the PLA has accepted what was imposed upon it indicates that it is conscious of the international trend towards peace and is trying to adapt to the new circumstances. Another major factor is the current transitional difficulties in the PLA's weapons R & D. Large numbers of new high-tech weapons designs have just passed the laboratory test and it will take many more years for them to become deployable. The top commanders know that this is not time to take action and are taking advantage of the West's engagement strategy toward China to further the country's defence modernisation.[32]

The post-Deng civilian leadership does not disagree with the PLA's perception of external threat to China's national interests. Discord arises in deciding how to handle the threat. This concerns the timing for a major counter-offensive, its intensity, and the way of retreating from a clash. Generally speaking, the military would like to see a hardline reaction to challenges to China's sovereignty, including the threat of military force. In contrast, the civilian leadership would have more to consider in a crisis—the economic consequences, international outcry, and the long-term effects on national interests. This discord is still more technical than fundamental at this stage. Civilian leaders have been successful in convincing PLA generals that if the Chinese military is not ready for a major action, it is in the PLA's best interests not to be dragged into a war prematurely. The question is how long the PLA will continue to accept this argument if it does not receive a firm commitment from civilian leaders to address the problem of military backwardness. The debate between a soft vs. hardline response to Western threat may escalate to the point where the overall direction of national development is altered. Recent world events, such as the enhanced US–Japan military alliance, Lee Tenghui's 'two-state' thesis, NATO's bombing of the Chinese embassy in Belgrade, and Chen Shuibian's election victory in Taiwan, have placed the civilian and military leadership at a crossroads.

The PLA will not always take whatever is imposed upon it by civilian leaders at any cost. As guardian of national interests it will have to raise its voice when it believes the civilian leadership has compromised too much. This is most vividly reflected in the PLA's attitudes towards Taiwan. The PLA missile launches in 1995–96 carried a clear message for the Taiwanese leadership: do not force our hand. Yet at the time, Jiang was still under illusions that the two sides could work out something peacefully. After Lee Tenghui's US visit in May 1995, Jiang was under pressure from PLA generals and state security personnel to revise the 'one centre, two basic-points' guiding principle set by Deng for China's modernisation. The military sought to add to Deng's 'one centre' (the economics in command) another centre, namely safeguarding national sovereignty and territorial integrity, which may mean a major military build-up. Indeed, Deng once told PLA leaders that the PLA should see protection of national sovereignty and territorial integrity as the state's primary task.[33] This provided PLA generals with a powerful weapon to demand a high level of preparedness.

The Politburo's Beidaihe conference in August 1995 put an end to the debate, for a while, and upheld Deng's non-confrontational diplomatic principle, after Jiang persuaded the participants that it was not time to confront the West.[34] The same Beidaihe conference in 1999, however, came to the new conclusion that NATO's bombing of the Chinese embassy exposed the bottom line of the West's policy toward China. Choice between peace and war was no longer in Beijing's hands. The civilian leaders, as pointed out by senior PLA officers, decided in a timely and resolute manner to enhance the intensity of military modernisation. The Party centre promised that the PLA would acquire the capacity to win a high-tech war with a major military power as quickly as possible. Obviously this would require a substantial increase in the national defence budget. Although promoting economic development is still the Party's central task, the civilian leaders' position in handling the contradiction between economic construction and military modernisation has tilted toward what the PLA has argued for all along.[35] The consequences of such a policy direction are profound. The Chinese leaders have now dropped Deng's assertion that major wars could be avoided. Their current assessment of the world order has been most pessimistic since the beginning of the 1980s. The bombing of the Chinese embassy has imposed great urgency on China's defence modernisation. In late 1999, Jiang issued orders on behalf of the Politburo to the participants of the PLA chief-of-staff conference that the PLA should accelerate military readiness for war.[36] While economics is still in command, more national resources will be devoted to military build-up.[37]

Yet it is interesting to note that, despite his supportive remarks on a quickened military build-up, Jiang has been reluctant to move China in a direction that can be interpreted as militarist. Whenever there are major international events damaging China's national interests he stresses the hard side of the policy. Whenever the tension eases, however, he retreats from his commitment to immediate war preparation. The same is true of Zhu Rongji. His tough talk in the April 2000 news conference, in which he addressed the question of Taiwan's presidential election, should be seen in the same light. Taiwan is a likely area where China's civilian and military leadership may differ in their policy emphasis for a long time to come.

## Conclusion

There has been a change in relations between the Party and the PLA in China. The passing of the first and second generation party and military leaders has reduced the scope of the intervention of the military in domestic politics. The PLA is increasingly presenting itself as a separate identity with distinctive corporate spirit and interests. Professionalism, as embodied in the slogan of winning the next major high-tech war, has been set as the ultimate goal for military modernisation. All this has made it possible for the PLA to transform itself from the tool of revolution to the guardian of national security. On the other hand, the PLA has no quarrel with the Party's command over the gun. Party control is seen as legitimate because the Party is the founder of the PLA in the first place. More importantly, the military sees benefits in protecting the Party, with which it shares vital vested interests. This has given rise to a relationship of give and take. If we observe this relationship in the longer term, however, we may see cracks in the relationship. As a highly professionalised organisation, the military will very likely outlive the CCP as a political party in power, which may either collapse if it cannot curtail its internal decay due to corruption or lose office to another new political party if fundamental political reform is introduced. Therefore the current Party–military relationship is undergoing transitory change, although this period of transition will necessarily be long.

The interaction between the military and the Party's third generation leadership is particularly indicative of the shared ties of give and take. In the last decade the military finally rid itself of the strongmen's personal control. As a result it has achieved a much higher level of autonomy. This is actually the most important reason for the PLA to accept Jiang Zemin, a political player who has never posed any threat to the PLA's vital interests. As far as civilian leaders are concerned, they will have to rely more on institutional power rather than personal authority to influence the military. The rules of the game are clearer than before. As a result relations between the Party and the PLA are easier to manage, but in the long run of time this trend will facilitate the divorce between the Party and the military in the form of a depoliticised and state-run military.

This progress does not preclude the possibility of the military taking hardline attitudes towards matters of national security. The efforts of professionalisation may focus the eyes of officers and men away from domestic concerns. The top mission of securing national interests may cause the PLA's external functions to be perceived as aggressive. Especially when the PLA is eager to fight for national territorial integrity, it may be viewed as sabre rattling. This is exactly the case with the Taiwan problem. The PLA will not initiate any action across the Strait without a reason because this does not serve the interests of China and the PLA. Particularly with the question of Taiwan, the choice between peace and war is no longer in the hands of the CCP leadership. Here the PLA may differ with its civilian commanders over an estimate of the geostrategic situation. Both of them may agree that more efforts must be made to empower the military and both of them may even agree that war may be inevitable, but, whereas the civilian leadership sees the possibility of prolonging the peace and the benefits of placing economic ahead of military needs, the military calculates its capability according to a worst case scenario and thus demands more inputs. So far there has not been a serious rift but that situation could easily change in a crisis. Eventually the civilian leadership will have to go along with the military, probably with the fourth generation of the Party core, because it dares not carry the blame of betraying national interests. We may see a Chinese military that will in the future become more assertive in assuming external missions.

## Notes

1 See for instance, Samuel Huntington, *Soldiers and the State*, (Belknap: Harvard Massachusetts, 1957).

2 Samuel Finer, *The Man on Horseback: the role of the military in politics* (Westview: Boulder, 1988).

3 There is a large body of literature on China's civil-military relations, although the bulk of it has become obsolete. See Jeremy Paltiel, 'PLA allegiance on parade: civil–military relations in transition', *China Quarterly*, no. 143, (September 1995); David Shambaugh, 'China's post-Deng military leadership', in James Lilly and David Shambaugh (eds), *China's Military Faces the Future* (M.E. Sharpe: Boulder, 1999).

4 Ellis Joffe first raised this issue of 'a separate army' in his 1993 article, 'The PLA and the Succession Question', in Richard Yang (ed.), *China's Military: the PLA in 1992/1993* (Taipei: Chinese Council of Advanced Policy Studies, 1993), 150.

5 See various chapters in Roderick MacFarquhar (ed.), *The Politics of China: the eras of Mao and Deng* (Cambridge: Cambridge University Press, 1997).

6 For more on this see You Ji, 'Jiang Zemin: struggle for the post-Deng supremacy', in Maurice Brosseau, Suzanne Pepper & Tsang Shu-ki (eds), *China Review 1996* (Hong Kong: The Chinese University of Hong Kong Press, 1996), pp. 1–28.

7 For a more detailed analysis, see You Ji,. *The Armed Forces of China* (Sydney, London & New York: Allen & Unwin and I.B. Tauris, 1999), 28–55.

8 Liu Yicang and Ku Guisheng, *You zhong guo tese de guofang jianshe lilun* [The national defence theory of the Chinese characteristics] (Beijing: the PLA Academy of Military Science Press, 1993), 216.

9 See Michael Swaine, *The Role of the Chinese Military in National Security Policymaking* (Santa Monica: RAND, 1996).

10 Harry Harding, 'The PLA as a political interest group', in Victor Falkenheim (ed.), *Chinese Politics from Mao to Deng* (New York: Paragon House, 1987), 213–14.

11 For a detailed analysis of the budget cut, see Shaoguang Wang, 'Estimating China's defence expenditure: some evidence from Chinese sources', *The China Quarterly*, no. 147 (September 1996); and, for its political consequences, see You Ji and Ian Wilson, 'Leadership by 'lines': China's unresolved succession', *Problems of Communism*, Vol. 39, no. 1 (January 1990), 28–44.

12 Michael Swaine elaborated the historical origin of the political-military factions in his book, *The Military & Political Succession in China* (Santa Monica: RAND, 1992).

13 Harding, 'PLA as a political interest group'.

14 On this cultural tradition, Ray Huang wrote an excellent chapter in his book, *1587: a year of no significance* (New Haven: Yale University Press, 1981).

15 Harding, 'PLA as a political interest group'.

16 See for instance, Yongnian Zheng, *Discovering Chinese Nationalism in China* (London: Cambridge University Press, 1998).

17 For a more detailed analysis of the PLA and RMA, see You Ji, 'Revolution in Military Affairs and the evolution of China's strategic thinking', *Contemporary Southeast Asia*, 21, no. 3 (December 1999), 325–45.

18 Guo Yongjun, 'Fangkong zuozhan ying shuli quanquyu zhengti fangkong de sixian' [Air defence should be guided by the theory of area and integrated defence], *Junshi xueshu*, no. 11 (1995), 47–49.

19 Shi Zhigang, 'Jiji fangyu zhanlue sixiang zai xinshiqi junshi douzheng de tixian' [The application of active defence strategy in the military preparation in the new era], *The Journal of PLA National Defence University*, (August–September 1998), 100.

20 Tao Bojun, 'Dangde sandai lingdao jiti yu keji jianjun' [The Party's three generation leadership and strengthening the armed forces through technological breakthroughs], *China Military Science*, no. 3 (1997), 65–73.

21 Xie Dajun, 'Qiantan zhishi jingji jiqi dui junshi gemin de yingxiang yu tiaozhan' [The influence and challenge of knowledge economy to RMA], *The Journal of PLA National Defence University*, (January 1999), 27.

22 Wu Jianhua, 'Wojun zhonggaoji nianqing zhihui ganbu peiyang de kaocha yu jishi' [The review of promoting young senior officers in our army and its lessons], *Journal of the PLA National Defence University*, no. 1 (2000), 51.

23 This class admits students at the level of the army commanders. Each year about 50 promising young major generals are enrolled in the course.

24 Yao Yanjin and Liu Jixian, *Deng Xiaoping xinshiqi junshi lilun yanjiu*, [Study of Deng Xiaoping's military theory in the new year] (Beijing: the PLA Academy of Military Science, 1994), 71–76.

25 Alastair Iain Johnston, 'Cultural realism and strategy in Maoist China', in P. Katzenstein (ed.), *The Culture of National Security* (New York: Columbia University Press, 1996), 251–68.

26 The PRC's largest loss of territory took place in the early 1950s when Beijing essentially watched India occupy 900,000 square kilometres of Chinese territory, obviously due to political and diplomatic reasons. See Mao Zhengfa and Zeng Yan (eds), *Bianfanglun* [Theory of territorial defence] (Beijing: The PLA Academy of Military Science Press, 1996), 132–34.

27 Li Gang and Wang Qi, 'Zhengque renshi shijie geju duojihua qushi' [Correctly recognising the multipolarity trend in the world order], *Journal of the PLA National Defence University*, no. 9 (2000), 26–27.

28 Zhao Kemin, 'Dui xinshiqi wojun sixiang zhengzhi gongzuo shijian de huigu yu sikao' [The reassessment of and reflection on our army's ideological and political work in the new era], *Journal of the PLA National Defence University*, no. 10 (1999), 22–25.

29 Meng Xiangqing, 'Jiang Zemin de anquanguan chutan' [An initial study on Jiang Zemin's theory of security], *Journal of Foreign Affairs College*, no. 2 (1999), 38–42.

30 Qu Xing, 'Shilun dongou jubian he suliang jieti hou de zhongguo duiwai zhengce' [China's foreign policy since the radical changes in Eastern Europe and the disintegration of the USSR], *Journal of Foreign Affairs College*, no. 4 (1994), 19–22.
31 I have made analyses of this exception in detail elsewhere, see You Ji, 'The China challenge in the new millennium', paper presented at the Strategic Update Conference, Parliament House, Canberra, 27 September 1999.
32 Xu Tao, 'Ruhe renshi woguo anquan liyi' [How to understand our country's security interest], *Journal of the PLA National Defence University*, no. 1 (2000), 16.
33 Peng Guangqian et al., *Deng Xiaoping zhanlue sixianglun* [On Deng Xiaoping's strategic thoughts] (Beijing: the PLA Academy of Military Science Press, 1994), 109.
34 See You Ji, 'Changing leadership consensus: the domestic context of war games', in Suisheng Zhao (ed.), *Making Sense of the Crisis Across the Taiwan Strait* (London: Routledge, 1999), 77–98.
35 Peng Rixuan, Ying Lin and Li Tao, 'Zhongguo jundui xiandaihua jianshe huigu yu zhanwang' [The review and forecast of the Chinese military modernisation], *Journal of the PLA National Defence University*, no. 5 (2000), 9.
36 Qian Guoliang, 'Quanmian luoshi silingbu jianshe gangyao gaobiaozhun zhuahao silingbu jiguan jianshe' [Comprehensively implementing the Guidelines for the Headquarters Construction], *Journal of the PLA National Defence University*, no. 6 (2000), 4.
37 Peng Rixuan et al., 'Zhongguo jundui', 9.

# 6
# China's participation in international organisations

**Ann Kent**

China's growing participation in international organisations provides a source and mark of its expanding power, and a measure of its increased global commitments and responsibilities.[1] Its effective entry into the global community occurred thirty years ago when, on 26 October 1971, the UN General Assembly adopted Resolution 2758 to transfer the seat of China in the United Nations from the Republic of China (ROC) on Taiwan to the People's Republic of China (PRC).[2] Following as it did a sustained period of Chinese isolationism and revolutionary paranoia, this development was universally hailed with relief, tinged with some lingering anxiety. Any initial concern within the international community about the potential problems associated with China's entry was, however, soon dispelled by the continuing domestic turmoil of the Cultural Revolution, then by the enticing prospects of China's market reforms and by China's modest, self-assigned role as a learner in global affairs. Despite its sudden international prominence, China was slow to participate in most of the UN's affiliated agencies—it did not join the World Bank, the International Monetary Fund (IMF), and the Conference on Disarmament (CD) or fully participate in the International Labour Organisation (ILO) until well after Mao's death in September 1976.

By the mid 1990s, only twenty years later, the scene had shifted. China was emerging as a great power, economically, politically and militarily, and one which was highly influential in international organisations. In terms of its increasing impact on international and regional politics and its influence in global issue areas of security, the environment, the international political economy and human rights, it even enjoyed the ascribed role of a superpower. As the international community began to feel the impact of China's burgeoning economic growth and its increased international assertiveness, scholars and statesmen alike began worrying about its place and role in a rapidly globalising world. Increasingly, they questioned the degree to which its domestic and international policies reflected an ability to co-exist peacefully and cooperatively with the international community.[3]

By 2000, China had become a member of over 50 intergovernmental organisations (IGOs) and 1,275 international non-governmental organisations (INGOs). This contrasted with the situation in 1966, when it was a member of only one intergovernmental organisation and 58 international non-governmental organisations.[4] In terms of numbers of IGOs, by 2000 China ranked seventh in the Asia Pacific region behind Japan, India, Indonesia, South Korea, Australia and Malaysia. In terms of its membership of INGOs, China was placed sixth in the region behind Australia, Japan, India, New Zealand and South Korea.[5]

It goes without saying that, for China, membership of international organisations is critical.[6] It is also critical for the global community, not only because of its implications for global power distribution but because, apart from their many other functions, international organisations are seen to contribute significantly to the international socialisation of participating states. International organisations and their treaty regimes not only ensure transparency, cut transaction costs, build capacity, and enhance dispute settlement, but also, through a process of 'jawboning', persuade parties to 'explore, redefine and sometimes discover' their own, and mutual, interests.[7] In this sense, they may be understood broadly as the institutional representations of interdependence, constituting a 'collective organising response to a multiplicity of 'traffic' control problems in a world of contradictory trends'.[8] Yet, for the same reason, they represent a challenge to the state. Participation in international organisations both confirms sovereignty and constrains it. Management of the problem of sovereignty is thus a highly complex matter. For each state it is a question of steering between the benefits for sovereignty that membership of international organisations and regimes entails, and the potential threat to sovereignty that it implies.[9] The power conferred on states by international organisational participation is balanced by the increased responsibility such participation entails.

The following overview of the goals underlying China's active engagement in international organisations, and of the means by which it pursues them, sheds light on its practical understanding of power and responsibility.

## China's approach to international organisations

While China's leaders appreciate that membership of international organisations enhances China's power and status and is essential to participation in globalisation and modernisation, they are also alive to the problems posed by international citizenship. President Jiang Zemin has both welcomed interdependence and warned of the threats posed by economic interdependence for North–South relations, the centrifugal and centripetal pressures that it exerts on the economy, the social and environmental ills that it entails, and the possible impact on China's economic growth rate. Yet he has also acknowledged the responsibility that interdependence places on China to broaden its understanding of the world.[10] Indeed, the extent of China's shift in this respect was reflected in Jiang's speech at a Royal Banquet in the United Kingdom (UK) on 19 October 1999, which expressed his pride and confidence in China's status as one of the five permanent members of the UN Security Council and revealed China's new readiness to view the United Kingdom, historically perceived as one of its oppressors, as one of its partners in international responsibility.[11]

However, other more defensive reactions within China stress the way in which international cooperation and interdependence protect and promote US hegemonic interests.[12] These reactions mirror the general ambivalence about globalisation (*quanqihua*) which, unlike the concept of modernisation (*xiandaihua*), is seen to place China at serious risk of losing control over its own policies.[13] This ambivalence explains China's insistence that interdependence and globalisation must not undermine state sovereignty. While formally recognising international organisations as subjects of international law, it has denied that they are 'supranational' or political entities in the same sense as sovereign states. On the one hand, it looks to international organisations to confer international prestige, status and domestic legitimacy[14] and to solve the problems inherent in globalisation. On the other hand, it prefers to use bilateral mechanisms for the resolution of interstate or intrastate conflict and views international relations from a realist, or, as some would have it, cultural realist, rather than liberal, perspective.[15]

## A China difference?

Samuel Kim has characterised China's attitude to international organisations as moving from a 'system-transforming' approach during the exclusion period of 1949–70 to a 'system-reforming' approach in the 1970s, to the 'system-maintaining and system-exploiting' approach of the 1980s and 1990s. Similarly, he has argued that China's international organisational behaviour is characterised by a 'maxi-mini approach', that is, a strategy of maximising the benefits of organisational participation through 'state-enhancing' rather than 'state-diminishing' functionalism and minimising normative costs and costs such as dependency and loss of sovereignty.[16]

Yet, is this behaviour an indication of a 'China difference'? It is important not to exaggerate the degree to which it is peculiar to China. A maxi-mini approach is adopted by most states, although most do not share the same history of attempting to transform the international system. Some scholars even appear to conclude that China has a negative attitude to interdependence simply because of its apparently self-interested motivation in acceding to treaties and joining international organisations. Yet most states ratify treaties and join international organisations for reasons of self-interest, or, conversely, do not, as instanced by the failure of the US Congress to ratify the Comprehensive Test Ban Treaty (CTBT) in October 1999 and by US rejection of an increasing number of international treaties in 2001. Moreover, the United States in particular claims special consideration and treatment in international organisations by virtue of its superior power and status.[17]

Nevertheless, the PRC's relative inexperience in the world of international organisations has meant that the last thirty years have involved a steep learning curve, mediated by its own ambitions, changing perceptions and unique perspectives. Its interaction has changed over the years, from the aloof posture of an outsider looking in and sizing up the game, to active participation and a lively, astute promotion of its national interests. China's complex identity as an incipient superpower, a permanent member of the Security Council wielding a veto, a member of the exclusive P5 (Permanent Five) nuclear club, a developing state which is the chief beneficiary of World Bank loans, and a socialist state previously exploited by imperialist powers, has given rise to conflicting concerns and idiosyncratic behaviour. Its Marxist principles and political culture continue to shape its particular motivations and perceptions, as well as its responses to international organisations. In particular, the doctrine of self-reliance and a fierce defence of sovereignty, if less egregious than in the Maoist years, remain constant influences underlying policy responses. Marxism coexists in the Chinese mindset with the more recent ideology of the laissez-faire market system—it has not been replaced.[18] Which particular reference point China invokes to justify its policy decisions depends very much on the context in which those decisions are made, on domestic political considerations and on the receptivity of the international community.

## Tactics

Reflecting this unique character, China adopts a number of historically effective tactics in international organisations. One of them is its self-constructed identity as a 'Club of One'. As Tian Jiyun has pointed out, '[i]n international relations, China adheres to nonalignment and does not engage in formation of military blocs, arms race and military expansion. China upholds an independent foreign policy of peace and a defensive national defence policy'.[19] Within this separateness, China creates a space for itself to bend, according to circumstance or need, towards either the developing or the developed world. The flexibility of its tactics mirrors the flexibility of its ideology. Separateness and ambiguity enhance China's power, despite Gerald Segal's claims to the contrary in his controversial thesis querying whether China 'matters'.[20] For instance, as Barry O'Neill has argued, of all the permanent members of the Security Council, China is the most powerful precisely because it stands alone with a veto at an extreme policy position. Thus, 'it is constantly using its veto or, rather, the threat to veto (actually or only implicitly), and so it is constantly making a difference'.[21] In contrast, the United States is also at an extreme point, but it is arguably less powerful than China because other Western veto members adopt similar policy positions.

China also has a tendency to free-ride where possible and to exploit its developing nation status.[22] Thus, for instance, although a member of the permanent five, China's contribution rate to the United Nation's regular budget is below 1 per cent. This rate, which in 1979 was reduced, at China's request, from 5.5 per cent to 0.79 per cent,[23] compares with the 25 per cent paid by the United States and the 19.9 per cent paid by Japan, a country which is not even a member of the permanent five. China, however, insists on adhering to the 'principles on contributions that we must follow'.[24] The United States is now attempting to increase China's contribution so that its own share may be reduced.

## Principles

Numerous China scholars have noted the importance of moral principles in China's international organisational behaviour.[25] These principles, which contrast with, but also buttress, pragmatic foreign policy goals, include the Five Principles of Peaceful Coexistence, and the rights to national self-determination and independence. Within the context of international organisations, the most important of the Five Principles is sovereignty, which China defines solely in terms of state power.

> China always maintains that all countries, regardless of their size, strength, and wealth, should be equal members of the international community. Peoples of various countries have the right to choose their social systems and development roads commensurate with their national conditions and should be able to decide the affairs of their own countries. All countries in the world must uphold the principles of mutual respect for sovereignty and territorial integrity, non-aggression, non-interference in each other's internal affairs, equality and mutual benefit, and peaceful coexistence.[26]

For this reason, China places heavier emphasis on Article 2, paragraphs 4 and 7, of the UN Charter, which emphasise state sovereignty, including in particular the requirement that 'nothing contained in the present Charter shall authorise the United Nations to intervene in matters which are essentially within the domestic jurisdiction of any state' (Article 2.7), than on Articles 56 and 55, wherein 'all Members pledge to take joint and separate action in cooperation with the Organisation' to promote, *inter alia*, 'universal respect for, and observance of, human rights and fundamental freedoms for all without distinction as to race, sex, language or religion' (Art. 55c). The Chinese formula is therefore far from the restrictive concept of sovereignty articulated by the UN Secretary-General.

> State sovereignty, in its most basic sense, is being redefined by the forces of globalisation and international cooperation. The state is now widely understood to be the servant of its people, and not vice versa. At the same time, individual sovereignty—and by this I mean the human rights and fundamental freedoms of each and every individual as enshrined in the Charter—has been enhanced by a renewed consciousness of the right of every individual to control his or her destiny.[27]

In contrast to its moral principles, China's pragmatic goals are basically to preserve an external environment conducive to its own internal development and to enhance its international status. Yet, the relationship between moral principles and pragmatic policies is also a symbiotic one. China's moral stance disguises its pragmatic goals and blurs the degree to which it is actually prepared to negotiate its sovereignty. Moral, particularly Marxist, principles also provide a bolt hole to which to return when domestic pressures and interests require a more assertive foreign policy stance.

China's emphasis on sovereignty is in part a product of the fact that its past is never very far from its present and future. Its perception of itself as the victim of the imperialist powers, even though it was never completely colonised, means that its foreign policy is strongly oriented towards, and motivated by, past grievances in a way that few other states' policies are. Over the decades, and in spite of growing international power, its sense of historical grievance has become a vehicle of the nationalism which sporadically erupts, primarily as a response to domestic pressures.

Emphasis on sovereignty is, moreover, a reflection of the extent to which China's international interaction carries with it considerable domestic, normative costs. For liberal democracies, cooperative behaviour and acceptance of interdependence is not as costly because such behaviour normally coheres with domestically observed standards and goals. In China's case, international cooperation and interdependence often conflict with the perceived needs of domestic stability, with the authority of Party leaders and with the norms of domestic culture. This explains the extreme sensitivity of China's international policies to the exigencies of domestic political pressures, whether they be disputes among political factions or manifestations of social instability. Even the most outward-looking of China's political leaders, like Premier Zhu Rongji, are alert to any signs that foreign or trade policies might have a negative domestic impact, and will change those policies accordingly. Needless to say, such sensitivity alters existing patterns of compliance, and, in particular, is likely to present problems after China's WTO accession. While routine activities in international organisations help stabilise the nature of China's participation, international bodies of a more political character often reflect the volatility of its policy shifts.

China's attitude to the international rule of law and its behaviour within international organisations is heavily influenced by its attitude to the domestic rule of law and to its political culture. The reliance of its domestic political culture on ethics rather than law, moral consensus rather than judicial procedure, and benevolent government rather than on checks and balances, has its resonances in China's international behaviour.[28] So too have domestic notions of hierarchy, power and personal relationships (*guanxi*). As in its domestic law, moreover, the force of precedent in its practice of international law is weak. Although China criticises other states for not following precedent, or for establishing an unacceptable precedent, in its own international organisational behaviour it often does not invoke the same standards of consistency.

Finally, while exercising increasing power and influence, and despite the gradual erosion of its Marxist convictions, China is still inclined to stress the North–South divide and to lament undue Western influence on the international system. Thus, in its participation in international organisations, it is not only motivated by a system-maintaining and system-exploiting approach, but also, paradoxically, as it has become more powerful and more confident, has effected a partial return to a system-reforming approach, which in its view redresses the imbalances and injustices of the past. It is also concerned to make a shift from the current unipolar concentration of global power to a multipolar world. International organisations have become one vehicle for this reform agenda.

The following sections of this chapter comprise an analysis of the state enhancing/protecting and global reforming aspects of China's participation in international organisations and, as evidence of the complex mix of power and responsibility in its global behaviour, a brief discussion of the process of its accession to the WTO.

## State enhancement/protection via international organisations

### Protecting and extending China's sovereignty

Membership of international organisations helps resolve issues of China's disputed sovereignty. Despite the universally recognised principle of self-determination, China's sovereignty over Tibet and Xinjiang is protected by the positions it takes in international organisations, such as the ASEAN Regional Forum, and through its veto power in the UN Security Council, on issues of self-determination and humanitarian intervention. The close connection between China's participation in international organisations and its reaffirmation of sovereignty over Taiwan has been well documented by Gerald Chan[29] and is illustrated in Taiwan's eighth failed attempt to enter the United Nations in August 2000, and its fourth failed bid to enter the World Health Organisation in May 2000. Equally, China's pressure on the United Nations in 1999 to restate its one-China policy was part of its push for sovereignty over Taiwan, as was its call in July 2000 for the inclusion of the 'One China' concept in a key text on its entry to the WTO. UN consciousness of PRC sensitivities has permeated all aspects of foreign policy, including the critical issue of humanitarian assistance for the Taiwan earthquake in September 1999. UN relief experts were even obliged to obtain China's formal prior approval before Taiwan's request for assistance could be met.[30] The only international organisations in which China has been prepared to adjust its stringent refusal to allow Taiwan joint membership have been Asia Pacific Economic Cooperation (APEC), the Asian Development Bank and the WTO.[31] In the finance and trade regimes, in other words, China is not as insistent on sovereignty as it is in the human rights, environmental and security regimes.

China's sovereignty is also protected by its participation in the negotiation of treaties or decisions with which it is not in agreement. For instance, one of the reasons given for its application to join the WTO was that it would enable China to 'take a direct part in formulating trade regulations and rid itself of the disadvantageous position of passive participation'.[32] Again, China chose to be closely involved in drafting the draft Optional Protocol to the Convention Against Torture, rather than simply failing to accede to it once it was formally adopted. Its strict position on sovereignty remained a barrier to drafting progress, since, together with Cuba, it insisted that the work of any investigatory UN mission to prisons and prisoners should be subject to national laws.[33] China was also closely involved in drafting the ILO's 1998 Declaration on Fundamental Principles and Rights at Work, despite its objections that the Declaration obliged members that had not ratified the relevant ILO Conventions to undertake the same obligations as those that had. After obtaining an assurance from the ILO that support for the Declaration would not mean that its standards immediately became applicable, China voted for it.[34]

China's preoccupation with protecting its sovereignty is also reflected in its use of international organisations to enhance the international legitimacy of domestic policies. For instance, both the World Bank and the United Nations Environment Programme (UNEP) have publicly endorsed a number of official Chinese economic and social programs which have been both internationally and domestically controversial. Although the Bank later withdrew its proffered loan to resettle Han Chinese in traditional Tibetan lands in Qinghai province, the program was initially supported by the World Bank despite international protest, while the domestically controversial privatisation of housing was defended by Klaus Topfer, Executive Director of UNEP and acting executive director of Habitat.[35]

## Projecting and enhancing international status

International organisations have promoted China's international status in various ways—through its chairmanship of UN conferences, and its hosting of international conferences, such as the Fourth World Conference on Women in Beijing held in September 1995, and the forthcoming APEC Leaders' Forum, to be held in Shanghai in 2001. As demonstrated in the recent election of Shi Jiuyong as Vice-President of the International Court of Justice (ICJ), Chinese officials have even been appointed into senior positions of organisations whose jurisdiction they do not accept.[36] China's superior status has also been reflected in its seniority and extensive voting rights in the World Bank and IMF.[37] At the same time, its aspirations for senior organisational positions within leading international organisations have had a constraining effect, leading it to modify its more extreme behaviour and to exhibit compliance in the interests of maintaining or obtaining organisational status. For instance, China's ambitions for executive status in the ILO have had a socialising impact on its participation in the ILO Governing Body Committee on Freedom of Association (CFA), increasing its readiness to accept core labour standards.[38]

## Maintaining China's strategic independence

China participates fully in the main international and regional nuclear non-proliferation and arms control organisations, the Conference on Disarmament (CD), the UN First Committee, the International Atomic Energy Agency (IAEA) and the ASEAN Regional Forum (ARF). In the CD, it exercises its dual role as a member of the five official Nuclear Weapons States and as supporter of the Non-Nuclear Weapons States. This enhances its ability to negotiate particular issues of concern, such as the prevention of an arms race in outer space, and, more recently, to oppose amendment of the Anti-Ballistic Missile Treaty.[39] It has also used the ASEAN Regional Forum to attack the US-proposed theatre missile defence system (TMD) for Asia and the national missile defence system (NMD) for the continental United States.[40] As evidence of its internalisation of the norms of the security regime, it has invoked the authority of international law and international treaties, particularly the ABM treaty, to critique the US proposal.[41]

Through its position as one of the permanent five of the UN Security Council, China also exercises its influence on major global issues of weapons proliferation, humanitarian intervention and peacekeeping. Of the 26 resolutions on which China abstained in the Security Council between 1990–95, 17 were explicitly enforcement measures taken by the Council under the authority vested in it under Chapter VII of the UN Charter. Three related to Iraq, three to the Federal Republic of Yugoslavia, six concerned Bosnia-Herzegovina, two Libya, one Haiti and two Rwanda.[42] In this arena, its policies have been more self-protective than proactive. As Nigel Thalakada observes,

> [t]he pattern that emerges thus far with regard to China's abstentions on Chapter VII resolutions is one of Chinese reluctance to condone the use of the Security Council's enforcement authority to undertake military action

> against a member state (as in the case of Iraq), apply sanctions against a member state (as in the cases of Libya and Yugoslavia), undertake peace enforcement and peacebuilding (as in the case of Bosnia, Haiti and Rwanda) and establish an international tribunal to prosecute widespread human rights abuses (as in the case of Rwanda).[43]

China's position on humanitarian intervention, which is primarily related to the protection of its own sovereignty, is of particular importance in the new era of concern about human rights in situations of domestic ethnic conflict or separatist movements. Its stance was crucial in the 1999 Security Council deliberations on East Timor. Although it finally voted in the Security Council in support of the INTERFET role in East Timor, had Indonesia refused to accept the entry of international peacekeepers into East Timor, the likelihood of China's veto of a Security Council resolution to introduce troops without Jakarta's permission may well have prevented any international assistance to the territory.

Therefore, the UN Secretary-General's path-breaking address on the challenges of humanitarian intervention to the UN General Assembly (UNGA) on 20 September 1999 represented a distinct challenge to China's concept of absolute sovereignty.[44] Reacting swiftly, China's Foreign Minister, Tang Jiaxuan, pointed out that the 'new interventionism of the so-called 'human rights over state sovereignty'' constituted 'hegemonism in essence'.[45] His response reflected China's increasing sensitivity about the possibility, in a new age of technological warfare in which war is 'fightable and easily winnable' without excessive casualties, of Western humanitarian intervention in China, particularly in the Chinese controlled regions of Tibet and Xinjiang and in Taiwan.[46] China subsequently opposed, if unsuccessfully, the resolution to set up a UN inquiry into violations of human rights in East Timor.[47] The recommendations in the Inquiry's report that the United Nations should set up a war crimes tribunal for East Timor were not endorsed by the Secretary-General, reportedly because Russia and China would be certain to exercise their veto rights.[48] True to expectations, on 1 February 2000, Chinese Foreign Ministry spokesman Zhu Bangzao announced China's opposition to the establishment of the UN tribunal.[49] This was despite the fact that the question of China's cooperation with the United Nations on matters of humanitarian intervention was one of the main topics addressed during the Secretary-General's visit to China in September 1999.

## Preserving an external environment conducive to its own internal development goals

China has long argued that a peaceful external environment is essential to the realisation of its economic modernisation. This instrumental use of international norms is also reflected in China's support for the value of 'cooperation', as opposed to 'confrontation', in international human rights organisations. The need for 'cooperation', for instance, has proved a useful rallying cry to deflect a resolution critical of China's human rights in the UN Commission on Human Rights, and has challenged the normal adversarial procedures accepted within the United Nations. Along with like-minded developing states, China also uses the concept of consensus, with its potential for stalemate, in international organisations to further its interests.[50]

## Promoting internal developmental aims through foreign investment, expanded trade, technology transfer, and developmental assistance.

The main forums meeting these needs are the International Monetary Fund (IMF), World Bank, Asian Development Bank (ADB), Asia Pacific Economic Cooperation Forum (APEC), United Nations Children's Fund (UNICEF), United Nations Development Programme (UNDP) and United Nations Conference on Trade and Development (UNCTAD). As will be seen, the World Trade Organization (WTO) is a less reliable forum for promoting its interests, because of the perceived risks its promotion of free trade entails for China's domestic stability.

China has been the World Bank's most acclaimed and successful client. It is regarded as a responsible, cooperative member and is presented as a model for other developing countries.[51] Since 1992, it has been the Bank's largest borrower of investment finance. Conversely, the Bank is China's largest source of long-term foreign capital. Its projects have supported China's economic reform process, targeting poverty alleviation, infrastructure development and human resources development. Cumulative lending to China by the World Bank Group between 1981 and 30 June 1999 is about US$33.2 billion, of which US$23.3 billion is from the International Bank for Reconstruction and Development (IBRD) and US$9.9 billion is from the International Development Association (IDA). This amounts to a substantial proportion of the total of US$400 billion lent to members (currently 180) since the Bank's establishment. The Bank has supported over 220 development projects in China, involving all major sectors of the economy and most Chinese regions. On the other hand, this amounts to only US$2.50 per person in China, representing the 'lowest proportion of lending per capita in the entire East Asia region'. [52]

China's loss of eligibility for International Development Assistance (IDA) loans, involving a drop in lending of about 25 per cent, has slightly modified this comfortable picture.[53] Reliance on IBRD loans will make it more difficult for poorer provinces to repay since the IBRD charges interest for loans, demands a shorter amortisation period, and has no policy for debt rescheduling. Despite this, the World Bank expects to lend China between US$5–7 billion in the next three years, of which at least US$1 billion will go to poor inland provinces.[54] In the new century, both the World Bank and the Asian Development Bank plan to intensify their cooperation with China in the area of poverty reduction and the environment.[55] The World Bank remains highly dependent on China's success as a role model for developing countries, and as a model client.

Since 1979, when China first accepted assistance from UNDP, that body has assisted China in 840 projects at a cost of US$500 million. The UN Children's Fund has cooperated on a total of 150 projects costing $300 million.[56] Moreover, despite the fact that China is not a member of Organisation for Economic Cooperation and Development (OECD), that organisation has described China as its 'most important cooperative partner'. The two sides have collaborated to study enterprise reform, train workers in the Chinese tax departments and analyse statistics, as well as cooperating in areas of agriculture, education, environment and investment.

China also exerts inter-organisational pressures to extend its economic power, exploiting any rivalries or functional overlap between organisations. Speaking at the United Nations General Assembly, the Chinese Foreign Minister called on the United Nations to hold a special conference on economic globalisation because 'the developing countries have the right to equal participation in world economic decision-making and formulation of relevant rules. In the new round of negotiations that will soon begin in the World Trade Organization, the reasonable demands of developing countries should be fully reflected'.[57] The overlapping jurisdictions of the World Bank and the ADB also allow China freedom to negotiate the terms and nature of the loan projects it selects from the ADB.

Finally, China benefits from (often conflicting) advice, information, technology transfer and research provided by international organisations. For instance, UNCTAD's advice on WTO was that China should resist opening its markets to any further international competition until it had undertaken further economic reforms.[58] The ADB supported China's entry, but argued its case on the basis that China's cautious approach to liberalisation of capital controls had insulated it from the worst of the Asian financial crisis.[59] It thereby differentiated its position from that of the IMF.[60]

International organisations are also sources of pressure for change. For instance, in September 1999, the IMF policy-setting interim committee asked India and China, as well as other developing nations, to accelerate 'key structural reforms' in taxation, banking and corporate sectors, establish an effective legal system, protect property rights and ensure 'greater transparency' and accountability in government activities.[61] In some cases, as its support for the WTO indicates, China has even looked to international organisations to impose the necessary external regulatory authority legitimising wholesale domestic reforms, which the Chinese leadership would be incapable of achieving through its own efforts alone.[62] Its readiness to import international norms and procedures and, by implication, to renegotiate the boundaries of state sovereignty, is more evident in the international political economy regime than, for instance, in the human rights regime.

The search for power can thus lead to widely varied outcomes. On the one hand, it can create obstacles to interdependence, and, on the other, it can give states a stake in the international system and create pressures for socialisation. Equally, sovereignty concerns can have an integrating effect, as well as constitute the source of non-cooperation. In China's case, however, power is not sought through conventional channels only.

## Global reform via international organisations

Because of China's increasing orientation to the market economy, its growing military and commercial power and its concomitant tendency to link its fortunes with the developed world and other major powers, China scholars have tended in recent years to downplay its earlier revolutionary aspirations, ascribing instances of non-cooperation with the international community to nationalistic rather than ideological wellsprings. Yet there are strong reasons to argue the continuing relevance of the Maoist heritage. China's leaders still appeal to Maoist principles of international law and still invoke its traditional, if now modified, identification with the interests of the developing world.

### Impacting on international law

China recognises the universal applicability of generally recognised international law, even if it underplays the importance of customary international law.[63] Yet, it still upholds Maoist principles which are seen not only to complement generally recognised international law, but even to be constitutive of international law. In a clear enunciation of China's policy on international organisations as it affected international law, former Chairman of the China International Law Society, Huan Xiang, pointed out in 1983 that, since 'Third World countries' were now in the majority, 'they have an important place in shaping and developing the principles, rules and regulations of international law'.[64] Participation in international organisations was seen as one way of ensuring this impact

> If the resolutions of international organisations, especially those of the UN General Assembly, are regarded as sources of international law, the position of the Third World countries as participants in the international law-making process is even more prominent, because they constitute a majority in international organisations and are playing increasingly important roles in the UN General Assembly. In fact, the resolutions containing legal documents of the General Assembly have all been initiated by Third World countries and approved with their support. Their backing has obviously given such documents greater legal significance and thus promoted the development of international law. The Third World countries have become new creators of international law both in name and in reality. As L. Henkin puts it, the new states are now both the new subjects of international law and its new masters.[65]

Huan saw the Third World as having impacted on international law in a number of ways. The most outstanding contribution of the Third World was seen to be the affirmation of national self-determination as a legal principle. The second contribution was the formulation of the Five Principles of Peaceful Coexistence as 'fundamental principles of international law'.[66] Moreover, the Third World had 'strengthened and developed' the principle of sovereignty, including the principle of economic sovereignty, or the principle of permanent sovereignty over natural resources. Apart from such fundamental principles, it had precipitated changes on the question of state responsibility and on the idea that the giving of economic aid is a 'legal responsibility' rather than a 'dispensation of favour'. It had emphasised the importance of 'territorial integrity' and had played a role in 'substituting a new law of the sea for the old' by developing 'the idea about the right over 200 nautical miles of sea areas'. It had opposed the unequal treaties imposed on them by colonial powers and had made contributions to the laws of war.[67]

These principles continue to animate Chinese international organisational policy and its attitude to international law. The Chairman of the National People's Congress, Li Peng, has argued the importance of a mastery of international law for a developing socialist state like China.[68] Contemporary scholars like Wan Xia and Lu Song, however, still claim not only that China adheres to, follows and applies international law, but also that it develops it. They argue that, because of the anomalies within international law and the development of new situations and problems, new 'rational' models of international law need to be established. The Five Principles of Peaceful Coexistence are still viewed as one of China's central contributions to international law. So too is Deng Xiaoping's notion of a new politico-economic international order (NIEO), based on state sovereignty, self-reliance, anti-hegemonism, equality, cooperation and the peaceful resolution of disputes.[69] Thus, President Jiang Zemin has insisted that the Five Principles should constitute the basis of the new international order and has reiterated support for Deng Xiaoping's goals.[70]

## Representing the Third World, redistributing international power, promoting a certain conception of international order and reorienting international norms

As a 'Club of One' in the United Nations, China is not the leader or spokesman of a group of developing states. Rather, it achieves a balance between promoting its own fundamental interests and representing those of the Third World. It does this by promoting Third World perspectives in the United Nations on issues in which it has a national interest—issues such as security, human rights, development and the environment. In the Conference on Disarmament (CD), for instance, it sees itself as supporting the NAM (Non-Aligned Movement) states through its non-first use policy, and through its identity as the only nuclear weapons state standing for the complete prohibition and destruction of nuclear weapons—a position it believes the Permanent 4 are now beginning to accept themselves. On the other hand, according to China, the

NAM states oppose possession of any nuclear weapons, a position China cannot accept. In addition, some NAM states fail to distinguish between the policies of the different states in the Permanent Five (P5), and propose a time-bound nuclear disarmament program which, China says, is 'not realistic'.[71] The NAM states have also been useful to China in advocating positions with which it agrees but which it does not wish to espouse openly. In the early years of its participation in the Conference on Disarmament (CD), for instance, it resorted to free-riding, falling in behind states like India and the Soviet Union. By contrast, its more recent disarmament diplomacy has been described as 'relatively open', involving frequent interventions in CD debates.[72]

Where China's interests do not cohere with those of the Third World, on the other hand, it remains silent. While it has vigorously supported Third World candidates for the secretary-generalship of the United Nations, for instance, it is not so outspoken about the formula for the reform of the Security Council, supporting the idea of greater Third World representation but not of an extension of access to the veto.[73] A Chinese diplomat at the United Nations has stated that only when developed and developing states have a 'more balanced representation' in the Security Council will the candidacy of Japan and Germany be resolved.[74]

Yet, withal their often divergent interests, the developing states represent an important power base for China in its effort to shift the current locus of global power from the United States to a more differentiated, multipolar world. For this reason, China has used its membership of multilateral financial and development institutions to attempt to redistribute international power in the interests of the developing world. For instance, Dai Xianglong, Governor of the People's Bank, has urged the IMF to take account in its reforms of the voices of developing countries.[75] China has also been attracted to regional solutions, partly with a view to securing its own backyard. For instance, it has been willing to consider Japan's proposal to establish an East Asia Monetary Fund, and has called for greater regional cooperation in trade, financial, investment, scientific and technological areas. At China's initiative, a Dialogue of Finance and Central Bank Deputies involving ASEAN,

China, Japan and the Republic of Korea (ROK) was launched in March 1999 under the auspices of ASEAN.[76] On 10 April 2000, China formally acceded to the Bangkok Agreement—Asia's only preferential tariff arrangement—thereby marking its debut in regional trading agreements.

China has likewise insisted on the responsibility of the developed states, as the chief agents and beneficiaries of environmental degradation, to assume the major burden of expenditure for the rehabilitation of the global environment. It has not, however, refused to contribute to the costs. Rather, it has disputed the amount and terms of its contributions, as well as arguing for the rights of developing states generally.[77]

In international human rights organisations, China has sought to promote the values of developing states and to question the universal applicability of international human rights norms. This is particularly the case in public and political forums like the UN Human Rights Commission, which not only provide a platform for China's projection of its moral principles, but which also have the potential to publicly threaten its sovereignty. At the normative level, in the 1993 UN World Human Rights Conference in Vienna, and yearly sessions of the UN Human Rights Commission and its Sub-Commission, China has stressed the principles of state sovereignty and non-interference, and the cultural relativist idea that each state has a right to its own interpretation of human rights. It has also emphasised the rights to subsistence and to development. Although the latter rights are important, China has seen them as prior rights, which must be satisfied before the realisation of civil and political rights. This conflicts with the UN principle, entrenched in numerous international instruments, of the indivisibility, interdependence and universality of civil, political, economic, social and cultural rights.

For a number of reasons, China has not been successful in its efforts to establish a new priority of rights. At the procedural level, however, through resort to the no-action motion to avoid resolutions against China in the Human Rights Commission and Sub-Commission, through its attack on non-governmental organisation (NGOs) and country situation resolutions, and its success in 1997 in bilateralising the multilateral Human Rights Commission process, China has helped undermine the principles of the non-selectivity and universality of the application of human rights norms.[78] Its sensitivity on issues of sovereignty has also made it reluctant in this regime, as in others, to allow international bodies to monitor conditions on Chinese soil.[79]

## Interdependence?

The complexity of China's mix of responsibility within the international community and its simultaneous concern to project its power, interests and national values, to maintain its independence, represent the interests of developing states and safeguard its domestic stability is no better exemplified than in the process of its accession to the WTO. The significance of its entry will not lie solely in its impact on the WTO and on the globalisation project generally. It represents China's most calculated gamble in the history of its entry into international organisations and its most unqualified leap into economic interdependence. Not only has China made sweeping concessions to the international community during its multilateral and bilateral negotiations, it has taken unprecedented steps to renegotiate the terms of its own sovereignty.

Why has China sought to join the WTO? Status, trading opportunities, the pressures of globalisation and the desire to deepen restructuring within China are all motives. The WTO is seen as an 'important carrier of globalisation', which will allow China to 'become a respectable member in the open international economic system' and enable it to enjoy equal trading treatment and take part in formulating trade regulations. The WTO will have the crucial function of opening up China's services industry. It will link China with the global economy, 'bring about rational allocation of resources', allow more Chinese enterprises out of the country and facilitate foreign investment in China.[80] Moreover, since China is not a member of any regional trading bloc, it will rely on the WTO to maintain its own competitiveness. Finally, China clearly hopes accession might facilitate better relations with Taiwan.[81]

In the interests of attaining these goals, however, China has had to, and will continue to, bear considerable costs. President Jiang Zemin has insisted, through his spokesman, that 'we absolutely will not sacrifice our national interests just for the sake of membership of the WTO'. [82] For this reason, throughout the fifteen years of accession negotiations, China has persisted in its request to receive the benefits due to a developing country in an incremental manner. Nevertheless, China's accession to WTO will subject it to the WTO Agreement, requiring it to enforce the WTO Understanding. China will become vulnerable to the WTO dispute system and to the courts. WTO membership will introduce enhanced competition within China and will further erode central control over commercial policy. It will require numerous policy changes, including significant reductions in tariffs, removal of nontariff barriers and quotas, the opening up of China's service sector, further protection of intellectual property rights and the elimination of many barriers to trade in agricultural products.[83] It will therefore create severe social strains and exacerbate the already existing unemployment problems. It will require increased legal transparency, and greater political openness and accountability. Moreover, under the bilateral agreement negotiated in November 1999 with the United States, China made asymmetrical concessions in favour of the United States.[84] In particular, the unparalleled, extensive and prolonged safeguards and anti-dumping provisions that the United States negotiated will be available to other WTO members under the Most Favoured Nation (MFN) principle.

Chinese economist Gao Shangquan has identified four challenges that WTO membership poses for China. It will constitute a challenge to the competitiveness of some Chinese industries and companies on the world market, a challenge to China's administrative system, a challenge to China's industrial structure, and a challenge to the Chinese government's macroeconomic control.[85] China's accession will bring challenges not only for China, but for the whole WTO system. In the process of implementing the rules, numerous obstacles will be met. These include problems of the insufficiency of WTO regulations to accommodate a non-market economy, including the inadequacy of existing surveillance machinery; problems of cultural mismatch between China and other WTO members, leading to differences in the interpretation of rules; the inadequacy of Chinese domestic financial and legal institutions; interference from, and non-compliance of, China's sub-national authorities; general problems of domestic implementation; and the danger that Western WTO members will initially engage in excessive dispute resolution with China.[86] The main variable throughout will be China's domestic stability. This is now a critical source of concern, in view of Zhu Rongji's failure to create a social welfare system funded through investments in capital markets to protect the unemployed and other groups rendered vulnerable by accession.[87] If during the process WTO members place too much pressure on China, if its economic restructuring is pushed too fast and social stability is imperilled, domestic turmoil will result. If, on the other hand, in the interests of domestic stability, China does not fully implement the reforms it has promised within the accepted timetable, it is liable to end up in constant dispute with other WTO members, and globalisation will be the loser.[88]

## Conclusion

In its participation in international organisations, China, like most states, seeks to maximise its power and interests. Again, like most states, it demonstrates some preparedness to accept the costs as well as the benefits of participation and to assume some responsibility within the international system. While its theoretical position on sovereignty may be absolute, in practice its approach to sovereignty is more flexible, except where debate concerns the right of the international community to enforce collective rights like self-determination. When national interest and the principle of absolute sovereignty are seen to coincide, China makes a theoretical statement about the absolute nature of sovereignty. But, in general its power is enhanced by its preparedness to negotiate its sovereignty, rather than to impose blanket vetos. For this reason, since 1981 it has preferred not to use its veto in the Security Council, but obtains numerous advantages from hinting it might do so.

China's need for moral stature and a good international reputation thus helps tone down the realism of its foreign policy, both in appearance and reality. In many cases, this does not mean that it has internalised international norms, but that it is prepared to be more pragmatic about its interests than its statements of principle would suggest. To that extent, it has been influenced by the rigorous process of participation in international organisations. Despite the costs it incurs, it continues to support international organisations and multilateralism and has acknowledged the inevitability of global interdependence, accepting that, just as the world needs China, China needs the world.

At the same time, China's readiness to accept the costs and responsibility of participation must be balanced against major problems it has experienced in implementing its obligations under international treaty and organisational rules. The first is its abiding concern with sovereignty, a problem permeating most of its decisions relating to organisational cooperation and causing intransigence in cases of alleged 'interference', such as proposals by international organisations to monitor Chinese conditions *in situ*. This is a particular problem in the human rights and security regimes. The second is its difficulty implementing in practice the domestic legislation which it introduces in compliance with its international obligations. This is a notable problem in the human rights and environmental regimes, and may well prove a problem in its relations with the WTO. Third is its tendency to free-ride where possible, using elements of its complex identity, such as its status as a developing nation, to plead special treatment.

However, the main obstacle to international cooperation, apart from an enduring preoccupation with domestic stability, lies in China's complex perception of its global responsibilities. While it is now tending to link its fortunes much more with the developed world and with other powerful states, it still recognises an obligation to act and speak on behalf of developing states. This is because identification with the interests of the developing world remains a constituent element of its own power. In other words, precisely because of considerations of power, China's sense of responsibility to the international community is double-edged.

While clearly committed to participation in international organisations and to being seen as a cooperative member, it still conceives a continuing responsibility to defend developing states, to forge new international norms, rules and procedures and to oversee the redistribution of power in the international system. The balance China achieves between power and responsibility is therefore unstable and dependent on time, issue area, foreign policy environment and domestic political pressures. Given the complexities of its motivations, reflecting a mix of self-interest, conformity and dissent, given the increasing dissonance between its international power and its domestic volatility, and in view of its deep-rooted political culture and the still essentially introspective focus of its foreign policy, the unpredictability that has characterised China's international organisational policies and behaviour over the last three decades is likely to persist.

## Notes

1. For a history of China's growing participation, see Wang Xingfang (ed.), *Zhongguo yu Lianheguo: jinian Lianheguo chengli wushi zhounian* [China and the United Nations: commemorating the 50th Anniversary of the founding of the United Nations] (Beijing: *Shijie zhishi* chubanshe, 1995); and *Shijie zhishi nianjian 1997/1998* [The Yearbook of World Knowledge, 1997–98] (Beijing: *Shjijie zhishi* chubanshe, 1998).
2. Speaking on the history of China's 50-year diplomacy in late 1999, China's Vice-Premier Qian Qichen identified the moment China's legal rights were restored in the United Nations in 1971 as marking the resumption of his country's status in the international community. See 'Chinese Vice-Premier on China's 50-Year Diplomacy', *Xinhua News Agency*, 24 September 1999, *Reuters China News*, 24 September 1999.
3. See also the excellent and informative study of China and international regimes, Elizabeth Economy and Michel Oksenberg (eds), *China Joins the World: progress and prospects* (New York: Council on Foreign Relations Press, 1999); David S.G. Goodman and Gerald Segal (eds), *China Rising: nationalism and interdependence* (London: Routledge, 1997); John R. Faust and Judith F. Kornberg, *China in World Politics* (Boulder: Lynne Rienner, 1995), 207–46; James V. Feinerman, 'Chinese participation in the international legal order:

rogue elephant or team player?' *China Quarterly*, no. 141 (March 1995):186–210; Jeannette Greenfield, *China's Practice of the Law of the Sea* (Oxford: Clarendon Press, 1992); Barbara J. Sinkule, *Implementing Environmental Policy in China* (Westport: Praeger, 1995); and Ann Kent, 'China, international organisations and regimes: the ILO as a case study in organisational learning', *Pacific Affairs*, 70, no. 4 (Winter 1997–98):517–32.

4 According to Union of International Associations (ed.), *Yearbook of International Organisations 1999/2000*, vol. 2 (Munchen: K.G. Saur, 2000), 'an organisation is intergovernmental if it is established by signature of an agreement engendering obligations between governments, whether or not that agreement is eventually published'. By contrast, according to ECOSOC Res. 288 (X), an international non-governmental organisation (INGO) is one not established by intergovernmental agreement. It must also be genuinely international in character. See Ibid., 1477.

5 For statistics, see Idem, *Yearbook of International Organisations 2000/2001*, vol. 2 (Munich: K.G. Saur, 2000), 1468–69. For specific, organisation-based monographs, see Samuel S. Kim, *China, the United Nations and World Order* (Princeton: Princeton University Press, 1979); Harold K. Jacobson and Michel Oksenberg, *China's Participation in the IMF, the World Bank, and GATT* (Ann Arbor: University of Michigan Press, 1990); and Ann Kent, *China, the United Nations and Human Rights: the limits of compliance* (Philadelphia, University of Pennsylvania Press, 1999). The main recent work on China and IGOs has related to the immediate problem areas of its relations with General Agreement on Tariffs and Trade (GATT), World Trade Organisation (WTO) and the non-proliferation treaty (NPT), or has been thematic, regime-based research.

6 The importance of the United Nations in particular was acknowledged in the lead up to celebrations for the fiftieth anniversary of the PRC, when China's Foreign Minister, Tang Jiaxuan, described the role of the United Nations in international affairs as 'irreplaceable' and observed that no matter how the international situation changed, the purpose and principles of the UN Charter and recognised international norms remained realistic and valid at present and in the future. See 'Chinese foreign minister meets UN Chief Annan', *Xinhua News Agency*, 24 September 1999, *Reuters China News*, 24 September 1999.

7 Abram Chayes and Antonia Handler Chayes, *The New Sovereignty: compliance with international regulatory agreements* (Cambridge: Harvard University Press, 1995), 5, 1–33.

8 Samuel S. Kim, 'China's international organisational behaviour', in Thomas W. Robinson and David Shambaugh (eds), *Chinese Foreign Policy: theory and practice* (Oxford: Clarendon Press, 1994), 405.

9 Kent, *China, the United Nations and Human Rights*, 27.

10 See Wang Yanjun, 'Xuexi Jiang Zemin guanyu xianghu yicun di lunshu' [Study Jiang Zemin's remarks on interdependence], in *Waijiao xueyuan xuebao*, no. 2 (1999), 36–40.

11 He stated, '[a]s permanent members of the UN Security Council, both China and the UK shoulder major responsibilities for world peace and development, and our two peoples should, together with other people of the world, make due contribution to the establishment of a fair and equitable new international political and economic order'. See 'Chinese President at royal banquet on fair and equitable new world order', *Xinhua News Agency*, 19 October 1999, *Reuters China News*, 20 October 1999.

12 See, for instance, Qin Yaqing, 'Guoji zhidu yu guoji hezuo—fanxiang xinziyou zhidu zhuyi' [International regimes and international cooperation–neorealism revisited], *Waijiao xueyuan bao*, no. 1 (1998), 45–6.

13 See the excellent analysis in Russell Leigh Moses', 'Chinese views on globalisation', *China Online*, available from http://www.chinaonline.com/commentary, accessed 26 June 2000.

14 Yoichi Funabashi, Michel Oksenberg and Heinrich Weiss, *An Emerging China in a World of Interdependence* (New York: The Trilateral Commission, 1994), 55.

15 Wang Jisi, 'International relations theory and the study of Chinese foreign policy: a Chinese perspective', in Robinson and Shambaugh (eds), *Chinese Foreign Policy*, 498; and Alastair Iain Johnston, *Cultural Realism: strategic culture and grand strategy in Chinese history* (Princeton: Princeton University Press, 1995).

16 See Kim, 'China's international organisational behaviour', 431, 425.

17 In particular, see John Braithwaite and Peter Drahos, *Global Business Regulation* (Cambridge: Cambridge University Press, 2000), 178–83, 196–98, 218–21.

18 See, for instance, Raj Bhala, 'China's WTO entry in labor surplus and Marxist terms', Paper Delivered at the Conference, 'China and the World Trade Organisation Conference', Faculty of Law, Australian National University, Canberra, 16–17 March 2001.

19 'Chinese parliament deputy advocates equality in international community', *Xinhua News Agency*, 11 October 1999, *Reuters China News*, 12 October 1999.

20 Gerald Segal, 'Does China matter?' *Foreign Affairs*, 78, no. 5 (September–October 1999):24–36.

21 Barry O'Neill, 'Power and satisfaction in the Security Council', in B. Russett (ed.), *The Once and Future Security Council* (New York: St Martin's Press, 1997), 75.

22 In addition, Elizabeth Economy and Michel Oksenberg list some other notable tactics—avoiding enduring commitments, making compliance with China's objectives the litmus test for friendly relations, mobilising support for China's position in developing countries; and capturing the moral high ground and placing the interlocutor on the defensive. See Economy and Oksenberg (eds), *China Joins the World*, 25.

23 Statistics in Kim, 'China and the United Nations', in Economy and Oksenberg (eds), *China Joins the World*, 65–68.

24 Greg Torode, 'Mission impossible for UN dues', *South China Morning Post*, 19 March 2000, *Reuters China News*, 19 March 2000.

25 In particular, see Shih Chih-yu, *China's Just World: the morality of foreign policy* (Boulder: Lynne Rienner, 1993); and Kim, 'China's international organisational behaviour'.

26 'Chinese parliament deputy advocates equality in international community'.

27 United Nations, 'Secretary-General presents his annual report to General Assembly', UN Press Release SG/SM/7136 GA/9596 (Washington, DC: United Nations, 20 September 1999).

28 Wang Jisi, 'International relations theory', 493.

29 Gerald Chan, *China and International Organisations: participation in non-governmental organisations since 1971* (Hong Kong: Oxford University Press, 1989).

30 Stephanie Nebehay, 'Foreign rescuers go to Taiwan as UN seeks okay', *Reuters China News*, 21 September 1999.

31 For instance, Taiwan joined the WTO after China's accession as 'Chinese Taipei' ('Zhonghua Taibei').

32 Gong Wen and Zhang Xiangchen, 'Zhongguo jiaru shimao zuzhi dashi shuping' [Comment on general trend of China's entry into WTO], *People's Daily*, 7 May 1999, 1.

33 Kent, *China, the United Nations and Human Rights*, 105–6.

34 Ibid., 138–9.

35 He observed that '[w]ith the introduction of market elements into the housing issue, people are stimulated to save more money and more flats will be built, the thorny problem of housing will be

solved gradually'. See 'China's environmental protection progressing, says United Nations official', *Xinhua News Agency*, 22 September 1999, *Reuters China News*, 22 September 1999.

36 China has never subjected itself to the jurisdiction of the ICJ since it resumed the China seat in the United Nations. See Kong Qingqiang, 'Enforcing WTO agreements in China: an illusion or reality?', Paper Delivered at the Conference, 'China and the World Trade Organisation', Faculty of Law, Australian National University Canberra, 16–17 March 2001.

37 For instance, in the IMF, China's vote constitutes 2.2 per cent of the total Fund votes, compared with the vote of 2.43 per cent commanded by the entire South Asia group of Bangladesh, Bhutan, India and Sri Lanka.

38 Kent, *China, the United Nations and Human Rights*, 136–39.

39 United Nations, 'Russian Federation, China stress importance of addressing prevention of outer space arms race in disarmament conference', UN Press Release DCF/390 (Washington DC: United Nations, 24 February 2000).

40 'US plan for missile defence system attacked at ASEAN regional forum', *Kyodo News*, 27 July 2000, *Reuters China News*, 27 July 2000.

41 For instance, Sha Zukang, Head of the Arms Control Department of the Chinese Foreign Ministry, reaffirmed China's support for the UN General Assembly resolution on 'Preservation of and Compliance with the ABM Treaty', and stated 'The strategic significance of the treaty goes far beyond the scope of the US–Russia bilateral relationship. It has been universally recognised as playing an indispensable role in maintaining global strategic stability, promoting nuclear disarmament and enhancing international security'. See 'China urges preservation of ABM Treaty', *People's Daily*, 21 February 2001.

42 Nigel Thalakada, 'China's voting pattern in the Security Council, 1990–1995', in Russett (ed.), *The Once and Future Security Council*, 88.

43 Ibid., 94–5.

44 In the face of failures in Rwanda, Kosovo and (potentially) East Timor, he defined the 'core challenge to the Security Council and to the United Nations as a whole in the next century: to forge unity behind the principle that massive and systematic violations of human rights—wherever they may take place—should not be allowed to stand'. He warned '[i]f the collective conscience of humanity—a conscience which abhors cruelty, renounces injustice

and seeks peace for all peoples—cannot find in the United Nations its greatest tribune, there is a grave danger that it will seek elsewhere for peace and justice'. See United Nations, 'Secretary-General presents his annual report'.

45 'Foreign Minister meets counterparts attending UN session', *Xinhua News Agency*, 21 September 1999, *Reuters China News*, 22 September 1999; and Evelyn Leopold, 'China castigates West on humanitarian intervention', *Reuters China News*, 22 September 1999.

46 You Ji, 'China's perceptions on the security of Northeast Asia', Seminar, Department of International Relations, Australian National University, 23 March 2001.

47 In the 27 September vote at the Special Session of the UN Commission on Human Rights to adopt a resolution on East Timor, China was one of twelve states which voted against retention of operative paragraph 6 of the draft resolution calling on the Secretary-General to establish a Commission of Inquiry to gather and compile information on possible violations of human rights in East Timor. By a ballot of 27 in favour and 12 opposed, with 11 abstentions, the Commission voted to retain the paragraph. The final resolution (E/CN.4/S-4/L.1/Rev.1) was approved by a roll-call vote of 32 in favor and 12 opposed, including China, with 6 abstaining. China's representative Liu Xinsheng, said that China was against the resolution, largely due to the proposal for an international inquiry. See United Nations, 'Special session of Commission on Human Rights adopts resolution on East Timor', UN Press Release (Washington, DC: United Nations, 27 September 1999).

48 Mark Riley, 'UN puts tribunal aside', *Sydney Morning Herald*, 31 January 2000.

49 Cited in Stephanie Ho, Voice of America, 1 February 2000, Human Rights Information Network, 1 February 2000.

50 See, for instance, Kent, *China, the United Nations and Human Rights*, 164.

51 Author's interviews with Bank officials, October–November 2000.

52 See World Bank, 'Regions and Countries', *World Bank online*, available at http://www.worldbank.org/html/extdr/regions.htm, accessed 1 August 2001.

53 'World Bank to slash lending to China', *Australian Financial Review*, 27 September 1999, 2.

54 'World Bank eyes $1 Billion in China Interior lending', *Reuters China News*, 17 March 2000.

55 'International organisations to enhance cooperation with China on poverty reduction', *Xinhua News Agency*, 16 May 2000, *Reuters China News*, 16 May 2000; and 'World Bank—China receives $360 million for two loans for flood protection and urban environment', *Reuters China News*, 30 June 2000.

56 'Unforgettable experience at UNDP', *Xinhua News Agency*, 6 August 1999, *Reuters China News*, 6 August 1999.

57 'China calls for economic globalisation conference', *Reuters China News*, 23 September 1999.

58 Just at the point when China was resuming its negotiations with the United States and the European Union for membership of the WTO, Jan Kregel advised it that empirical studies had shown that for a developing country to benefit fully from globalisation, it needed to have a robust domestic economy that could effectively counterbalance any increase in imports that came from lowering trade barriers. China's economy was seen as weak, particularly in the banking and state enterprise sector and consequently it was advised to hold back, (see Sheel Kohli,'UN offers recipe for reforms', *South China Morning Post*, 22 September 1999, *Reuters China News*, 22 September 1999).

59 'ADB—China's entry to WTO to benefit itself and region', *Xinhua News Agency*, 26 April 2000, *Reuters China News*, 26 April 2000.

60 'IMF warns of strains in slowing Chinese economy', *Reuters News Service*, 22 September 1999.

61 'IMF asks China and India to speed up structural reforms', *Reuters China News*, 28 September 1999.

62 For example, the *People's Daily* pointed out that WTO membership would provide an opportunity for the Chinese economy to become a part of standard and fair international competition and would even enhance China's economic security, (see Gong Wen and Zhang Xiangchen, 'Comment on general trend', 1).

63 See Kong Qingqiang, 'Enforcing WTO agreements in China'.

64 Huan Xiang, 'Strive to build up New China's science of international law', in Chinese Society of International Law (ed.), *Selected Articles from Chinese Yearbook of International Law* (Beijing: China Translation and Publishing Company, 1983), 21.

65 Ibid., 24.

66 These are: mutual respect for territorial integrity and sovereignty, mutual non-aggression, non-interference in each other's internal affairs, equality and mutual benefit, and peaceful coexistence.

[67] Huan Xiang, 'Strive to Build Up', 24–40.

[68] 'Parliament leader Li Peng urges study, use of international law', *Xinhua News Agency*, 29 April 2000, *Reuters China News*, 4 May 2000.

[69] Wan Xia, 'Huigu yu zhanwang–gaige kaifang 20 nian guojifa zai Zhongguo di fazhan' [Looking back and ahead: the development of international law in China during twenty years of opening and reform], *Waijiao xueyuan xuebao*, no. 2 (1999), 63; and Lu Song, 'Guojifa zai guoji guanxi zhong de zuoyong' [The role of international law in international relations], *Waijiao xueyuan xuebao*, no. 1 (1997), 14.

[70] 'Chinese President calls for fair New World Order', *Xinhua News Agency*, 12 April 2000, *Reuters China News*, 12 April 2000.

[71] Author's interviews, Geneva, August 1998.

[72] Author's interview with Rebecca Johnson, Geneva, August 1998.

[73] See discussion in Kim, 'China and the United Nations', 57–60.

[74] 'China said not ready to support Japan's UN Security Council entry', *Kyodo News Service*, 28 June 2000, *Reuters China News*, 28 June 2000.

[75] Although he acknowledged that the IMF had always occupied a key position in the international monetary system and that its role was not replaceable by any other institution, he insisted that it should allow developing countries to join in decisionmaking, and take into account their ability to sustain the strains, instead of forcing them to reform their economic structures according to the standards of developed countries. He argued that the international community should create conditions to increase the distribution and application of special drawing rights and strengthen the IMF's function in providing international liquidity, (see 'Governor of People's Bank of China on IMF, financial policy', *Xinhua News Agency*, 27 September 1999, *Reuters China News*, 29 September 1999; and 'Developing countries call for New World Financial Order', *Xinhua News Agency*, 16 June 2000, *Reuters China News*, 6 June 2000).

[76] See 'Chinese Premier urges greater regional cooperation at recent ASEAN summit', *Xinhua News Agency*, 28 November 1999, *Reuters China News*, 30 November 1999; and 'China 'willing' to consider East Asia Monetary Fund', *Xinhua News Agency*, 25 November 1999, *Reuters China News*, 26 November 1999.

[77] Lester Ross, 'China and environmental protection', in Economy and Oksenberg (eds), *China Joins the World*, 317–18.

[78] Kent, *China, the United Nations and Human Rights*, 242–43.

[79] Exceptions have been the visits to China of the UN Special Rapporteur on Religious Intolerance, the UN Working Group on Arbitrary Detention, the UN High Commissioner for Human Rights, Mary Robinson, and the invitation to the UN Special Rapporteur on Torture.

[80] Gong Wen and Zhang Xiangchen, 'Comment on general trend', 1–2.

[81] See Shi Guangsheng, Minister of Foreign Trade and Economic Cooperation, reported in 'China's stance on WTO accession unchanged', *People's Daily*, 13 March 2001.

[82] Vivien Pik-kwan Chan, 'Opening up markets 'a double-edged sword'', *South China Morning Post*, 12 September 1999; and 'China won't sacrifice national interests to join WTO', *Kyodo News*, 3 September 1999, *Reuters China News*, 3 September 1999.

[83] For instance, under the agricultural agreement, brokered in Washington in April 1999, the United States won substantial concessions—the average tariff for agricultural products will be cut to 17 per cent from 21.2 per cent, with the average tariff for US priority products falling to 14.5 per cent. All tariffs will be phased out by 2004. Quantitative restrictions, except for those on major agricultural products such as wheat, rice, corn, cotton and table sugar, will be eliminated. See Paul Mooney, 'Post-WTO shocks for China's farmers', *China Online*, 17 January 2000, available online at http://www.chinaonline.com/issues/wto/NewsArchive/secure/2000/january/C00011721.asp, accessed 1 August 2001).

[84] According to US Trade Representative Charlene Barchevsky it 'secures broad-ranging, comprehensive, *one-way* trade concessions on China's part, granting the United States substantially greater market access across the spectrum of industrial goods, services and agriculture' [my emphasis], see 'Barchefsky on China WTO, Congressional trade status vote', *China Online*, 29 February 2000, available online at http://www.chinaonline.com/commentary_analysis/wtocom/currentnews/secure/C00022920.asp, accessed 1 August 2001.

[85] 'Chinese reform expert proposes countermeasures for WTO challenges', *Xinhua News Agency*, 7 March 2000, *Reuters China News*, 7 March 2000.

[86] See Pieter Bottelier, 'The impact of WTO membership on China's domestic economy, Part 1' *China Online*, 3 January 2001, available online at http://www.chinaonline.com/issues/wto/NewsArchive/

secure/2001/January/c01010160.asp; Idem, 'The impact of WTO membership on China's domestic economy, Part II' *China Online*, 4 January 2001, available online at http://www.chinaonline.com/commentary_analysis/wtocom/NewsArchive/secure/2001/January/c01010260.asp, both accessed 1 August 2001; and Zhao Wei, 'China's WTO accession: commitments and prospects', *Journal of World Trade*, 32 (1998), 51–75. For particularly valuable insights, see proceedings of conference, 'China and the World Trade Organisation', Faculty of Law, Australian National University, 16–17 March 2001.

87 See Economist Intelligence Unit, 'Financial Reforms Delayed' carried in *China Online*, http://www.chinaonline.com/issues/wto/NewsArchive/cs-protected/2001/February/c01020957.asp (accessed 20 September 2001); and Zhu Rongji, 'Report on the work of the government', 5 March 2000, Part VII.

88 See Bottelier , 'The impact of WTO membership'.

# 7
# China's diplomacy in North and Northeast Asia: norms and practice

**Stuart Harris**

Over the last decade or so, western discussion about the major powers in Northeast Asia has tended to take two different approaches. Drawing on lessons from the history of the rise of Germany and Japan (but seemingly not of the United States), the first argues that the dramatic transformations of economics and power among the major states in the area, notably the rise of China (and the decline of the USSR), pose enhanced risks of conflict. This, realists argue, leads to power balancing by the major powers (building up militaries, leading to arms races in competitive attempts to dominate militarily or, for smaller powers, the formation of alliances). The second puts weight on the increasing evidence of cooperative approaches among the countries of the region as well as within a larger Asia Pacific cooperative framework. This implies some adherence to implicit if not explicit norms and rules of behaviour.

In this chapter, I look at aspects of China's diplomacy in North and Northeast Asia within a general framework of how that diplomacy fits with the second approach—cooperative relationships in compliance with generally accepted international norms. Precisely what such compliance means is not always clear. Norms are principles and standards of behaviour that may be explicitly specified—as in the UN Charter or in international agreements. They may, however, simply be generally understood and accepted standards defined less specifically in terms of what constitutes responsible international behaviour.[1] They are thus often imprecise and changing and capable of varying interpretations.

For most countries, at present, they would include peaceful resolution of disputes, respect for sovereignty, non-interference in the internal affairs of a state, adherence to the underlying principles of international institutions such as those of the United Nations, and of specific institutions and agreements such as the International Monetary Fund (IMF), United Nations Convention on the Law of the Sea (UNCLOS), United Nations High Commissioner for Refugees (UNHCR), the Non-proliferation Treaty (NPT) and the Comprehensive Test Ban Treaty (CTBT), and cooperative rather than confrontational participation in international affairs. China would put particular emphasis on sovereignty and other UN principles such as non-interference in the internal affairs of a state, would argue that it adheres to the peaceful resolution of disputes and that in general it complies with the other universally accepted norms and rules. It would add, however, the further norms of equality and mutual benefit.

In North Asia, China borders Russia, Mongolia, North Korea and several members of the Commonwealth of Independent States (CIS). It has anxieties about separatist influences in the autonomous region of Xinjiang, in part encouraged externally, and interests in economic exchanges with Russia and the CIS. In Northeast Asia, as well as its interests across the Taiwan Strait, China also interacts with the two other major powers—the United States and Japan—and with the two Koreas. The size and strategic importance of the countries in these areas is considerable. Most have large military capacities, three are nuclear powers and the fourth (Japan) could become one without much difficulty. Three are permanent members of the United Nations Security Council, and three (not including China) are in the G8. Our interest in those relationships comes primarily from the capacity they have to disturb substantially the economic viability and/or the strategic stability of the region. Moreover, relations with the three powers, Japan, Russia and the United States, can be seen as the focus of China's identity.[2] How China interacts with them is central to regional analyses but, more importantly, to an understanding of the likely nature of China's future diplomacy.

In the West, notably in the United States, attention tends to be directed to China's growing relationship with Russia, which from 1996 has been termed a 'strategic partnership'. An exaggerated if not singular US commentary suggested 'The alliance is all but signed'.[3] China has specific concerns over developments in the US–Japan relationship. Japan would not welcome too close a relationship between Russia and China, and worries when relations between China and the United States appear too close but also when too cool. Where the Koreas (separate or unified) fit is also a matter of economic as well as strategic interest. Yet, whatever the concerns experienced in the North Pacific, they do not seem to have stimulated significantly changed policies leading to power balancing, arms races or to significant alliance formation. Rather than a build up of military capabilities in the border areas there have in fact been quantitative reductions (although at times accompanied by qualitative modernisations) not only among the four major powers but also in South Korea. Apart from the strengthened US–Japan alliance, whether there are alliances or even substantial alignments is also in question, although frequent shifts are discernible from time to time among the major players as they see benefits from reordering their interests among the bilateral relationships involved.

Broader economic issues also arise beyond the growing trade and investment interrelationships. Demand for energy in particular is growing in the region. Various estimates of future regional energy requirements point to large increased needs. In the midst of the Asian economic crisis, when earlier optimistic economic forecasts had been revised downwards, a Shell spokesperson said, nevertheless, that in the next 20 years Asia Pacific oil demand would double and gas demand quadruple.[4] One estimate of China's imports of oil is for an increase from some 40 million tonnes in 1999 to 390 million tonnes in 2020.[5] Such projections and the implications for energy security are exercising policy thinking in the various regional states, as well as stimulating some alarmist conclusions in the West.[6]

China's diplomacy in North and Northeast Asia has a range of objectives. The argument of this chapter is that its priority objectives are concerned with power relationships with neighbours. Other objectives, such as its economic objectives, are important but secondary to, or supportive of, its priority objectives although China's access to Russian military equipment and technology has grown in importance. Its global objectives, concerned with global power relationships, are high on the agenda from time to time as external circumstances require but do not dominate as a major continuing factor.

To understand China's links with the major powers we need to look briefly at the bases of China's relationship with each of the major powers.

## China–Russia

The PRC's history of relations with Moscow is of ideological links that soured in the 1960s. That souring, and an exhaustion of China's willingness to play a subsidiary role, led to consequent ideological conflicts, major border disputes, threats and substantial military build ups on both sides of the very long (7000 or so kilometres) China–USSR border. This ultimately resulted in military confrontations on a small scale, and fears of armed confrontation on a large scale. From this emerged China's shift towards the United States in the 1970s and what some saw as an implicit alliance with the United States against the USSR into the 1980s. This close relationship fell away as the Cold War and the US need for an alignment against the USSR wound down, and then as a result of the Tiananmen Square repression. With Gorbachev's 'new thinking' from 1986 on and ultimately the 1991 break up of the USSR, Washington's relations with Moscow improved considerably. China came to feel isolated, however, as Russia gradually moved towards Europe and became, for a while, part of the Wester-led international community. This, and the gradual increase in economic exchanges between Russia and China, were reinforcing but not key factors in Beijing's move to seek rapprochement with Moscow.

In looking at what did bring about the warming of China's relations with Russia, it is useful to consider what motivates China and what motivates Russia. Given its domestic priority of economic development, China was concerned to negotiate solutions to its long-standing border disputes with neighbours. In addition, with Russia in particular, it wanted to reduce military threats and tensions through reducing troop emplacements and to enter into confidence building measures (CBMs), especially on border military activities. Gorbachev's *glasnost* and the 1989 normalisation of bilateral relations made this possible to contemplate. Since China's hesitant acceptance of CBMs went with a view that they would only work if there were a broad based relationship, attempts to establish confidence across a broader range of economic, political and strategic issues were regarded as important. The break up of the USSR also raised new questions about the respective interests of Russia and China in the CIS states.

After 1986, and particularly following Gorbachev's visit to Beijing in 1989, the previously tense bilateral relations improved and made possible bilateral meetings between leaders of the two countries in most years from 1991 onwards. A series of bilateral agreements, joint statements and understandings resulted, that led to the withdrawal of military forces, development of military CBMs, border negotiations and trade, with the relationship being institutionalised through annual leaders' meetings and in other functional ways. The agreements also reaffirmed Russia's support for the Chinese position on Taiwan. These led subsequently both to the adoption of the terminology of 'strategic partnership of cooperation'[7] and to the initiation of meetings of the Shanghai Five—China, Russia, Kazakstan, Kyrgyzstan and Tajikistan.

The main Chinese interest in these broader meetings was border management, military cooperation on the border and cooperation against cross border secessionists, religious extremist activity, terrorism and drugs. From these meetings, the first in 1996, came two broader agreements. The first was the Shanghai Agreement signed in 1996. This provided for non-aggression, non-use of force, de-targeting of nuclear weapons, notifications preceding military exercises and manoeuvres, and limits on the types of exercises permitted within the 100 kilometre zone on both sides of the border. The second was the Moscow Agreement signed in May 1997 dealing with troop reductions within 100 kilometres on both sides of the border.[8] In a further bilateral agreement in April 1999, China and Russia completed the negotiations of a common border.[9]

As well as settling border disputes and achieving force reductions, China's access to Russia's advanced military technology has been important given that, following the 1989 events, alternative sources, notably the United States, have been unavailable to it. Thus there have been substantial sales of advanced military equipment both of aircraft (SU 27s and SU 30s) and naval craft (nuclear submarines and destroyers). Russia was originally concerned not to provide the latest technologies but this seems to have relaxed somewhat with the sale of SU 30s,[10] although criticism of the arms relationship remains in Russia. How far sales of more sophisticated equipment reflected a Russian strategic decision, rather than a need for foreign exchange (and the need to keep the Sukhoi company afloat), is unclear. Claims have been common that military cooperation has greatly expanded, notably since Kosovo and following General Zhang Wannian's visit to Moscow in June 1999.[11] Despite talk of a prospective 'defence' accord,[12] however, outside of defence procurement, the training that goes with such sales, and limited naval exchanges, the extent of such cooperation has been limited.

The other major functional links are concerned with Xinjiang, which is dealt with under CIS states below, and with economic exchanges. Russia, in particular, initially expected economic exchanges to be a major functional benefit of the bilateral relationship. Results have fallen far short of expectations despite efforts to stimulate trade and, to a degree, investment. Total two-way trade in 2000, some US$8 billion, was the highest since 1993, but well below the target of US$20 billion. In 1999, in particular, major efforts have been made on both sides to improve the economic exchanges and to give an added stimulus to energy cooperation. China currently imports some 60,000 tonnes of oil a year from Russia and an increasing concern for energy security in China provided an added motive. Moreover, for China, a further stimulus was the belief that the political links needed to be buttressed by significant economic exchanges.

These bilateral factors were the main drivers behind the Chinese interest in closer links. As the internal Russian economic picture started to seem less promising, blamed in part on pressures from the West, support in Russia for its closeness to the West fell away. More generally, China and Russia came to share a common worldview, reflecting the international imbalance that had emerged from the end of the Cold War. Specific factors that led to closer relations include 'a perceived threat of Eurasian encirclement' from the enlargement of NATO in the West and the United States and its alliances in the east,[13] US unilateralism, NATO's involvement in Kosovo, and the US development of Theatre Missile Defence (TMD) and National Missile Defence (NMD) with the likely abrogation of the Anti Ballistic Missile (ABM) treaty.

Although, since 1996 in particular, global factors have led to an added interest in joint cooperation, the level of coordination has not always been good, as Russian commentators have noted. For example, although Yeltsin and Jiang agreed in principle their general position on Iraq, in practice, at the time of the December 1998 crisis, China, unlike Russia, did not put its troops on alert, withdraw its US and UK ambassadors, or withdraw citizens from Iraq. While the Russian Duma moved to evade United Nations sanctions, China stressed that all members of the United Nations, particularly the United States and United Kingdom, should adhere strictly to the UN Charter.[14] Moscow's sensitivities over NATO's enlargement were partly alleviated by compensating memberships of the G8 and APEC and a place at the NATO table. The West's approach to Iraq and then to Bosnia, however, raised concerns which created divisions within Russia between those more Western inclined, including Yeltsin, and an opposing group that included Primakov, notably when foreign minister and then as prime minister. The assault on Serbia brought these divisions out more clearly. Vladimir

Putin, the present president, has been variously portrayed as both more and less Western oriented than Yeltsin, although he has stressed a balanced approach that continues to place weight on the bilateral links with China and on Asia's importance generally.

Were the United States and Russia to agree on amendment of the ABM treaty, this could test the relationship given China's concerns while China's only qualified opposition to missile defence worried some Russian observers.[15] For both countries, however, the relationship with the United States is still the priority. There is a sense, nevertheless, in which the value of the bilateral relationship increases for each as it experiences particular difficulties with the United States.

Yet, overall, Russia's positive response to China's interest in closer political links is not just to ensure the border security of the Russian Far East but also a way of reasserting itself as a Great Power, including as a Great Power in Asia. Russia's efforts to join APEC, its resentment at being excluded from the talks on the Korean peninsula, and its initiative for six-party talks on issues on the peninsula and in North Asia reflect this.

While Kosovo raised particular anxieties for China, as Western military aid to a secessionist ethnic minority, it was a greater problem initially for Russia. Russia, attempting to cope with its fall from international leadership, was left out of the processes involved, with the UN Security Council bypassed explicitly as a way of sidelining Russia. Although initially unhelpful, the Russian involvement ultimately in brokering a Kosovo peace settlement, against the hard line position of Primakov and others in his ministerial team, was welcomed by China. The interests, however, could have diverged. Victor Chernomyrdin reportedly visited Beijing to ensure that China would not block the Russian-brokered UN agreement in the Security Council.[16]

The important bilateral issues have been addressed primarily in the meetings of the Shanghai Five, and in bilateral summits Jiang has had with Gorbachev, Yeltsin and Putin. Most important on the agenda has been resolving border differences and border management of fundamentalist and secessionist incursions. A major added item, however, was economic and energy cooperation and Russia certainly sees energy projects as a key element of the relationship, as we note below.

While China's global priority remains its relations with the United States, links with Russia provide a safeguard, if not a card to play, to discourage US unilateralism. Too much of a lean to Russia, however, would be unproductive and would be criticised domestically as contrary to Deng Xiaoping's 'independent foreign policy'.[17] Chinese leaders have been concerned about the management of Russia's economy, its large financial borrowings from international institutions and the elements of chaos and corruption in the Russian system, reflected in particular in the 1998 economic deterioration. While Kosovo will have encouraged a shift back to Russian links, Russia's weakness and political instability is recognised in China as limiting their value.

In the longer term, although it probably over estimates it, China is concerned at what it sees as incipient Russian nationalism. More importantly, China assumes that Russia at some stage is likely to recover its strength and grow in influence and will then be capable of actions adverse to China's interests. Chinese analysts see this, however, as a long-term factor. Jiang himself is reported as saying 'Russia would not pose a political or strategic threat to China for the next 30 years at least'.[18] However accurate the citation, the substance has support from many Chinese analyses, and the need to engage with Russia to influence its long-term political development, in ways compatible with Chinese interests, is broadly accepted.

According to one source, of some 1500 Chinese companies in Russia, 1200 (approximately US$200 billion of investment) are in the Russian Far East (RFE), concerned primarily with RFE's raw materials.[19] This poses potential for problems since there are already fears of an eventual Chinese absorption of the RFE. Local difficulties have already arisen over illegal migration and Beijing has cooperated with Moscow in regulating the border to contain and reduce the problems.[20] Anti-Chinese rhetoric is not limited to the RFE but local politicians, greatly exaggerating the concerns about illegal Chinese migration into the area, have used Russian nationalist arguments, fears of massive Chinese migration, and 'yellow peril' xenophobia for local political purposes, mainly against Moscow. Nevertheless, in the longer term, the demographic imbalances pose potential bilateral problems for the two countries. These potential problems have been recognised by President Putin, who has observed that, without more effective domestic development of the RFE, even the indigenous Russian population of the region 'will soon speak mostly Japanese, Chinese or Korean'.[21] Yet, development of the RFE's resources would require substantial amounts of labour, which would be difficult to get other than from China.

The RFE has been the area where most difficulty has been experienced in resolving border disputes, including a rejection for some time by the local leadership of the agreement reached by Moscow on the eastern section of the border. There has also been vigorous opposition in the RFE to the idea of being simply a supplier of raw materials for China among others, an opposition expressed more widely by Russian nationalists.

The bilateral relationship has been buttressed by a number of joint declarations and statements; and these have been incorporated in a formal Sino-Russian Treaty of Good Neighbourly Friendship and Cooperation is expected to be signed in 2001. This is seen by China as an important development affirming more formally many of the border, force reduction and other bilateral agreements, and Russia also wants to formalise border and other agreements with China, notably with respect to the RFE. Although there are elements within the Russian élites who would support closer links with China, Russian and Chinese spokespersons have distanced themselves from the idea of an alliance.[22] The bilateral relationship is not anti-Western. This does not mean, however, that taking common positions contrary to specific actions of the United States and its supporters in the United Nations and elsewhere will not continue from time to time. Nor does it rule out the possibility that, should China be in conflict, limited intelligence or other indirect assistance might be given by Russia. Among the common interests, particularly in the long term, would be the aim to counterbalance Western influence over the energy resources of the CIS, although even that might depend upon where the large financial requirements might be sourced.

Suggestions have also been made of the possibility of a three-way linkage with China, Russia and India. This idea was first raised by Yeltsin during his visit to India in 1993 and again by Primakov when prime minister and subsequently by Putin.[23] There would be difficulties to overcome were this to be pursued beyond rhetorical agreement to seek multipolarity in global relationships. A Russian correspondent in Beijing noted that this idea ignored the emerging nuclear capacity of India, 'an age old adversary of the PRC', and the massive deliveries to India of Russian aircraft superior to the SU 27s delivered by Russia to the PRC.[24] China and India have improved their relations, despite China's continuing links with Pakistan, but India's positive response to the Bush administration on NMD poses a constraint and India's wish for closer links with the United States might limit its concerns over US unilateralism.

Overall, therefore, and despite reservations, continuing elements of mistrust among important groups on both sides, and its limitations, China's diplomacy has sought to build up the substance of the bilateral relationship with Russia. In stimulating its desire to establish a substantial relationship, ideology has been replaced by a range of more practical interests. For China, its interest in the substance of the Shanghai and Moscow agreements, ultimately a formal treaty and also the Chinese belief that these need to be buttressed by a wider range of bilateral and multilateral relationships to build confidence, reflect more practical interests than geopolitical concerns with US attempts to press its own agenda on China.

In the short to medium term, the relationship with Russia has direct and more substantive security and functional than geopolitical benefits for China despite the occasional coordination of positions in the UN Security Council and in other global contexts. Although China and Russia wish for a multipolar world, and see the long-term trend towards multipolarity as inevitable, there is a general acknowledgement that this is some decades away.[25] Nor, despite its expressions of concern, is China's anxiety strongly felt. Jiang, at the 1999 Bishkek meeting, said that since the end of the Cold War 'the international situation generally speaking has tended to become relaxed'.[26]

Over the long term, China seems to have accepted that its interests tend to be best pursued through following international norms. Within a series of bilateral and multilateral meetings, over a long period from 1986 to 2000, China and Russia peacefully negotiated a common border, in a context where animosities have been intense for centuries. It covers southeast Siberia—territory disputed since the seventeenth century and fought over as late as 1969—as well as disputed territory in Central Asia, also fought over in 1969.

Although these developments reflect behaviour consistent with many of the norms and rules outlined earlier, its actions against rising separatist sentiment and religious extremism reflect considerations, for China as well as Russia, of the balance between reducing the threat of violent terrorism and supporting international human rights norms. China's handling of secessionist activities is harsh and conflicts with what would be widely seen as the appropriate norms. On the other hand, the West's new post-Kosovo interventionist doctrine remains a greater concern for Beijing in Xinjiang than for Russia in Chechnya and Dagestan for several reasons, including the particular politicisation in the United States of China's human rights behaviour. Nevertheless, the cautionary note in the Bishkek meeting of the 'Shanghai Five' in 1999 that human rights should not be a pretext for outside interference reflected a shared interest.[27]

## CIS states

For China, the border issues, already a major factor before the collapse of the USSR in 1991 became more so after that. The independence of the CIS nations, with regional unrest in southern Russia and with activists in the new CIS nations that threaten to undermine China's control of its western province, posed added potential problems. China, which promptly recognised the newly independent Kazakstan, Kyrgyzstan and Tajikistan, soon sought to enter into border negotiations with them.

The border issue was not only important in itself but relations with the new CIS nations were crucial for controlling ethnic separatism and preventing inroads from Islamic fundamentalism, international terrorism, drugs and other international crime. These issues have become more crucial with the growing influence of the Taliban in Afghanistan. China recognises that the potential exists to undermine its largely Muslim province of Xinjiang, and for Uighur separatist elements to challenge Beijing's control. That, like China, a number of CIS nations fear the influence of Islamic fundamentalism internally facilitates cooperation. In 2000, Uzbekistan was, for the first time, an observer in the meeting of the Shanghai Five, held in Dushanbe, the Tajik capital. It became a full member of the group in its more substantive form as the Shanghai Cooperation Organisation (SCO) in 2001.

Xinjiang was a source of dispute with the Soviet Union in the 1960s when the USSR tried to foment secessionist activities and earlier, in the 1950s, when the CIA sought to destabilise the province. It is now important to China in terms of sovereignty as well as security and economic interests because of its location—central to its links with Russia, the CIS nations and the Middle East. Although it has a potential role in meeting China's energy needs, either from its own apparently rich resources, or as a site for pipelines from other energy supply sources, instability poses problems for the security and continuity of oil and gas supplies through Xinjiang, notably from Kazakstan. To some extent the increased efforts by Beijing to ensure stability in Xinjiang have come from these interests.

The CIS nations are torn between a sense of a Chinese 'threat', including the threat of a large Chinese migratory flow in Kazakstan and political influence applied by Russia. While most CIS nations are under Russian military protection in accord with their Collective Security Treaty, there is a fear of undue dominance by Russia. Kazakstan in particular seems to be fretting under Russian pressure. The CIS nations' interest in greater cooperation with China is therefore in part for its economic benefits but also as a balance against the pressure on their independence from Russia, which sees the CIS nations as within its area of influence. Although irritations between the two countries may occasionally result from these conflicting pressures, both Russia and China have sufficient interests in stability in the CIS nations to be likely to manage adequately this potential for conflict.

## China and Japan

China's relationship with Japan remains less than warm but is carefully managed by both sides. The economic relationship in particular continues to grow, with China moving gradually toward a generally non-discriminatory and liberal trade and investment regime and accepting the implications of economic interdependence with Japan. In 1999, during Prime Minister Obuchi's visit to Beijing, agreement was reached on the bilateral negotiations between Japan and China for China's accession to the WTO. Japan's aid to China became a political debating point within Japan after China's nuclear tests in 1996 and has remained so as Japan's economy has weakened. Zhu Rongji, in his visit to Japan in 2000, was careful to acknowledge the value to China of Japan's aid, thereby countering a major Japanese criticism that there was no gratitude from China for the help given by Japan.

China has also accepted changed Japanese aid priorities. These include greater emphasis on projects to limit the environmental effects of its economic growth on Japan, particularly of acid rain. This is also a factor in Japan's interests in China's energy policies. Beyond simply wanting to substitute gas for coal in China's energy use for its environmental benefits, however, Japan is concerned at the effect of growing Chinese demand on Asia Pacific oil and gas markets and, therefore, on Japanese energy costs.[28] Japan has demonstrated an interest, therefore, in a common energy strategy to increase energy production worldwide, without which competition among East Asian economies will lead to increased Japanese costs. Some commentators have seen this competition for energy supplies as leading to conflict between China and Japan,[29] but these conclusions did not seem probable then and seem even less so now, given China's efforts to integrate itself into the global energy market, and given the acceptance by China of the logic of economic interdependence. It is also reflected explicitly to a degree in China's energy strategy, which looks for greater reliance on natural gas, one reason for which is to contain the sources of acid rain affecting China's neighbours, South Korea as well as Japan.

There are many issues, mostly stemming from the history of the bilateral relationship or war settlements, that remain irritants in the relationship and surface from time to time. These include arguments about the degree of acknowledgment of war guilt, which continues to rise and fall in intensity. Zhu's visit to Japan in 2000, however, was clearly more successful than Jiang's the year before in taking some of the heat out of the issue.[30] The nationalist revision of Japanese school textbooks in 2001, however, and Prime Minister Koizumi's proposed visit to the Yasukini Shrine put some of it back in.

China and Japan are also in dispute over the Senkaku (Diaoyu) Islands. During the 1978 peace treaty negotiations, a large demonstration of Chinese fishing boats in support of the Chinese position was regarded as an attempt to pressure Japan at a time when discussions had broken down. Eventually, China agreed to defer the issue of sovereignty over the islands 'to the following generation'. The question of sovereignty over the islands has recurred from time to time but more particularly between Japanese and Taiwanese authorities. In 1997, when Japanese nationalists sought to stir the issue, Beijing moved to prevent direct involvement from the mainland.

Difficulties in negotiating on ocean border issues remain but are unlikely to cause major problems. This is in part because they are technically difficult and also because of caution on both sides since any resolution in one context sets precedents for other contexts and negotiations with other countries. They are additionally complex because of the unresolved issue of Taiwan and its claims over ocean borders. [31]

More broadly, Japan can hardly feel threatened by China, although it does feel uncertain about China's military modernisation in the long term. Japanese public opinion reacted adversely in 1996, however, to China's missile exercises at the time of Taiwan's presidential election and again to China's delay in ceasing nuclear tests and acceding to the CTBT.

Nuclear issues have been a long-term and major factor in the relationship. They emerged in particular in the 1990s as Japanese opposition to China's nuclear testing grew in Japan, with proposals to cut Japanese aid to China as a consequence. In 1996, China announced the suspension of testing and foreshadowed its eventual signing of the CTBT. While public feelings ran high in Japan, both governments managed the issue with some care. China gave advanced notice of tests and tried to explain itself to the Japanese public. China also responded positively to Japan's decision to dispose of a large volume (700,000) of chemical artillery shells left in China by Japan after the Pacific War. The resolution of practical problems associated with the disposal suggests a cooperative approach on that issue by the two countries. China's accession to the CTBT, despite the US decision not to do so, also reduced the adverse Japanese reaction to China's nuclear testing.

As problems have arisen in the relationship they have usually been resolved through diplomatic negotiations, often after top level Beijing–Tokyo discussion. Thus, in 2000, Japan reacted strongly to evidence of Chinese research vessels entering the Japanese Economic Exclusion Zone (EEZ) without prior notice. Although formally legal, China and Japan agreed peaceably in February 2001 on how the issue should be handled in the future.[32] Although some breaches still seem to occur, the problem appears generally to have been handled satisfactorily.

For China, the question of Taiwan, rather than the fear of a resurgence of Japanese militarism, has again become a central issue in the relationship. While that fear is not absent, China is mostly concerned by developments in Japan's role as a partner for the United States in containing China. Central to this is Japan's closer alliance with the United States, notably the passage of legislation for a revised set of defence guidelines and Japan's agreement to participate in the development of a US theatre missile defence system.

In the past, the US–Japan defence treaty has sometimes been an issue, but only occasionally a major one for China–Japan relations. China's hostility has emerged with the development of new guidelines for Japan–US defence cooperation, which came into law in 1999, as they conceivably envisage Japanese support for the

United States in any clash that might occur with China over Taiwan. It may be argued that just for that reason, Japan is likely to be more cautious and urge that increased caution on the United States in any crisis over Taiwan. It was uncharacteristically prompt in responding adversely to President Lee's 'state to state' statement in July 1999. Japan's participation in TMD has similarly been strongly criticised by China because of the implications for Taiwan, in this case seen as encouraging a sense of security for Taiwan that may lead it to pursue independence.

More generally, despite their long history as enemies, despite the lack of mutual trust, but perhaps in part because of the past history of aggression, the principle of non-aggression seems likely to continue to have a powerful restraining effect on both countries. Japan has become more cautious about the Taiwan issue given what it sees as a more assertive US approach under President Bush because of the implications for Japan's possible involvement in a cross-strait conflict.

## China–United States

It is not intended here to deal with China–US relations as a whole but merely with those aspects that relate to North and Northeast Asia and China's diplomacy in that context. Nevertheless, it is relevant, as background, that since 1999 the Cox Report, Kosovo, the US–Japan security guidelines and, most particularly, the Belgrade embassy bombing and the surveillance plane incident have damaged China–US relations. Continuing promotion of NMD has not made improvement easy subsequently, nor has the US shift towards Taiwan or China's treatment of Falun Gong adherents. My assumption is, however, that, short of a bad mistake by the United States, China or Taiwan, the general relationship will remain basically sound if subject to sizeable swings in warmth or coolness. It has yet to be seen what overall policy stance towards Northeast Asia will eventually emerge under the Bush administration but Secretary of State Powell has restated support for the 'one China' policy and for the three communiqués that have been the basis of US–China relations under previous administrations.

It is also relevant that US administration policies towards China have consistently given weight to a belief that increased economic interchange provides disincentives to military conflict and encourages internal reform. These principles, which are seemingly held by President Bush if not by all his supporting élites, had the advantage of gaining strong business support in the United States, and for the most part fit with China's current priorities.

Nevertheless, China's priorities and policies are increasingly predicated on a belief that international competition among nations in the future will be based on economic and technological power rather than simply on military power and that economic modernisation has to remain the priority. The inability of Russia to overcome its economic and political weakness is one factor that encourages China to work to maintain its links with the United States. Another is a lesson drawn by some Chinese analysts from the collapse of the USSR—that to be dragged into a Cold War with the United States would result in a similar Chinese collapse.[33] China's approach to the United States is based primarily, however, on the belief that good relations with the United States are necessary to enable the modernisation that will give China economic and technical power. For that reason, US–China relations are likely to remain its top priority.

As with Russia, ideology has ceased playing a major role in China's relations with the United States. What remains relevant, apart from the vestigial remains of Cold War ideology in the US Congress, is what China sees as the US ideological concern to spread US 'values' to China by way of 'peaceful evolution'.

In the North Pacific, the United States, while acknowledged as greatly superior to each of the other major powers, has not actively sought leadership beyond military security, as with the handling of the North Korean nuclear problem—to that extent the North Pacific is structurally multipolar. The US role has been essentially reactive and compartmentalised—whether over Taiwan or North Korea, or with respect to missile defence. It sees its Northeast Asia policy largely in bilateral terms based most particularly on its alliances with Japan and South Korea. It has a particular interest in Chinese attitudes to developments in the area, including the potential changes on the Korean peninsula, such as China's attitudes towards a continuing US presence in Korea should reunification occur. China has not pronounced firmly on those possibilities and much would seem to depend on circumstances and the shape of China–US relations at the time. In their dealings with North Korea the Clinton administration, at least, seemed to have accepted that China had largely been constructive.

It is possible, however, that China's pursuit of energy linkages in Russia and the CIS may be seen as competitive with, and potentially threatening to, US financial and energy interests.[34] Given China's size, the rise of its economy and its increased participation in global markets, including the energy market, it will obviously challenge existing market participants. This should not be a surprise. The United States has been encouraging China to integrate itself into the international energy market—and encouraging investment and technology transfer to this end. In large part, as we note later, this seems to have worked.

## China-Korea

China's prime interests on the Korean Peninsula are that it remain peaceful and stable and that its border with North Korea remain secure. It would seem to prefer continuation of a divided, but non-conflictual, peninsula but seems willing to accept moves towards peaceful reunification. It also wants to maintain its influence on the peninsula. In pursuing these interests, it has managed the changing circumstances on the peninsula and its relations with both Koreas with some care. It maintains its traditional links with the North, supporting its economy and encouraging peaceful reconciliation while developing vigorously its links with South Korea, initially in economic terms and then in political and strategic terms. It accepts that normalisation of North Korea's relations with the United States and Japan on balance is generally likely to be helpful in reducing its own commitments but is also likely to affect its own influence.

China has a sizeable border with North Korea and is concerned that instability within North Korea will lead, among other things, to outside interference and to large refugee flows into China. It is generally uneasy at the prospect of a nuclear North (or South). According to one report, China's foreign minister was to advise North Korea against its nuclear program on a foreshadowed visit.[35] China has aimed to maintain its relationship with North Korea for strategic reasons, to maintain its influence and to satisfy its domestic (mainly older PLA) constituencies. It has given support, however, to the broad elements of US policy towards North Korea, including the Agreed Framework although it has remained outside of the Korean Peninsula Energy Development Organisation (KEDO). It has reaffirmed that support in the uncertainty of the Bush administration's policy towards North Korea. It recognised belatedly that the first firing by North Korea of the Taepodong missile to launch a satellite certainly provided a basis for Japanese military developments, and for close US-Japanese military cooperation including TMD programs, about which South Korea seems ambivalent. Further North Korean missile tests would have a major impact on China's regional neighbours which would be adverse to its interests.

From South Korea's perspective, a willingness had been evident to move closer to China for a number of reasons, including growing economic relations, but also the ability of China to play a mediating role between North and South Korea. China has participated in the various US discussions within the Four Party framework. Although there have been suggestions that China could do more to influence North Korea, it has generally been seen by South Korea as constructive in these discussions. President Kim recently noted that China had played a crucial role in dissuading North Korea from firing another missile, and encouraging the North to strike a deal with the United States on the missile issue.[36] On the other hand, there are South Korean views against moving too close to China, and South Korea is managing its relations carefully to avoid leaning too far to one side or the other. Yet, although it has substantially improved its links with Japan, South Korea's feelings towards Japan and the continuing, if diminishing, fears of Japanese militarism—not helped by its anger over the 2001 Japanese textbook issue—will mean that some leaning towards China is likely.

Fishery competition has been a traditional area of dispute in the regional seas and, with Law of the Sea developments, disputes over territorial waters and offshore mineral and fishery rights have become increasingly important in the North Pacific. China and South Korea still have to define finally their EEZ borders arising from their ratification of the UN Law of the Sea. They have signed a fisheries agreement as an interim arrangement in the Yellow Sea until the zonal boundaries are settled.[37] This agreement seems to have been more readily achieved than South Korea's fishing arrangements with Japan. China, for its part, had signed a new agreement on fisheries with Japan in 1997, which similarly provided for a joint control zone in the central part of the East China Sea, carefully avoiding the issue of the disputed Senkaku (Diaoyu) Islands.

Energy cooperation between China and South Korea is expected to grow as a consequence of the oil and gas developments within Russia and the CIS being discussed in North and Northeast Asia. South Korea is also to be involved in nuclear power plant development in China.

## Mongolia

Western analysts often question China's adherence to the norm of non-aggression. One motivation for China's aggression has been that of sovereignty—still threatened in the case of Taiwan and argued by some Western analysts, with some limited evidence, over China's activities in the Spratly Islands. For those that believe China wishes to restore the borders of its earlier imperial days, Mongolia provides something of a test.

Certainly, among China's concerns over its territorial integrity and sovereignty is its Mongolian Autonomous Region (or Inner Mongolia). What was once Outer Mongolia, however, obtained its independence after the Soviet collapse and now has an elected government. It was previously a site for the positioning of large Soviet forces (now removed). Fears that China, when strong, would seek to recover what had once been claimed as its territory, or at least to bring it under its dominant influence, seem not to have materialised nor to be likely. The example of a successful democratic and independent Mongolia clearly offers risks to China's control of its own Mongolian population. Generally, however, China appears to have come to terms with the situation. Sino-Mongolian relations are, for China at least, satisfactory though not without tensions, as there are some Mongolian fears of economic domination, since economic exchanges with China have growing substantially. Mongolia knows, however, that significant irredentist activity could risk less cooperative Chinese relations.

## Regional cooperation

China regards the multilateral meetings of the Shanghai Five, now the SCO, as a particularly important element of its northern diplomacy, which to date has provided substantial benefits in terms of security and stability in the area. For others of the SCO this is similarly important although a desire to develop links with Europe is suggested by membership of the NATO's Partnership for Peace with Tajikistan finally joining Kazakstan, Kyrgyzstan and Russia as a member.

Apart from the multilateral processes of the Shanghai Cooperation Organisation, North and Northeast Asia is lacking in regional multilateral institutions. China has not been active in looking to develop regional institutional arrangements but neither has it sought to establish institutions to rival those of the international system. Nevertheless, many informal multilateral groupings have emerged in which China has participated, with official encouragement, seeking to deal with such things as security, economics, management of ocean resources, transport and the environment and, most especially, energy developments.

Cooperation in the transport area, including on a Eurasian rail link, has been associated with the rapid growth of trade among the regional states that constitutes a major incentive for cooperative relations in Northeast Asia. This cooperation has often taken forms that reflect natural economic linkages rather than political linkages, such as South Korea's emphasis on investment in China. There have been efforts by the United Nations Development Programme (UNDP) to stimulate cooperation among China, North Korea and Russia along the Tumen River. These are actively supported by China's Jilin province in providing access to the Sea of Japan but, despite being originally a Chinese idea, the project has received a lower priority from Beijing,[38] and development is moving at best very slowly.

In the security field, Russia has proposed from time to time a collective security arrangement among the six regional countries of the North Pacific. South Korea has proposed a six-party official dialogue process. China seems unenthusiastic about multilateral security cooperation at the official level, despite being pressed by Kim Dae-jung during his 1998 Beijing visit to support something like the Organisation for Security and Cooperation in Europe (OSCE).[39] China, although opposing any OSCE-type process as likely to intervene in domestic matters, has accepted that a semi-official process could be acceptable. It is comfortable at present, however, with the Four Party talks dealing with the Korean Peninsula. Japan would no doubt go along with a broader multilateral arrangement but is at the moment also seemingly satisfied with the Four Party talks. It has also seen the ASEAN plus 3 (Japan, China and South Korea) meetings as providing an opportunity for the principal Northeast Asian leaders to meet and discuss common interests.

In the energy field, considerable dialogue has taken place. In this field, a number of cross-cutting issues come into play. China's interests in Central Asia's energy economy are substantial but so are Russia's interests in controlling that economy. While, in this respect, China's and Russia's interests are likely to be competitive, in both cases other motivations are important. In some respects these other motivations are compatible—both want to control religious extremism, terrorism and transborder crime. In others, Russia's objectives, whether for political, strategic and economic dominance or control of energy sources and transport may not always fit China's interests. In the short run, Russia's weakness will limit its capacity to dominate but in the long run the situation could change.

Given China's large potential future requirements for energy, the question has been raised of its strategy for meeting those needs. What that strategy will be and how it is prosecuted has important regional implications. The options posited are reliance on the market or territorial acquisition.[40] It seems apparent that China will basically rely on the market, formulating strategies to compete actively in the market. In practice, therefore, China is becoming substantially integrated in the world energy market. Thus the Chinese National Petroleum Corporation (CNPC) has been investing extensively in oil and natural gas fields and in energy related enterprises globally in order to provide for supply security and to reduce its dependence upon the Middle East. It is also a way of obtaining technology—but Chinese companies have also become joint venturers in providing services to the global oil and gas industry. For obvious reasons, however, it has a particular interest in Russia and the CIS as alternative energy suppliers to the Middle East.

Russia and the CIS have larger proven gas reserves than the Middle East. The nature of the energy sector in Russia and the CIS, however, with very large investments required in development and in pipeline transport as well as passage rights commonly makes multilateral rather than bilateral cooperation inevitable. Much of the discussion of such cooperation has been at the company level (many of which have been government companies, as in China's case), but governments have increasingly become involved, particularly in the case of China and Russia. No multilateral forum has evolved, however, at the official level as distinct from the unofficial level.

There are a variety of projects under consideration, some regional pipeline projects involving virtually all the regional states, the main objective being to bring Russian, Kazak and Turkmen oil and gas to China, Japan and South Korea. While much has still to be worked out, the attraction for China is the diversification and long-term security of supply and environmental benefits. China's CNPC has two development projects in Kazakstan, won in competition with US and Russian bidders. Plans for the development of Irkutsk's Kovyktinskoye gas field and construction of a pipeline by a consortium of countries including China, involving supply to

China, are at an advanced planning stage; progress has also been made on plans to pipe gas from western Siberia to Xinjiang and from Turkmenistan also to Xinjiang.

In other areas, much of the discussion, and many of the announcements of deals signed or projected have not proceeded very far and when they have they are often conditional, as with China's oil investments in Iraq. Often the announcements or agreements are little more than symbolic. Decisionmaking is slow, technical problems are major and political differences arise, such as over where processing should take place, a factor not only important in the RFE but also between China's support for a processing industry in Xinjiang and the Kazak wish not simply to supply raw materials. But the joint Chinese-Russian gas exploration and pipeline project in Irkutsk in Eastern Siberia seems to have progressed further than this.

For energy cooperation with China's north, a multilateral approach appears to be 'an inescapable necessity'.[41] Given the large costs involved in energy development and transport, the economic viability of projects will normally require participation of other gas or oil consumers, notably Japan and South Korea. This will require the development of stronger cooperative ties between China and these countries.

Despite China's efforts to reduce dependence upon the Middle East through its closer links with Russia and the CIS, it will remain heavily dependent upon the Middle East. While it will no doubt want to gain a particular edge in the competition for energy from that area, it also has an interest in stability in that region and energy interests will no doubt be an increasing influence in China's strategic policy. It also makes it evident that the concern at sea lane security that Japan and others have often expressed will be more likely a concern shared by China rather than China being seen as a possible threat.

## Conclusion

It is a commonplace that China must play by the rules and norms of the international system if it is to be integrated into global society. China might reasonably ask who wrote the rules or formulated the norms, and who judges compliance with norms? The evidence of its diplomacy in North and Northeast Asia does not suggest, however, that China rejects the general propositions nor the legitimacy of international norms that are genuinely international, and not simply the policy preferences of a relatively small, if powerful, group of countries. In the region at least, China has been following most of the universal norms and has benefited in security, stability and economic terms from their pursuit and, indeed, reaffirmation.

Human rights is the obvious area where it still has a long way to go. While it is also argued that this is true of proliferation of weapons of mass destruction, this is not a major issue in China's northern diplomacy and, in any case, it is increasingly difficult to substantiate evidence in what has become a highly politicised context. There have been signs, moreover, of its sharing international opinion and understanding of the interdependence of security as well as of its recognition of its own national interests in arms control. Support for the ABM treaty remains as strong in China as in its northern neighbours.

We noted earlier that norms are changeable. China has argued that internationally accepted norms should be preserved—by which they mean that sovereignty should be respected and that intervention in the internal affairs of another country should only be within UN auspices. In the Shanghai Five context, it has reasserted its support for these norms.

In North and Northeast Asia, some norms are more important than are others. Peaceful resolution of territorial and other disputes, non-interference in domestic affairs and cooperative handling of relations are most relevant and have been important in influencing China's North Pacific diplomacy.The related emphasis on confidence building has reinforced this approach. Although success in the economic field, seen as important in building confidence as well as on its own merits, has been limited, economic linkages among the North Pacific countries are likely to grow. China's efforts in the north are not primarily motivated by anti-US sentiment as such. Although unilateralist US policies and the policies of NATO have added to areas of common interest in arguing for a multipolar world, links with the West remain central for China and Russia in particular. Bilateral issues with China's northern neighbours are important enough, however, to need cooperative relationships.

The scope for cooperation in the North and Northeast Asia region is large in regional security, economics, transport, energy supply and environmental management. That cooperation may fail or be slow for many reasons, including a lack of governmental capabilities among the major states involved. The evidence does not suggest that the barrier will be that China's intentions conflict with international norms.

## Notes

1 As Keohane has argued, they are normally less specific than rules and regulations but the two categories overlap at the margin. Robert Keohane, *After Hegemony: cooperation and discord in the world political economy* (Princeton: Princeton University Press, 1984), 57–58.

2 A point emphasised by Rozman. See Gilbert Rozman, 'China's quest for great power identity', *Orbis*, 43, no.3 (Summer, 1999), 383–402.

3 'Kosovo conflict accelerates formation of Russia–China strategic alliance', *Stratfor Special Report*, 25 June 1999, available online at http://www.stratfor.com/asia/specialreports.

4 *Oil and Gas Journal*, May 4, 1998, 42.

5 *Tai Kung Pao* (Hong Kong), 24 November 2000, carried in FBIS-CHI-2000-1109.

6 See, for example, Kent Calder, *Asia's Deadly Triangle: how arms, energy and growth threaten to destabilize Asia Pacific* (London: Nicholas Brealey, 1996), chapter 3.

7 Defined as more than a simple bilateral relationship but less than an alliance.

8 The two agreements are discussed in Yuan Jing-dong, 'Sino-Russian confidence building measures: a preliminary analysis', Institute of International Relations, University of British Columbia (processed).

9 *Agence France Presse*, Beijing, 28 April 1999. There are, however, still two islands in the Amur River, near Khabarovsk, and an islet in the Erguna River, where boundaries are unresolved.

10 Although Russia now has more advanced SU 37s.

11 *Stratfor*, 'Kosovo conflict'; *Segodnya*, (Moscow) 15 June, 1999; Wei Jen in *Tai Yang Pao*, (Hong Kong), 28 June 1999.

[12] *Agence France Press*, Moscow, 22 February 2000.

[13] Robert Scalapino, 'The People's Republic of China at fifty', *NBR Analysis*, 10, no.4 (October 1999), 8.

[14] *Nezavisimaia gazeta*, 23 December 1998.

[15] *Izvestia*, 3 March 2001.

[16] Bin Yu, 'NATO's unintended consequence: a deeper strategic partnership…or more', *Comparative Connections*, (July 1999), 3, available online at http://www.csis.org/pacfor/cc/992Qchina-rus.html, accessed 1 August 2001.

[17] *Chen Ming* (Hong Kong), 10 October 1998, FBIS-CHI-98-292; *Ming Pao* (Hong Kong), 13 May 1999, FBIS-CHI-1999-0512.

[18] Attributed to Jiang Zemin in justifying a proposed US$15 billion aid package to Russia. Ibid.

[19] Li Lingjie, 'Sino-Russian relations in Asia Pacific', in Koji Watanabe (ed.), *Engaging Russia in Asia Pacific* (Tokyo: Japan Centre for International Exchange, 1999), 54–66.

[20] See, for example, Elizabeth Wishnick, 'Chinese perspectives on cross-border relations', in Sherman Garnett (ed.), *Rapprochement or Rivalry: Russia–China relations in a changing era* (Washington, DC: Carnegie Endowment For Peace, 2000), 227–56.

[21] Cited in Alexander Lukin, 'Russia's image of China and Russian-Chinese relations' *CNAPS Working Paper* (Washington, DC: Center for Northeast Asian Policy Studies, Brookings Institution, May 2001), 16.

[22] Statements by the Russian deputy foreign minister, Karasin, that the two countries 'are not willing to, or planning to, form any alliance', *Interfax*, Moscow, 1 October 1999, and repeated in *Xinhua* domestic service, FBIS-CHI-99-295. The response to queries about the Bishkek meeting was that 'a new bilateral alliance was neither discussed nor is on the table'. *Interfax* (Moscow), 26 August 1999, FBIS-CHI-1999-0826.

[23] *Associated Press* (New Delhi), 29 January 1993; *The Pioneer* (New Delhi), 16 January 1999, FBIS-NES-99-016; *Xinhua*, FBIS-CHI-2000-1001, 1 October 2000.

[24] Pavel Spirin, *Nezavisimaia gazeta*, 23 December 1998.

[25] Lu Nanquan, deputy director of CASS, cited in interview in *Ta Kung Pao*, (Hong Kong), 19 July 1999, FBIS-CHI-1999-0716.

[26] *Xinhua* (Domestic Service), 26 August 1999, FBIS-CHI-1999-0825. A similar view was expressed by Qian Qichen, *Xinhua*, 28 September 1999, FBIS-CHI-1999-0924.

[27] Mike Collett-White, *Reuters*, Bishkek, 27 August 1999.

28 Gaye Christofferson, 'China's intentions for Russian and Central Asian oil and gas', *NBR Analysis*, 9, no.2 (March 1998).

29 Gerald Segal cited in Christofferson, 'China's intentions', 29; Kent Calder, *Asia's Deadly Triangle*.

30 The history issue is discussed in detail in Gregory Austin and Stuart Harris, *Japan and Greater China: political economy and military power in the Asian century* (London and Honolulu: Hurst and University of Hawaii Press, 2001).

31 See Greg Austin, *China's Ocean Frontier: international law, military force and national development* (Sydney: Allen and Unwin, 1998), 197–99.

32 *Reuters* (Tokyo), 13 February 2001.

33 Lu Nanquan in *Ta Kung Pao,* (Hong Kong), 19 July 1999, FBIS-CHI-1999-0716.

34 When, in 1997, China's was the successful bid for an oilfield in Kazakstan over US and Russian competition, the specialist US press indicated some alarm, the *Asian Wall Street Journal* talking of 'resource warriors', *Asian Wall Street Journal*, 23 July 1997; others referred to the new 'Great Game'.

35 *Hong Kong Standard*, 5 October 1999.

36 Lee Chang-sup, *Korea Times,* 20 September 1999.

37 *Seoul Yonhap,* 10 November 1998, FBIS-EAS-98-314.

38 James Cotton, 'China and the Tumen River: Jilin's coastal development', *Asian Survey*, 36, no.11 (November 1996), 1086–101.

39 *Korean Herald,* 23 October 1998.

40 Stephen Blank, 'Energy, economics and security in Central Asia: Russia and its rivals', Strategic Studies Institute, US Army War College, Carlisle, March 1995 (processed).

41 Vladimir Ivanov, 'The energy sector in Northeast Asia: new projects, delivery systems, and prospects for cooperation', *North Pacific Policy Papers 2* (Vancouver: Institute of Asian Research, University of British Columbia, 2000), 29.

# 8

# Power, responsibility and sovereignty: China's policy towards Taiwan's bid for a UN seat

**Baogang He**

China's power in international relations has been growing in the last two decades, particularly following the handover of Hong Kong in 1997 and of Macau in 1999. Beijing's current political agenda is to unify Taiwan with China. A realist would argue that a Great Power like China can set its agenda for dialogue, that the idea of political equality is irrelevant in settling the Taiwan question, and that the United States will also cease its support of Taiwan if China becomes more powerful in the next two decades. A realist would also be pleased to note that all major political parties in Taiwan except the Democratic Progressive Party (DPP) went to Beijing in 2000 to express their 'loyalty' in the face of the increasing military, political and economic power that China enjoys. All the above views share one key idea—it is power that matters, power that decides Taiwan's fate, and power that settles the Taiwan question. This chapter does not endorse this view of power politics, instead it argues for the politics of responsibility.

The basic idea of the politics of responsibility is that the greater power a state has, the more responsibility it has to take. The international community now expects China to take greater responsibility in international affairs in accordance with its increased power. China is expected to demonstrate responsibility not only for the interests of its own people, but also the interests of other states and peoples affected by China's policy. This is because, in an increasingly globalised world, the impact of domestic policy often extends beyond borders. Indeed, people in Southeast Asian countries—particularly Singapore—and in Australia are seriously concerned about China's Taiwan policies and their actual and potential impacts. Ignoring the impact domestic policy has beyond one's borders is a form of narrow collective egoism and is likely to invite protests and condemnation from the international community. As a result, responsibility is not only a moral issue, but a real political matter. Failing to take responsibility can damage a state's reputation and weaken its place in the international community. The key question for China is whether Beijing can develop a Taiwan policy that is not only responsible to the Chinese people on the mainland, but also to the people of Taiwan, East Asia, Southeast Asia, and the international community as a whole.

In recent years, China's foreign policies have generally been restrained and responsible. China has, for example, stopped its nuclear tests in response to international pressure. China has cooperated with the international community in pursuing a peaceful settlement in Cambodia and supporting international peace-keeping efforts in East Timor.

China's Taiwan policy has also been restrained and responsible recently, notwithstanding the military exercises it conducted in the Taiwan Straits in 1995–96. Chen Shuibian's policy has also been restrained. In his presidential address in May 2000, Chen pledged that he would not declare independence, change the national title, or push for the inclusion of the so-called 'state-to-state' description in the constitution. Chen further pledged that he would not promote a referendum on Taiwanese independence if the CCP regime had no intention of using military force against Taiwan. Although Beijing was dissatisfied with Chen's ambiguity about the one-China principle, it responded to Taiwan's goodwill in a positive way. In the politics of defining one-China, Beijing made a compromise—although Beijing insisted that Taiwan stick to the one-China principle, it did not define China as the People's Republic of China and left open the question of what constitutes China.[1] Apart from the absence of military conflict, three mini-links were established, and DPP officials were invited to visit China. Nevertheless, though pragmatic compromises are being made, substantial rethinking of the principle of sovereignty is still lacking. A responsible Taiwan policy must deal with the question of sovereignty.

This chapter attempts to reexamine the fundamental question of sovereignty by examining China's policy toward Taiwan's bid for UN membership. It calls for the development and adoption of a new construct and practice of sovereignty that is acceptable to both sides. The chapter argues for a more flexible and responsible policy regarding Taiwan's UN ambitions.

## China's opposition to Taiwan's bid for UN membership

The Republic of China (ROC) government launched its seventh bid to join the United Nations on 12 August 1999. Twenty nations supported its proposal to the UN steering committee. The number of countries that opposed Taiwan's bid, however, increased from 40 to 48. In particular, the United States, United Kingdom and France, all of which had chosen to stay away from the issue in the past, stood against the ROC in 1999.[2] The ROC launched its eighth bid to join the United Nations in August 2000. On 3 August 2000, only twelve UN members submitted a joint proposal to the UN Secretary-General requesting inclusion of the proposal to consider the ROC seat as a supplementary item in the agenda of the fifth plenary session of the General Assembly in September 2000.

Of course, Beijing saw Taipei's bid as a separatist action and stood firm against the move. China's blockade of Taiwan's bid for UN membership is understandable given the general perception of the United Nations as an intergovernmental organisation of sovereign states. According to international norms, whoever joins the United Nations is regarded as an independent state. In other words, UN membership is an international criterion for independent statehood.

It is also easy to understand China's opposition to Taiwan's entry to the United Nations in the light of the deep-rooted Chinese ideal of Great Unity, which holds that there can be but one sovereignty, just as there is one sun. As far as China is concerned, there is only one China, and China can only speak with one voice and can only be represented by one seat in the United Nations.[3]

There is another important reason why China is against Taiwan's UN membership. It might be thought of as a mentality, a centre–province mentality. To China, Taiwan is but a province, and as such it cannot join the United Nations separately. This mentality, however, ignores the historical fact that Taiwan has been autonomous for fifty years. The PRC has to realise (however irritating it would be to admit it publicly) that Taiwan is politically, economically and militarily more independent of other powers than many nation–states whose populations and land areas are smaller than Taiwan's.

Given the strength of Taiwan's political, military and economic power, it is not certain that China will be able to prevent Taiwan from joining the United Nations in the long term. Taiwan's UN membership will repeatedly present itself in this new century as a thorny political issue. So far, Taiwan has been recognised by 28 countries. It has never stopped expanding its 'living space' by establishing flexible, substantive international relations. It is only logical that Taiwan will continue to push this agenda as its economic strength grows. Pressure from China can only result in a backlash in Taiwan—the stronger the pressure, the stronger the backlash. In trying to hurt the Taiwanese government politically and diplomatically, China hurts the feelings of ordinary Taiwanese people. As a result, the very notion of reunification is losing its appeal to many Taiwanese.

## Institutional innovation

An alternative mode of thinking and search for an institutional innovation is now urgently required. A substantive issue is Taiwan's position in the world. Is it possible that China might stop trying to push Taiwan out of the international community and switch to mutually and multilaterally inclusive policies? Does a peaceful unification policy require Beijing to renounce the use of force and agree to Taiwan's membership of the United Nations and intergovernmental cooperation?

If Hong Kong enjoys international recognition and a special status in international organisations such as Asia Pacific Economic Cooperation (APEC) and the World Trade Organization (WTO) , Taiwan should enjoy more international space and recognition than Hong Kong if a reunification takes place. There is every reason to explore flexible options that are sympathetic to the will of the Taiwanese people while at the same time laying an inclusive political foundation for reunification. A critical speculative question is whether it is possible for China to welcome Taiwan to the United Nations voluntarily.

Importantly, it is possible for China to negotiate with the United Nations about the status of Taiwan. Taiwan may first become an observer in the United Nations, just as twenty other states or organisations (including Palestine) have done. Then, Taiwan may obtain associate membership. Ultimately, Taiwan may gain a seat in the United Nations under the name China–Taiwan, similar to the arrangement of China–Hong Kong in APEC. Even the name People's Republic of China is open to discussion and change. It should be stressed that China's support for Taiwan's UN membership would be conditional on Taiwan's commitment to an eventual union. If Beijing were to make such a move, a crucial precondition for the resolution of the Taiwan question would be some concession by Taiwan to its claim of sovereignty. Independence-related activities must take into consideration the interests of China and the feelings of the Chinese leadership and people. Taiwan and the PRC need to pool their sovereignty to form a loose federation and share their sovereignty in the United Nations.

Territorial communities like Taiwan have come to enjoy considerable international status. As Michael Davis argues,

> Beijing should recognise that affording an autonomous constituent community a substantial degree of international participation would help to gain its trust in any agreed arrangement. For a confederal Taiwan, this

> might even include participatory rights normally enjoyed by states. Taiwan's leaders will be reluctant to agree to anything less'.[4]

The old idea that one sovereignty enjoys only one seat is counterproductive in dealing with the Taiwan question. The new idea, that one sovereignty can be represented by two asymmetric seats in the United Nations, is capable of satisfying both Taiwan's desire for international space and China's one-China policy. That is, Taiwan would be a part of China, while enjoying special status in the United Nations. This 'dialectic' politics would achieve reunification through supporting an 'independence' policy that welcomed Taiwan into the United Nations.

The UN system does provide such institutional flexibility. As a sovereign state, San Marino is associated with Italy but controls its own foreign policy and has UN membership. Liechtenstein shares a number of powers with its dominant neighbour, Switzerland, but retains its status as a sovereign state.

The proposal of UN membership as a possible solution to the Taiwan problem might sound 'unrealistic', but this is only because the current Chinese leadership is unlikely to accept the idea of democratic federalism, or the idea of a separate UN seat for Taiwan. The current Chinese leadership rejects such liberal or democratic lines of thought. Qian Qichen, for example, has said that any attempt to change the status of Taiwan through a referendum in Taiwan would pose a serious problem.[5] Tang Shubei, Vice-Chairperson of the Association for Relations across Taiwan Strait, has also asserted that democracy is not an essential question and that democratic reform should not constitute an obstacle to negotiations on the reunification question. He stressed that Taiwan should not impose democracy on China, nor should China impose socialism on Taiwan.[6]

Nevertheless, such a proposal is certainly not far removed from reality. Top leaders in Beijing have reportedly considered recognising Taiwan as a political entity.[7] In a new initiative, Beijing has promised that it would not appoint senior Taiwanese officials as it does those of Hong Kong and Macau, that Taipei could maintain some quasi-diplomatic functions, and that the united country need not be called the People's Republic of China.[8] The proposal becomes even more feasible if we take into account the international practice of dual seats in the United Nations, the costs and benefits of recognising Taiwan's seat, changes in Chinese practice of sovereignty, and the development of post-modern state sovereignty. Importantly, dissidents within the Party have already proposed new policies toward Taiwan. For example, Fang Jue writes that

> the People's Republic of China and the Republic of China should have equal status under international law. Each has its own territory and citizens. In reality, neither entity has ever had legal and administrative jurisdiction over the other. The above statement should be the starting point for an understanding between people on both sides of the Taiwan Straits and for the international community. If mainland China and Taiwan conduct political negotiations, they should be carried out only on an equal basis between the government of the People's Republic of China and the government of the Republic of China.[9]

## Comparative lesson

China's current opposition to Taiwan's UN bid is predicated on the assumption that UN membership means independence for Taiwan. This is not a well-grounded assumption. When there is a dispute over national identity, or the question of divided nationhood, the United Nations allows for dual representation.

Let us look at this from a comparative perspective. The two Germanies were admitted to the United Nations in 1973 and unified in 1990. The Yemen Arab Republic joined the United Nations in 1947, the People's Democratic Republic of Yemen became a UN member in 1967, and the two Yemens merged in 1990. It was proposed that UN membership be granted to the two Vietnams, but this did not occur due to the formal unification of Vietnam in 1976.[10] The sovereignty of the Soviet Union was represented by the Soviet Union, Ukraine and Belarus.[11] Both the Democratic People's Republic of Korea and the Republic of Korea became UN members in 1991. As of the end of 1991, 153 countries had established official diplomatic relations with the South and 112 with the North. Today, Korea—the cultural motherland of the Korean nation—is represented by both South Korea and North Korea.

One of the most important things that these cases tell us is that state sovereignty is not necessarily represented by one seat in the United Nations. It is clear that Beijing's notion of 'one sovereignty–one seat' does not equate with the way in which sovereignty is construed in the cases of the two Yemens, the two Koreas, the two Germanies and the Soviet Union, Ukraine and Belarus. China's opposition to Taiwan's UN membership might be justified historically in the sense that Taipei and Washington successfully blocked Beijing's bid for UN membership in the 1950s, but it finds little support from comparative politics.

In the context of dual seat arrangements, China's one seat policy seems to be the exception in international rule. If the two Germanies, the two Koreas, and the two Yemens were able to have dual seats in the United Nations, why is a similar arrangement denied to Taiwan? One explanation is the asymmetric power relations between China and Taiwan. As a greater power in East Asia, China is able to block Taiwan's bid to enter the United Nations, whereas North Korea was in no position to block the South's entry to the United Nations in spite of its initial objection to the idea of dual UN seats. Here, it is China's greater power that renders the idea of dual seats improbable. For this reason, it is imperative (as a precondition to the settlement of the Taiwan question) that China use its greater power wisely. It is this asymmetric power relation that necessitates the power of the United States as a balancing force to create power equilibrium and the current stability of the region.

## A cost-benefit analysis

Now let us look at the potential benefits if China agrees to Taiwan's UN membership. First, it can ensure peace and break the cycle of tension and relaxation across the Strait, and reduce the possibility of military conflict. It will also reduce Taipei's motivation to buy defence hardware from the United States.

Second, the economic cost for both sides can be greatly reduced or saved as the need to compete for diplomatic recognition is removed.[12] It would be far more beneficial to the peoples of Taiwan and the mainland if the money consumed in diplomatic wars were wisely used on cross-Strait relations.

Third, Taiwanese UN membership might be helpful to reunification in the long run. If China welcomed Taiwan to the United Nations, the two could potentially create an economic union. This could in turn provide a foundation for political union. Let us now look at this issue from a comparative perspective. Dual seats did not prevent the final unification of the two Germanies (bear in mind that they had separate seats in the United Nations for 17 years) and the two Yemens. It is political arrangements based on mutual recognition, as in the case of the two Germanies, that actually promoted the final unification. In the case of the two Koreas, independence is a non-issue since both are members of the United Nations. For them, the only issue is reunification.

One reason why independence is on Taiwan's agenda is that it is deprived of UN membership. If Taiwan were to become a member of the United Nations, the independence problem would disappear. This would leave reunification as the only issue, and this could only improve cross-Strait relations.

A lesson from the experience of the European Union is that member countries have conceded some of their national sovereignty for the sake of political and economic union so as to compete more effectively with Japan and the United States. If China and Taiwan are locked into the nineteenth century notion of national sovereignty, they are less likely to play a major role in global politics other than as a 'trouble spot' for the international community.

To achieve unification, the sequence of action is important. The rigid view that any action cannot appear to move away from the goal of unification is unhelpful. It might be a better sequence to allow Taiwan to join the United Nations and be autonomous before pursuing reunification. Reunification, like a marriage, should be a voluntary bond. Reunification is less likely if goodwill in Taiwan is damaged as a result of political pressure from the mainland. Moreover, as a result of China's threat towards Taiwan, Taiwan's unification advocates cannot speak out strongly. If Taiwan were admitted to the United Nations, however, they could develop into a more dynamic force for unification.

A fourth benefit of China being more positive about Taiwan's UN membership is that a contradiction in cross-Strait relations could be resolved—the contradiction between cultural/economic convergence and political divergence manifested in political antagonism. While cultural/economic contact and exchange are increasing between Taiwan and the mainland, the two entities are drifting further apart politically.

Fifth, recognition of Taiwan will enhance China's international status and demonstrate that China is a good international citizen. The idea that losing Taiwan will undermine China's status is myth. The idea that the CCP will collapse if it loses Taiwan is another myth. When China treats Taiwan unequally and violently, it invites international condemnation. If China respected Taiwan as an equal partner, it would also gain respect from the international community.

What is the cost to Beijing of Taiwan becoming a member of the United Nations? The greatest cost is Taiwan's independence. Two seats for one sovereignty means a reduction of one party's claim of sovereignty over the other. Moreover, a substantial cost in the eyes of the Chinese military is that Taiwan's independence poses threats to China's sea power and to China's domestic politics in that it sends a signal to secessionists in Tibet and Xinjiang. Complete independence should, however, be distinguished from the form of 'independence' implied in the proposal for a Taiwanese seat in the United Nations. As stated above, the recognition of Taiwan's UN seat is a special arrangement—it requires Taipei's commitment to unification in return. But recognising Taiwan would only mean 'nominal' independence anyway because Taiwan has already gained its political autonomy. Moreover, what Beijing would like to have is only 'nominal' unification—it has promised that Taiwan would retain its army, currency and government if unification went ahead. Beijing would not have the right to control Taiwan's people or land, nor could it impose taxation. If that is the case, China should not continue its rigid opposition to Taiwan's international move.

The second cost for Beijing would be the loss of the legitimacy upon which their political authority relies. In Chinese nationalist thinking, the Taiwan question is a potential and actual source of legitimacy for the government. In reality, however, if the CCP could reduce the tension, save diplomatic costs, and benefit both the Taiwanese and mainlanders, this would greatly bolster its legitimacy.

The third cost for Beijing is the reduction of China's privilege in the United Nations. The exclusion of Taiwan helps China maintain its status and privilege in the international community in that only Beijing represents China.

Beijing must also consider the greatest potential cost of all—a war against Taiwan's independence. A war would seriously damage the domestic economy, evoke opposition from Asian countries and the West, and delay modernisation in China. The cost of war would far outweigh the cost of making concessions to Taiwan. Of course, there are other perceptions of costs and benefits. Some military officers in China may see great benefit in waging war against Taiwan. They imagine that a war would free China from the influence of Japan and the United States, and from the disintegrative forces associated with Taiwanese independence.

The above analysis contains an economic rationalist account of the Chinese politics of membership. It stresses that membership is merely a political 'commodity'. China is on the supplying side. To allow Taiwan a seat in the United Nations would not cost China anything, but would return enormous benefits. Why not trade sovereignty for economic interests? A pragmatic approach would take such a trade-off seriously. Some countries sell membership or national licenses for economic interests. Conversely, Beijing uses economic incentives to secure China's 'integrity'. It allows some countries to access China's markets, but, in return, asks those countries to respect Beijing's one-China policy. Compellingly, however, China will not trade sovereignty for economic interest.

Can economic logic extend to the political sphere of sovereignty? As far as territorial sovereignty is concerned, Beijing has kept a rigid line, rejecting any compromise over Taiwan. This way of thinking is characterised by a move from principle to reality, rather than the other way around. This is an ideological obstacle to the peaceful settlement of the Taiwan question. For Beijing, unification is the goal. Rhetorically, Beijing insists that there can be no compromise on sovereignty; sovereignty is sacred.

## Adjusting, negotiating and 'trading' Chinese sovereignty

The key issue here is sovereignty. In its Taiwan policy, the Chinese government consistently attempts to defend its sovereignty.

The notion of sovereignty is complex and subject to different interpretations. Simply put, sovereignty denotes a state's entitlement to control the population within its national territories. It is reflected in border control, legal jurisdiction, representation in international organisations, the ability to set the agenda in policymaking, and the capacity to control exchange rates and tax policy.

Several questions need to be considered. First, must sovereignty be exclusive? Can sovereignty be shared and inclusive? Has Chinese sovereignty remained intact or has it been diminished as a result of increasing globalisation? Is there a link between the nature of the political regime and the idea of sovereignty? Democracy entails popular sovereignty, thus respecting the people's consent over the boundary question, while authoritarian regimes rely on an absolute idea of sovereignty as a basis for their existence. Is there a linkage in China between the decentralisation of power and the dilution of its sovereignty?

China has become integrated into the international community by participating in the world economy, joining international organisations, and signing and ratifying international treaties. Integration and the pressures of Great Power relations, the global economy and technological innovation are forcing China to adjust its conception and practice of sovereignty. The Chinese government has tried hard to maintain what it considers a proper balance between state autonomy and integration into the world community.

Where economic interests are involved, China is willing to make more concessions or place less emphasis on sovereignty. Yongnian Zheng's phrase 'perforated sovereignty' precisely describes the situation wherein the Chinese central government is no longer monolithic in all aspects of foreign affairs and provincial governments are increasingly becoming paradiplomatic actors in China's foreign trade.[13] It is imperative for China to attract foreign investment in the highly competitive international economy. To do this, China has gradually opened some economic sectors, such as banking and insurance. In doing this, it has given up *some* of its economic sovereign power by ratifying international treaties and making concessions to global economic forces. Beijing has given up more economic sovereignty in order to join the World Trade Organization (WTO). China allows foreign companies to bypass the Chinese judicial system for a fair trial if an economic dispute occurred. If economic interests outweigh the desire to retain national sovereignty, China may have to consider the option of sacrificing more of its sovereignty to the WTO.[14]

The human rights discourse in China has shifted from an emphasis on domestic issues to recognition of universal issues. Although the Chinese government insists that human rights cannot override sovereignty, many books and articles have been published in China advocating the predominance of universal human rights. One article discusses the tendency towards declining state sovereignty and the increasing internationalisation or globalisation of human rights, and elaborates the conditions under which international intervention on human rights is justifiable.[15] Importantly, a new conception of a fundamental basis for government legitimacy has emerged—a genuine protection of human rights. Any government that denies or violates human rights is regarded as illegitimate. As Zhang Chunjin put it, '[h]uman rights are the greatest politics. All activities of politics should take human rights as central, or be guided by the human rights principle. Without human rights, politics become hypocritical and cheating'.[16]

In the battle over sovereignty and human rights, Beijing seems to be in a losing position in the sense that it has to make concessions under pressure while still insisting on the sacredness of sovereignty. In practice, China has signed international treaties on human rights, entered the international human rights regime, and has thereby accepted a derogation of national sovereignty (despite this, the question of whether and to what extent China subscribes to the international human rights regime remains). International protection of human rights implies that states do not have supreme authority over the way in which they treat people within their territory. On a fundamental level, the human rights discourse has made it immoral and impractical to view the world as consisting of territorial units each exerting supreme authority within their own borders.

Significantly, a quiet change has taken place in China's policy toward international intervention. China objected to NATO's intervention in Kosovo, but supported the UN peacekeeping force in East Timor by sending some police. This implies that Beijing recognises that sovereignty is not sacrosanct and that international intervention can be allowed to override national sovereignty. That said, Beijing's approach certainly has a different emphasis. For example Beijing believed that the NATO intervention in Yugoslavia was illegitimate because the Federal Republic of Yugoslavia had sovereign power over Kosovo, while UN intervention in East Timor was legitimate because it was invited by the Indonesian government and Indonesia did not have well-established sovereignty over East Timor. Nevertheless, China has changed its position, from a strong one that holds that no intervention is allowed as far as sovereignty is concerned, to a weak position that holds that international intervention may be allowed if injustice occurs and the intervention is under UN auspices.

In other areas, the PRC has suppressed extreme nationalists and discouraged any debate on the sovereignty over Senkaku (Diaoyu) Islands. China's policy toward conflict in the South China Sea is also characterised by an emphasis on mutual benefit rather than sovereignty. In the early 1970s, the Chinese government opposed not only joint development of the East China Sea but also the idea of putting aside the question of sovereignty. Beijing changed its policy in the 1980s. In 1988, Wang Yingfan, Chinese ambassador to Manila, suggested that Beijing had decided to temporarily shelve the question of sovereignty over the Spratly (Nansha) Islands. This, however, does not mean that China has given up its claim to sovereignty over these Islands. Chinese scholars also object to the Antarctic model being applied to the South China Sea.[17]

The notion of 'One country, two systems' in Hong Kong demonstrates the complexity of Chinese sovereignty over Hong Kong. On the one hand, China's sovereignty is symbolised by its military garrison in Hong Kong, the state's monopoly of violence, and the central appointment of the chief executive through a symbolic election process. The latter gives rise to tension between sovereignty and accountability: to whom are the elected politicians and the non-elected government officials accountable—Beijing or the citizens of Hong Kong?[18] On the other hand, China has shown great flexibility in aspects of its sovereignty over Hong Kong. For example, Beijing does not impose taxation—one key element in the traditional practice of sovereignty—on Hong Kong. The people of Hong Kong are allowed to have two or more different passports, implying tacit recognition of dual nationality by Beijing. This undermines the exclusivist notion of Chinese citizenship, which is a part of the Chinese practice of sovereignty. Border controls between China and Hong Kong prohibit ordinary Chinese from freely entering Hong Kong. Moreover, Hong Kong enjoys special status in some international organisations, such as APEC.

Looking back, China has made a great deal of concessions over Hong Kong. Such compromise is now widely accepted in China. It should be emphasised that it was Deng Xiaoping's innovation and determination that convinced his fellows to make such a compromise with regard to sovereignty. Today, China needs a similarly innovative and capable leader to implement a deal with Taiwan.

The Chinese government has considerable flexibility on some practical issues in Taiwan Straits relations. Beijing negotiated a treaty with Taipei to deal with PRC citizens who hijack aeroplanes in order to reach Taiwan. The negotiation initially broke down on issues of sovereignty, such as whether Taiwan has the jurisdiction to decide if hijackers are to be sent back to mainland China. Eventually, Beijing compromised and ratified the basic agreement on hijackers.[19] Taiwan has already been a member of the Asian Development Bank and APEC. Thus, China's Taiwan policy already implies a divided notion of sovereignty. Although Chinese sovereignty would ideally be realised through formal unification of mainland China and Taiwan, Taiwan would keep its own army, police force, currency, and parliament. Under this arrangement, China's national sovereignty would be reflected by two *different* systems with separate armies, parliaments and currencies.

## Against an absolute right of national sovereignty

Clearly, China is flexible enough to adjust its practice of sovereignty even though it often rhetorically insists on the sacredness of sovereignty. The issue is whether Beijing is flexible enough to allow Taiwan to have a seat in the United Nations, in effect allowing China's sovereignty to be represented by dual seats.

Here, new political thinking is needed. The outdated assumption that sovereignty must be safeguarded by force must be abandoned. A modern marriage or union can be maintained only by mutual caring, not force. Also questionable is the tendency to regard territorial integrity as sacred and place it ahead of economic interests and culture. Sovereignty in the modern world is not sacred, but is a commodity that has an exchange value. Sovereignty can be used in bargaining. Compromises on sovereignty can be made for the sake of economic interests. Here, what is required is political pragmatism, and this can be found in Deng Xiaoping's policies with a functional emphasis. Thorough political pragmatism contains the notion that economic interests can override symbolic sovereignty. In other words, symbolic sovereignty can be traded as a commodity for economic benefits. In the South Pacific, for example, the earliest trade in 'tokens of sovereignty' was in postage stamps sold to overseas collectors (Pitcairn Island funds 20 per cent of its budget in philatelic sales). Tonga licenses other countries to use the geostationary satellite slots it controls as a member of the International Frequency Registration Board and Tuvalu has leased out its internet domain code 'tv'.[20]

Nevertheless, Chinese pragmatism contains some elements of symbolism, or seemingly 'irrational elements'. But this symbolism is functional in terms of providing moral justification and serving political aims. This is the contradictory function of Chinese political pragmatism. Failure to understand this amounts to failure to understand Chinese politics.

It is now useful to hark back to Mencius, who said that 'the people are the most important element (in a state); the sprites of the land and grain are secondary; and the sovereign is the least'.[21] In the context of China's foreign relations, if this ancient idea of people is combined with a democratic notion of popular sovereignty, it amounts to the principle that people should be given priority in cross-Strait bickering and that they should have a say. If the first priority is the interests of the people on either side of the Taiwan Strait, and if peace is in the best interests of the people, then territorial integrity and state sovereignty can be negotiated. Sovereignty cannot be detached from the interests of the people. The use of force is certainly not beneficial, whereas flexible policies in the spirit of magnanimity will better serve the interests of the people.

The nationalist idea of absolute sovereignty must be rejected. The nationalist approach emphasises the power of the state to do whatever is necessary to preserve the integrity of national boundaries and endorses the use of force to defend the superiority of national interests and national territory. As Hertz remarks,

> [t]he idea of the national territory is an important element of every modern national ideology. Every nation regards its country as an inalienable sacred heritage, and its independence, integrity, and homogeneity appear bound up with national security, independence and honor. This territory is often described as the body of the national organism and the language as its soul.[22]

If the state regards its right of sovereignty as absolute and maintains it over dissident secessionist groups or nations, and if an independence group asserts an uncompromising right of secession on the part of any community that calls itself a nation, no solution is possible except the destruction of the state or the suppression of secession.

The idea of absolutist national sovereignty cannot provide a solution to the Taiwan question.[23] The Taiwan issue can be resolved only if national sovereignty is compromised, negotiated, traded and shared. Compromise should be made by both sides. While China needs to reconsider its conception of sovereignty, Taiwan's pro-independence groups must also make a compromise in their claim over sovereignty. Independence groups must not view the right to self-determination as absolute. It is unlikely that a compromise over Taiwan's UN seat can be reached if the DPP continues to stress Taiwanese sovereignty and the right of the people of Taiwan to decide their future.[24]

## Toward post-modern sovereignty?

According to Cooper, pre-modern states, such as Somalia, Afghanistan and Liberia, are characterised by chaos and anarchy. Modern states are concerned with state sovereignty issues and its corollary—non-interference by one country in another's internal affairs.[25] China, alongside Russia, Indonesia and Malaysia, best fits this description of a 'modern' state in defending territorial sovereignty. The Shanghai Five Agreement reflects the common ground that state boundaries are sacred and human rights should not be a pretext for outside intervention. On this matter, Segal has pointed out that 'East Asia is reminiscent of 19th-century Europe: its sovereign nations have strong ideas of self-interests but little idea of how to resolve these interests when they come into conflict with each other'.[26]

Modern states value their sovereignty and feel threatened by post-modern intrusion. According to Cooper's theory, post-modern states have 'largely shed their hang-ups about sovereignty'.[27] Post-modern states are open to mutual inspection and interference as a means of building trust and confidence between states in order to deter fighting. As such, these states attach different values to sovereignty. As Cooper points out,

> [t]he post-modern system does not rely on balance; nor does it emphasise sovereignty or the separation of domestic and foreign affairs. The European Union, for example, is a highly developed system for mutual interference in each other's domestic affairs, right down to beer and sausages.[28]

It seems that national sovereignty has been eroded and reduced in post-modern states such as in the European Union. Sovereignty has declined with the introduction of one unified market and currency, the establishment of the European parliament and court, the emergence of European citizenship, and the absence of visa requirements for European citizens within the European Union. Moreover, supra-national organisations are required to deal with regional and/or global issues (global ecology, nuclear threats, international immigration) and conflicts among nations. Importantly, the idea of legitimate sovereignty has been developing. Sovereignty is not merely decided by a seat in the United Nations. States will be considered full members of international society only if they respect human rights and practice democracy.[29] The place of sovereignty in global society and its way of operation have changed but sovereignty still exists. The exclusive practice of sovereignty, the sacredness of sovereignty, and the use of force to defend sovereignty all belong to a nineteenth-century notion of sovereignty.

It is too early for China to accept the post-modern view of sovereignty. Yet, Jiang Zemin has shown his new thinking regarding security. Replying to a question regarding Canberra's military alliance with the United States, Jiang said, 'The...concept of basing security on military alliance and strengthening security through military build-up, a concept that prevailed during the Cold War period, has become obsolete'.[30]

Since it took China a century or so (and at great cost) to learn Western notions and practices of sovereignty, it will be extremely difficult to persuade China to unlearn them and accept post-modern notions and practices of sovereignty or the thesis of the end or erosion of sovereignty. China has finally come to grips with the original Western notion of sovereignty, only to find that the West has moved on to a new game with a new set of rules.

There are three possible reactions to this new development. One response is that the doctrine of the end of sovereignty is a construct of neo-imperialism, and an intellectual design for Western domination. The second response is to defend the sovereignty principle. Indeed, Beijing is adopting just such an approach in international arenas at the moment, and would like to represent the South, the Third World, to maintain the existing boundaries. The third response calls for 'link up with the world'. This response argues that it is imperative that China learn a new set of international rules that regard sovereignty as questionable. It will take time for China to make adjustments to its understanding of post-modern sovereignty and adopt flexible policies. The adjustment seen in its Taiwan policy is evidence of the learning process. A major issue for China is the cost of learning. If China can adopt flexible policies toward Taiwan, the cost will be lower; refusal to adapt to the post-modern notion of sovereignty is likely to cost China dearly. It is also important for China to learn the new practice of sovereignty from the European Union rather than the United States, which lags behinds on this matter.

## Conclusion

It is imperative for China, as an increasingly important power in the Asia Pacific, to develop responsible policies regarding Taiwan, one of which is to welcome Taiwan into the United Nations. The main obstacle comes from Chinese sensitivity to its national sovereignty, but China's rhetorical stress on the sacredness of sovereignty contrasts with its practical application of sovereignty—China has actually been flexible in ceding some sovereignty. Will

Beijing accept the idea of 'one-sovereignty, two-seats' in the United Nations? Can Chinese leaders take an innovative approach to overcome the structural limits of narrow nationalism and the absolute concept of sovereignty? Both the potential for conflict and the way out of a potential war are clear to us, but we do not know when and where a solution will be proposed, accepted and implemented. It will be a great tragedy if there is no political will to implement a responsible Taiwan policy. Must it really take a war to bring both sides to the negotiating table?

## Acknowledgment

The author would like to thank Zhang Yongjin, Guo Yingjie, Lou Qi, Sheng Lijun, Chen Dongrong, Peter Kien-hong Yu, Eric Zhang and Aw Beng Teck for their useful comments, suggestions and help, and to all participants at the International Conference on the PRC at Fifty: Power and Responsibility, 28–29 October 1999, ANU, Australia. A different version of the paper appears in *China Perspective*, March–April, 2001.

## Notes

1 *United Daily News*, 14 July 2000, 1; 19 July 2000, 3.

2 See *The Free China Journal*, 20 August 1999, 1; 23 September 1999, 2; and *The Peoples' Daily* (Overseas edition), 17 September 1999, 1.

3 *The Peoples' Daily* (Overseas edition), 17 September 1999, 1.

4 Michael C. Davis, 'The case for Chinese federalism', *Journal of Democracy*, 10, no. 2 (1999), 135.

5 *Peoples Daily* (Overseas edition), 29 January 1999, 1.

6 *Peoples Daily* (Overseas edition), 28 January 1999, 5.

7 *Central Daily News*, 28 May 1994.

8 *South China Morning Post*, 5 January 2000.

9 Fang Jue is a former Chinese government official presently living in China. On 20 November 1997 he issued a document entitled 'China needs a new transformation: program proposals of the democratic faction', which has been distributed to members of the Central Committee of the Chinese Communist Party. See his article, 'Liberal voices from China II: a program for democratic reform', *The Journal of Democracy*, 9, no. 4 (1998), 18.

10 On November 16, 1976, the United States used its eighteenth veto in the Security Council to prevent the admission of the Socialist Republic of Vietnam. However, Washington dropped its objection to Vietnamese membership in July 1977.

11 The Soviet Union, Ukraine and Belarus had seats in the UN in 1945 (when the Soviet Union demanded two extra seats for its republics in order to increase its influence in international affairs).

12 It is reported that Taiwan will pay up to $US2.5 billion in exchange for Papua New Guinea's diplomatic recognition of the ROC. *The Australian*, 22 July 1999, 6.

13 Yongnian Zheng, 'Perforated sovereignty: provincial dynamism and China's foreign trade', *The Pacific Review*, 7, no. 3 (1994), 309–21.

14 In India, opposition parties opposed to the government's sacrifice of the country's sovereignty to GATT. See *Economist*, 2–8 April 1994, 26.

15 Li Lin, 'Guoji renquan yu guojia zhuquan' ['International Human Rights and State Sovereignty'], *Chinese Studies of Law*, no. 1 (1993), 37–44.

16 Zhang Chunjin, *Renquanlu* [On Human Rights] (Tianjin: Tianjin People's Press, 1989), 19.

17 Chen Hurng-yu, 'A comparison between Taipei and Peking in their policies and concepts regarding the South China Sea', *Issues and Studies*, 29, no. 9 (1993), 45, 48.

18 Jane C.Y. Lee, 'The exercise of PRC sovereignty: its impact on Hong Kong's governing process in the second half of the political transition', *Issues and Studies*, 29, no. 12 (1993), 88–111.

19 *Central Daily News*, 20 December 1993, 1; 22 December 1993, 1.

20 I am grateful to Peter Lamour for this.

21 Fung Yu-lan, *A History of Chinese Philosophy*, Vol. 1, trans. by Derk Bodde, (Princeton: Princeton University Press, 1952), 113.

22 F. Otto Hertz, *Nationality in History and Politics: a study of the psychology and sociology of national sentiment and character* (London: Kegan Paul, 1945), 150–51.

23 In discussing the secession of Nagorno-Karabagh, Khachig Toloyan also arrives at the same conclusion about the limits of sovereignty, see Khachig Toloyan, 'National self-determination and the limits of sovereignty: Armenia, Azerbaijan and the secession of Nagorno-Karabagh', *Nationalism and Ethnic Politics*, 1, no. 1 (Spring 1995), 86–110.

24 *Lianhe Zaobao*, 17 July 2000, 22.

25 Robert Cooper, a British diplomat, discusses the post Cold War period in terms of pre-modern, modern, and post-modern states. See his book, *The Post-Modern State and the World Order* (London: Demos, 1996), 19.

26 Gerald Segal, 'An un-Pacific Asia', *The Economist*, special edition on the world (1996), 71.

27 'Not quite a new world order, more a three-way split', *The Economist*, (20 December 1997), 41–43.

28 Robert Cooper, *The Post-Modern State and the World Order*, 23.

29 Rosemary Foot, 'Chines power and the idea of a responsible state', chapter 2 in this volume.

30 Cited in S.P. Seth's article, 'Potential for trouble ahead as Canberra courts Beijing', *The Free China Journal*, 23 September 1999, 6.

# 9
# China and arms control: a learning process

**Gary Klintworth**

Any discussion of China's approach to arms control policy, in terms of whether or not it has acted responsibly, needs to be placed in context. And the proper context is Sino-US relations and US attitudes towards China as a great power. It is only the United States that has vigorously scrutinised China's arms control behaviour. It is only the United States that has accused China of not complying with its arms control commitments and it is only the United States that has the capacity to make life difficult for China on arms control issues. Looking at the material on China and arms control, most of it comes from the US government or *The Washington Post.* And indeed, it is only the United States, with its national technical means of intelligence (that is, high resolution satellites) and its intelligence network in China that has the ability to tick or cross the boxes on China's compliance with arms control regimes like the Missile Technology Control Regime (MTCR). Sometimes the United States gets it right and sometimes, relying on circumstantial evidence, it gets it wrong.

As a general observation, it is safe to say that China has moved from a position of disinterest and opposition in the 1950s and 1960s to a strong commitment to arms control and non-proliferation of weapons of mass destruction (WMD) by the 1990s.

Why did China make this shift? The simple answer to the question, and I believe the best one, is that China wants a safer world, with a reduced risk of tension and conflict so that it can restrain its defence budget and concentrate scarce resources on domestic economic reform, reconstruction and modernisation. That goal requires global peace and stability. Of course, there may be a long-term strategic imperative behind China's modernisation, with arms control merely an interim ploy pending China's attainment of superpower status. China, after all, is pressing ahead with the acquisition of modern Russian weapons and military technology at a quickening pace.[1]

But for the moment I am not inclined to the view that China's interest in arms control stems solely from concerns about *realpolitik*, defined in terms of a concern about China's global image and a desire to rein in the power of the United States and the former Soviet Union.[2]

Michael Swaine and Alastair Iain Johnston suggest that China is 'acutely sensitive to its international image as a peaceful leader of less-developed countries and a strong advocate of complete WMD disarmament'. They canvass a possible shift by China towards acceptance of the value of a common security approach to arms control but conclude that China's approach is dictated by the *realpolitik* interests of a relatively weak state.[3] There may be some truth in this but I think China was and is interested in the same common security values as the United States, and that means getting along with the United States.

China therefore seeks to avoid the threat of sanctions and the embarrassment of adverse publicity about proliferation deals with states regarded by the United States as so-called rogue or outlaw states. It wants to avoid fuelling the already combustible anti-China lobby in the US Congress because that would mean a possible loss of US technology and cooperation. This would have seriously adverse consequences for China's survival, development and modernisation. China wants to preserve diplomatic and commercial relations with the United States at almost any cost (leaving aside the question of Taiwan). That means restricting the export of strategic missile and WMD technologies to states not well-regarded by the United States and Israel, such as Iran, Iraq, Syria, Saudi Arabia, Algeria, Libya, North Korea and, more recently, Pakistan.

Robert J. Einhorn, Deputy Assistant Secretary of State for Nonproliferation has acknowledged China's willingness to engage with the United States on nonproliferation 'frequently and at various levels'. He judged that China had become a leading participant in such forums as the Conference on Disarmament (CD) and that the Chinese appreciated, like everybody else, that Beijing's national security interests were not served by the spread of dangerous military capabilities.[4]

## China's record

Until 1964, China had no real policy on nuclear weapons and arms control. It was rather more concerned about building a credible nuclear capability. It considered attempts to limit testing and proliferation as discriminatory but, after its first atom bomb test on 16 October 1964, it did propose, and has proposed ever since, a no-first use treaty and support for regional nuclear weapons-free zones.[5] China started to participate actively in the global arms control process with the commencement in 1978 of an open door foreign policy and engagement with the rest of the world. China joined the Geneva Conference on Disarmament in 1980. It stopped atmospheric tests in the same year. It joined the International Atomic Energy Agency (IAEA) in 1984. It put forward working papers and proposals on nuclear disarmament. In later years, China signed the Inhuman Weapons Convention, the Antarctic Treaty, the Outer Space Treaty, the Biological Weapons Convention (BWC), the Seabed Treaty, the Non-Proliferation Treaty (NPT), the South Pacific and Latin America Nuclear-Free Zone Treaties, and the Chemical Weapons Convention (CWC) and the Comprehensive Test Ban Treaty (CTBT). All these treaties were related to controls on the use and deployment of nuclear weapons, nuclear proliferation and nuclear testing.

## Comprehensive Test Ban Treaty

China conducted its first nuclear test in 1964. Fourteen years later in 1980, it was committed to the values of a nuclear arms control regime. It joined the Conference on Disarmament in Geneva. It announced on 21 March 1986 that it would cease nuclear tests in the atmosphere (although it actually stopped in October 1980). It participated in the negotiations for a CTBT from the beginning (January 1994) and pursued a CTBT that was fair, reasonable and verifiable, with universal adherence and unlimited duration. China's representatives played an active role negotiating at the CTBT conference table. They presented many working papers and suggestions regarding the draft text and dealt with a series of critical issues in the Preamble, Basic Obligations, Organisations, Verification and Entry into Force sections of the treaty.[6] China announced a moratorium on all nuclear tests as of 30 July 1996. It signed the CTBT on 24 September 1996 despite reservations about the absence of provisions on no-first use of nuclear weapons, a timetable for Russia and the United States to dismantle their huge nuclear arsenals, unsatisfactory procedures relating to inspections and the need to permit tests for peaceful nuclear purposes.[7]

China also claims that by signing the CTBT it paid the highest price because technically, with just 46 tests (compared to over 1000 conducted by the US, 800 by Russia and 200 by France), it had not completed all the tests it needed to ensure the reliability and safety of its arsenal. In other words, the technical gap between China and the other nuclear powers has been frozen by the CTBT, but even so, China was prepared to sign the CTBT in the interests of global arms control and its responsibilities as a nuclear power.[8]

According to a PLA officer, China made 'the great sacrifice' in the interests of 'preserving world peace' and eliminating the threat of nuclear war.[9] That is, China claimed it was acting for reasons of what Alastair Iain Johnston calls *idealpolitik* although, in his view, China actually signed up primarily for reasons of *realpolitik*—that is, its image as a responsible peace-loving global citizen.[10]

## Nuclear Non-proliferation Treaty

China ratified the NPT on 9 March 1992 and helped secure an indefinite extension to the Treaty in May 1995. China may have signed the NPT primarily for reasons of *realpolitik* just like the United States, Britain and the former Soviet Union but it signed it nonetheless, the fourth nuclear weapon state to do so, and five months ahead of France. Zachary Davis suggests that the reasons were to correct China's poor international standing after the Tiananmen massacre in June 1989, to access Western nuclear technology, to avoid the loss of MFN (Most Favoured Nation) treatment in the United States, to avoid being left out of the NPT club, and only lastly to reduce the risk of nuclear proliferation.[11]

In April 1996, China became the 18th country to ratify the IAEA's International Convention on Nuclear Safety.

China's publicly stated position has consistently been that it does not engage in nuclear proliferation activities and will not advocate or encourage nuclear proliferation and does not engage in developing, or assisting other countries to develop, nuclear weapons.

China claims that it has consistently approached the question of the transfer of sensitive materials and military equipment with the utmost gravity and that it supports the NPT goals of preventing the spread of nuclear weapons and accelerating nuclear disarmament. Beijing claims that is has always stood for the complete prohibition and thorough destruction of nuclear weapons, pursuing a policy of not supporting, encouraging or engaging in the proliferation of nuclear weapons and not assisting any other country in the development of such weapons. China, however, maintains that these aims should not prevent other countries, especially the developing ones, from being able to make peaceful use of nuclear energy.[12]

As a weapon state party to the NPT, China is prohibited from helping a non-weapon state develop nuclear weapons. Moreover, it must make any nuclear-related transfers to non-nuclear weapon states subject to the safeguards of the IAEA.

China has consistently denied that it has ever helped Pakistan develop nuclear weapons. Although an allegation was made in 1983 that China had given Pakistan sufficient highly enriched uranium for two bombs, there is as yet no evidence that China supplied either plutonium or highly enriched plutonium to Pakistan or indeed to any other non-nuclear weapon state.[13] Pakistan has imported nuclear technology from China but has never acquired any nuclear weapons technology from China, according to the Pakistani Foreign Office.[14]

China claims it wants neither tension nor an arms race in South Asia. That is logical and sensible for China. It has pursued the same goals as the United States on the non-proliferation of nuclear weapons in South Asia. It condemned the May 1998 nuclear tests conducted by India and Pakistan and urged both states to stop their nuclear testing, to abandon plans to arm themselves with nuclear weapons, to sign the CTBT and the NPT unconditionally and accept the IAEA full-scope safeguards.[15]

China has worked closely with the United States to help defuse tension in South Asia. On 27 June 1998, Presidents Jiang Zemin and Bill Clinton issued a joint statement reaffirming that their common aim was to prevent the export of equipment, materials or technology that could in any way assist programs in India or Pakistan for nuclear weapons or for ballistic missiles capable of delivering such weapons.[16] According to US Deputy Assistant Secretary of State Susan Shirk, China actually led the UN Security Council—with US help and support—to coordinate efforts within the Security Council to devise ways to prevent a nuclear arms race in South Asia.[17]

China has turned down requests from Libya for nuclear technology.

China is alleged to have at least contributed to North Korea's nuclear weapons research program, but there is no evidence to support this claim.[18] China has a shared interest with the United States in ensuring the Korean peninsula, and by extension Japan, remains non-nuclear. Indeed, Beijing put a lot of time and effort into urging North Korea to ratify the NPT's full-scope safeguards agreement in 1992. In the last decade, moreover, China has resisted North Korean requests for military assistance and has played a constructive role in finding solutions and restraining North Korea from pursuing the nuclear and missile option. China's key role in helping the United States convince North Korea to freeze and eventually dismantle its nuclear program has been acknowledged by senior US officials.

China has attracted criticism from the United States because it supplied a nuclear reactor to Algeria and has since cooperated with Algeria on nuclear energy research. Both China and Algeria have denied any collaboration on nuclear weapons. But US intelligence experts alleged that the reactor was larger than would be required for routine nuclear research and US Senate Foreign Relations Subcommittee Chairman Joseph Biden claimed it was evidence that China was becoming a rogue elephant.[19] It would appear, however, that what China is doing in Algeria complies with the inspection requirements of the IAEA—the project was approved by the IAEA and was subject to supervision and inspection by IAEA experts during its construction and test operation. Furthermore, China persuaded Algeria to place its nuclear facilities under IAEA safeguards in 1991.[20]

In the case of Iran, China argued that what it was doing was consistent with the NPT in that it was helping Iran safeguard a uranium conversion facility. The United States, however, was concerned that Iran could divert material from the conversion facility into a clandestine weapons-related centrifuge enrichment program with nuclear weapons potential.[21] In the end, however, in October 1995, China withdrew authority for the sale of two 300,000 kW nuclear reactors to Iran after talks between then US Secretary of State Warren Christopher and then Chinese Foreign Minister Qian Qichen.[22] China also cancelled the sale to Iran of a uranium conversion facility and turned down an Iranian request for a heavy water moderated research reactor. That is, China complied with US prodding to stop helping Iran with its nuclear program, notwithstanding China's energy-derived interest in building up goodwill in Tehran and elsewhere in the Middle East. Admittedly, the offset was billions of dollars of US nuclear reactors, equipment and technology for peaceful nuclear programs that China might not otherwise have been licensed to receive.[23]

## Biological Weapons Convention (BWC)

China ratified the Biological Weapons Convention in November 1984 and there has been no suggestion of a breach, even by the US Congress, despite growing concerns expressed by the US Director of Central Intelligence for Nonproliferation.[24] In 1998, China agreed to work with the United States to negotiate an enforcement protocol for the BWC.[25]

## Landmines

In 1982, China signed the 1980 United Nations (UN) Convention on the Prohibition of Certain Indiscriminate Conventional Weapons with its associated Protocol II on landmines. China took an active part in the amendment of the Landmine Protocol and, in 1996, signed a revised version of the Protocol prohibiting the transfer of landmines that are undetectable and that do not contain self-destructive devices. Like the United States, however, China is not in favour of a complete ban on landmines. Beijing regards them as indispensable defensive weapons for a country with long land borders and 'an uncertain security environment'. Thus, according to China's former Disarmament Ambassador in Geneva, Sha Zukang, China reserves the right to use landmines on its own territory until alternative means of defence are found.[26]

## Chemical Weapons Convention (CWC)

China signed the CWC in January 1993 and ratified it in December 1996 despite reservations about provisions for challenge inspections.[27] But China has a mature chemical warfare capability and has produced and weaponised a wide variety of agents according to the US Department of Defense.[28]

China is alleged to have at least contributed to North Korea's chemical weapons research program. However, there is no public available evidence to support this claim or any firm evidence that China has breached its undertakings under the CWC.

In July 1993, there were accusations that China was supplying Iran with chemicals. Then, US intelligence sources accused China of selling Iran thiodiglycol and thionyl chloride—chemical precursors for making mustard and nerve gases. In August 1993, the US Navy—with the agreement of the Chinese government—searched the *Yin He*, a Chinese container ship in the Gulf of Hormuz only to find nothing to support the allegation. According to Robert J. Einhorn, Deputy Assistant Secretary of State for Nonproliferation, Department of State, US intelligence was good and the Chinese were just lucky not to be caught out.[29] Nonetheless, the US State Department expressed appreciation for China's cooperative and forthright assistance in resolving the dispute in the interests of nonproliferation of goods and technology that might be used in WMD.[30]

In May 1997, the United States imposed sanctions on seven Chinese chemical companies for allegedly assisting Iran's chemical weapons program.[31]

According to Gary Milhollin, Director of the Wisconsin Project on Nuclear Arms Control, US officials were of the view that China had been exporting poison gas ingredients, equipment and technology to Iran since at least 1992 and that such exports, including entire factories, were continuing.[32] However, the chemicals involved were dual use items with civilian applications, and China held up the supply of raw materials to an alleged chemical weapons factory.[33]

Significantly, China subsequently agreed to strengthen controls over the export of dual-use chemicals and it expanded the list of chemical precursors that will be under those controls.[34] But it is not easy for China to audit the thousands of enterprises and laboratories that might be engaged in the manufacture of dual-use chemicals.

According to the US State Department, citing the positive Chinese response to a proposed sale by a Chinese entity of a chemical—anhydrous hydrogen fluoride—to the Isfahan Nuclear Research Centre in Iran, 'the US is firmly of the view that there has been a sea-change in Chinese policies and practices on nonproliferation and that China is moving towards the kind of relationship that advances and protects the security of the United States, its interests and its allies'.[35]

## Strategic arms reduction

On strategic arms reduction, China's position is fairly well known. According to China's White Paper, *China: arms control and disarmament*, the United States and Russia must take the lead in 'drastically reducing their stockpiles of all types of nuclear weapons and means of delivery' and commit themselves to a treaty of no-first use, a formula that suits China's relatively weak strategic circumstances. Only after the United States and Russia reduced their stockpiles by 50 per cent, would China participate in discussions on strategic arms reductions.[36] Given the overwhelming superiority of the US strategic arsenal (6000 to China's 200–300), it is difficult to argue that China's case does not have some merit.

In the United States, however, this is regarded as 'free riding'—that is, China prefers measures that advantage China's relatively weak position and gives least support to measures that impose constraints on China.[37] In my view, this is simply a case of China practising some *realpolitik*.

## Missiles

During the Iran–Iraq war in 1981–85, China sold both sides over US$4 billion worth of arms, such as tanks and tactical missiles such as the Silkworm, (a slow, old-fashioned anti-ship cruise missile). But China did not sell Scud missiles to Iran and Iraq, despite claims to the contrary (the Scuds came from the USSR). In 1987, China sold 36 now obsolete Dong Fang 3 or CSS-2 Intermediate Range Ballistic Missiles (IRBMs, range 3000 km) to Saudi Arabia for US$3 billion, a deal that may been the carrot for Saudi Arabia to switch diplomatic relations from Taipei to Beijing in 1990.

China may have helped North Korea reverse engineer Soviet Scud missiles in the late 1970s, but there is no evidence that China helped North Korea develop its Nodong or Taepodong missile.[38]

In 1989, China agreed to sell 48 M-9 missiles (range 600 km) to Syria.This deal was cancelled by China in January 1992 after lengthy negotiations with the United States involving the threat of commercial sanctions relating to computers and satellites and possibly offers of assistance from Israel to fill critical gaps in China's defence technology.

In March 1992, China reached a bilateral agreement with the United States to abide by the guidelines and parameters of the Missile Technology Control Regime (MTCR), established by the United States in 1987). MTCR, it should be noted is a voluntary agreement, has no international legal authority, and China is not a member. China also agreed to the five-power Arms Control in the Middle East (ACME) forum limiting arms sales to the Middle East.

The MTCR was upgraded in July 1992 to deny the export of any system suspected of being used as a delivery system for WMD. Category II also requires case by case evaluations for exporting complete unmanned delivery systems that do not meet the Category I threshold (300 km) but which can fly more than 300 km with a minimal payload (such as biological weapons), as well as dual use components, materials and other commodities. These expanded guidelines were designed to counter Chinese moves to operate on the fringe and circumvent the original MTCR guidelines through piecemeal technology transfer. In October 1994, China signed an agreement with the United States to comply with the 1987 version of the MTCR, that is, to not export complete missiles that are inherently capable of reaching a range of 300 kilometres with a payload of 500 kilograms.

There is no evidence that China has violated its pledge not to export such missiles. On 21 November 2001, China declared that it would not assist other countries in any way to develop ballistic missiles capable of delivering nuclear weapons, a move welcomed by the Australian government.[39] But so far China has not agreed to stop exporting the missile technologies or shorter range systems armed with conventional warheads. MTCR, moreover, still leaves open the door for China to claim it has received assurances from the recipient that the equipment or technology supplied will not be used to develop a proscribed missile system.

China also interprets the MTCR differently to the United States. The United States claims the 'inherent capability' of a missile should be used to see if it is covered by MTCR guidelines. That is, regardless of its payload, the question is whether the missile can reach 300 kilometres if its payload is adjusted. China's view is that if the missile is below the 300 kilometre threshold, it is not caught by MTCR guidelines. Thus, when China sold CSS-8 missiles (range 150 kilometres) to Iran it argued that they were not covered by the MTCR, and that China had signed the contract with Iran in 1988 which was prior to its agreement to comply with the MTCR.

A similar process took place with regard to US concerns about China selling some C-801 and C-802 anti-ship missiles to Iran. The C-801 has a range of 50 kilometre. The C-802 has a range of 120 kilometre. Both are subsonic. They are not the kind of missile that ought to be covered by MTCR. Despite this, US Congressman Christopher Cox, Chairman of House Republican Policy Committee complained that US forces stationed in the Gulf—the 15,000 men of the US Fifth Fleet—were within range of the Chinese missiles and that the United States therefore, should apply the Gore–McCain Iran–Iraq Arms Nonproliferation Act of 1992. This Act requires the President to sanction nations that transfer 'destabilizing numbers and types' of advanced weapons to outlaw nations like Iran.[40]

Even though China was not threatened with sanctions over the missiles, it nonetheless promised to stop supplying additional anti-ship cruise missiles, including those under contract, or the technology to achieve over-the-horizon capability or indigenous production.[41]

So far, China has stuck to its general MTCR Category I undertakings although many reports to the contrary have appeared in *The Washington Post*.

The United States would like China to become a full member of MTCR and tighten its missile technology controls for example; with regard to Pakistan.[42] I note however that Swaine and Johnston argue that the United States does not want China to become a member of MTCR because it would have to share sensitive intelligence information and membership would exempt China from sanctions.[43]

## Pakistan

Pakistan is something of a special case for China and is often mentioned as one of the exceptions to China's promises to abide by its arms control commitments. For China, Pakistan balances India's quest for hegemony in South Asia and, bearing in mind China's Muslim region of Xinjiang, Pakistan is a useful ally for China to have on side as insurance against Islamic fundamentalism in Central and Inner Asia.

Pakistan has been one of the largest markets for Chinese conventional arms and equipment such as fighter aircraft and tanks. China is Pakistan's most reliable and extensive source of conventional arms.[44] China therefore has a historical and strategic interest in helping Pakistan, an old friend and tacit ally since China's war with India in 1962. For China, a strong Pakistan presents a potential second front to India vis-à-vis the latter's rivalry with China. So, while China advocates nuclear and missile nonproliferation, it is under some obligation to help Pakistan if and when India appears to be getting the upper hand, for example, with the development of its Agni and Privthi missiles.[45]

It would not be surprising, therefore, to find that China has been the source of Pakistan's missile technology even though China has not provided Pakistan with actual missiles. In 1988, China contracted to supply Pakistan with up to 40 M-11 missiles, with delivery to commence in 1991. According to the Chinese, the 290 kilometre range of the M-11 meant it was not covered by the MTCR whereas the United States claims the M-11 has a range of 309 kilometres and is therefore caught by MTCR.[46]

According to US intelligence sources, China shipped launchers and key components of the M-11 missile to Pakistan in November 1992. Following pressure from the United States, however, the deal either lapsed or another solution was found because there was and is no evidence that completed missiles were ever shipped to or even assembled in Pakistan, notwithstanding allegations that US satellite intelligence had spotted M-11 missiles in crates at a Pakistani airbase at Sargodha.[47]

There is an assumption that Pakistan used the M-11 technology or components to build the Hatf-III but it remains an assumption because nobody has seen a Hatf-III. Nor is there any conclusive evidence to support the allegation that China helped Pakistan build an M-11 production facility in Rawalpindi.[48] However, according to Senate Foreign Relations Committee Chairman, Jesse Helms, the CIA's *National Intelligence Estimate on Military Threats to the US* was 'absolutely clear that there is zero doubt about China having transferred M-11 missiles to Pakistan'.[49]

China reportedly refused to sell Medium Range Ballistic Missiles (MRBMs) to Pakistan. On the other hand, Pakistan's Shaheen I Short Range Ballistic Missile (SRBM) looks remarkably like China's M-9 or Dong Fang DF-15 (range 600 kilometres). It has the same nose shape, the same fins, the same length and diameter and no country makes a similar missile. Oddly, however, despite all the fuss about the M-11, the United States has not yet expressed complaints about the Shaheen I.

Meanwhile, Pakistan has in fact been looking at North Korea's Nodong missile technology to build its Ghauri I or Hatf-V (range 1500 kilometres) to match India's Agni SRBM (range 2000 kilometres), possibly because China was not forthcoming with the technology or parts.

China has also helped Pakistan build a complete 300,000 kW nuclear power station at Chashma, 260 kilometres from Islamabad under a 1992 agreement. China provided the assistance on the basis that it would be a use of nuclear power for peaceful purposes. It claims that the transfer is subject to IAEA safeguards. Beijing claims that any suggestion that it is helping Pakistan develop nuclear weapons is groundless.[50] The equipment was made in Shanghai and included high and low pressure heaters, condensers, water tanks, and other non-nuclear devices.[51]

China has also been helping Pakistan develop nuclear technology at the Khan Research Laboratories (KRL) in Kahuta. In 1995, the United States objected to China's sale of 5000 ring magnets to KRL (ring magnets are used to make enriched fuel for nuclear bombs as well as civilian-use fuel rods). The ring magnets were sold to Pakistan by a company in Shanghai, the China Nuclear

Energy Industry Corporation (CNEIC). The Chinese government pleaded that it did not know about the sale until the United States raised the matter and that the ring magnets were not part of the Nuclear Suppliers Group's trigger list, that they were not prohibited and, in any case, they had civilian uses. Since it upset the United States so much, however, the Chinese National Nuclear Corporation undertook to prevent any further exports to unsafeguarded facilities and introduced even stronger controls on the Nuclear Suppliers Group dual list as well as the Zangger Committee's trigger list. China also agreed to consult with the United States in future on other export control arrangements for nuclear related technologies.

China accommodated the United States because, it has been argued that under a 1994 US law—the Nuclear Proliferation Prevention Act—the United States can deny bank loans, credit and insurance to any country that wilfully aids states to acquire unsafeguarded nuclear material. If the United States decided that China had 'wilfully' helped Pakistan, companies like Westinghouse and Bechtel might suffer. But the truth of the matter is that the central government in Beijing probably had no idea that a Chinese company in Shanghai was selling ring magnets to nuclear facilities in Pakistan.

## Weak export controls in China

In an effort to placate the United States, China claimed that it established a Military Sales Leading Group in 1989 to oversee arms exports, chaired by Army chief, General Liu Huaqing, with representatives from the General Staff Department (GSD), the Central Military Commission (CMC) and the Foreign Ministry. In April 1992, it claimed to have created several monitoring groups, such as the State Military Exports Administration Commission, to stop unauthorised arms sales.

If China did supply countries like Pakistan and Iran with missiles, components and technology, the problem may have arisen in part at least because China does not have an effective national control system. Thus, even when Beijing is willing to exercise restraint, its ability to do so is inadequate, especially in the area of chemical export controls.[52] According to another observer, China had in effect two export control systems, one civilian and one military, with a gap between the two that sometimes allows unauthorised items to slip through.[53]

In some cases, the State Council and the Ministry of Foreign Affairs may not know what a distant branch of China's huge military-industrial complex is doing or selling. In fact, it would appear that the US intelligence community has a better grip than China's central bureaucracy on what China's provincial industries are or are not exporting in terms of chemical precursors and nuclear and missile technology, or related bank account transactions.

Generally, the Chinese Ministry of Foreign Affairs, the Ministry of Foreign Economic Relations and Trade and the Chinese National Nuclear Corporation have made genuine efforts to implement a responsible WMD and missile-related export control system. They understand the broader principles of non-proliferation and have sought to ensure China's compliance with its arms control obligations. The Foreign Ministry recognises compliance is an important and sensitive issue in Sino-US relations and that preserving that relationship is more important than earning a small amount of cash, important as that might be to some chemical factory in Shenzhen or Shanghai.

Bureaucrats in Beijing, however, do not have a list of every company producing dual-use technologies like ring magnets or dual-use WMD components in the chemical industry. There were until recently something like 10,000 military-owned enterprises such as the China Poly Group and the China Precision Machinery Import and Export Corporation. They have an estimated turnover of US$10–18 billion and function more or less autonomously. Industries might sell equipment without consulting the central government. In the case of the ring magnets—very unsophisticated devices—they were treated under China's export control system as routine general commercial goods.

In November 1995, China's State Council released a White Paper titled *China: arms control and disarmament.* It stated that arms exports must be used for the legitimate defence of recipients, not for aggression, and must not harm regional peace and security. The White Paper stated that any corporation or individual who transferred weapons or military equipment without examination and approval by the government would be strictly dealt with according to law.

As it turned out, the person responsible for the sale of the ring magnets to Pakistan was dismissed.[54] Of course, it might not have been irrelevant that a company like China Great Wall Industrial Corporation, at the forefront of China's space industry, stood to lose billions of dollars in business and, more importantly, access to critical US technologies if sanctions were imposed, all for the sake of ring magnets worth a mere US$70,000.[55]

On the other hand, some conservative PLA leaders might feel China needs to placate Pakistan and the oil-rich Muslim states in the Middle East and Central Asia. In the view of this constituency, if the United States misbehaves in areas of great sensitivity to China, such as selling F-16s and missile defence related military technology to Taiwan, despite a commitment (in Beijing's view) under the Taiwan Relations Act not to do so, they see no reason why China should not reciprocate in kind in areas of great sensitivity to the United States, that is, to Muslim states in the Middle East or old friends of China's like Pakistan.[56]

This attitude—and I am speculating—might explain the CNEIC's subsequent sale and installation at unsafeguarded nuclear facilities in Pakistan of a special industrial furnace and high-tech diagnostic equipment 'with military applications' (the furnace could be a vacuum or skull furnace used to melt plutonium and uranium for nuclear bomb cores and titanium for missile nose cones and other critical missile parts). According to a top secret CIA memorandum dated 14 September 1996, paperwork had been falsified to disguise the final destination of the technology but senior Chinese leaders probably approved the illicit sale.[57] The US State Department made its concerns known to Beijing but, according to another report, US State Department spokesman Nicholas Burns stated that he was 'absolutely confident' that China had not violated the commitment it had made on 11 May 1996.[58]

A similar problem arose in March 2001 after US allegations that Chinese firms were helping Iraq improve its air defences by installing fibre-optic cables, contrary to UN-imposed sanctions. China's Foreign Minister Tang Jiaxuan strenuously stated the allegations were unfounded. He claimed that the Chinese government was 'very serious, very strict and always responsible in implementing UN resolutions on Iraq' and that Chinese businesses were prohibited from engaging in trade or other economic activities in Iraq that were contrary to UN Security Council resolutions.[59]

## The black view of China

The suggestion of bureaucratic ineptitude as an explanation for China's problematic record is not accepted by many influential people in Washington. While it is generally true that some sales of Chinese technology and products associated with WMD to Iran and Pakistan were undertaken by semi-autonomous entities without Beijing's approval, there was 'convincing evidence' that other deals were negotiated and executed with Beijing's knowledge and tacit approval, according to Mitchel B. Wallerstein, a Deputy Assistant Secretary of Defense for Counterproliferation Policy in the US Department of Defense.[60]

In 1997, in testimony to the US Congress, Gary Milhollin, Director of the Wisconsin Project on Nuclear Arms Control, alleged that China was not fulfilling its 1994 commitment to comply with MTCR and, citing US officials, he alleged that China was continuing to export missiles and missile technology to Pakistan, including assistance with an M-11 missile production plant. He also alleged, citing US officials, that China had been exporting poison gas ingredients, equipment and technology to Iran since at least 1992 and that such exports, including entire factories in 1996, were continuing.[61] He claimed that the ring-magnet sale to Pakistan was no accident and represented China's ongoing support for Pakistan's nuclear weapons program, beginning in 1980. He claimed that, because the ring magnets were made specifically to go into centrifuges that make enriched uranium for nuclear weapons and because they were sold to Pakistan by the China National Nuclear Corporation, an arm of the Chinese government, it amounted to a violation of the NPT. Milhollin made similar allegations with regard to China's nuclear assistance to Iran—Chinese inputs directly assisted Iran's nuclear weapons program. According to Milhollin, China was a rogue state and the United States would not be able 'to stop a rogue state from being a rogue state by treating him like a non-rogue'.[62]

Likewise, the Director of US Central Intelligence, George Tenet, said in his report to Congress in June 1997, that China was the most significant supplier of WMD-related goods and technology to foreign countries. He alleged in January 1998, that 'there is no question that China has contributed to WMD advances in Pakistan and Iran'.[63]

In a similar vein, the Chairman of the US Senate Foreign Relations Committee, Jesse Helms, and Senate Intelligence Committee Chairman, Richard Shelby, alleged that China was and is an irresponsible Great Power and that it had a 'long record of proliferation of the most dangerous weapons technologies—frequently in violation of earlier commitments and international norms and obligations—combined with a history of denial, deception, evasion and lying about these activities'. They cited the CIA's Non-Proliferation Centre as stating in June 1996 that China was 'the most significant supplier of weapons of mass destruction-related goods and technology to foreign countries and the primary source of nuclear-related equipment and technology to Pakistan and a key supplier to Iran'.[64]

The Cox Report, commissioned by the US Congress in June 1998 (Select Committee on US National Security and Military/Commercial Concerns with the People's Republic of China) was released on 25 May 1999. Three hundred pages were regarded as too sensitive for release. The Cox Report capped a crescendo of allegations about China's record on arms control and alleged that China was one of the leading proliferators of complete ballistic missile systems and missile components in the world and had possibly proliferated the world's most sophisticated nuclear weapons technology to nations hostile to the United States. China, according to the report, had sold complete ballistic missiles to Saudi Arabia and Pakistan, and components to a number of countries, including Pakistan. The report alleged that China had proliferated military technology to Iran, Pakistan and North Korea, and that China had not accepted the revised MTCR guidelines. It alleged that China was providing assistance to the missile programs of Iran (guidance components, solid propellant missile technology, the CSS-8 surface-to-surface missile with a range of 150 kilometres, and the C-802 anti-ship cruise missile with a range of 120 kilometres), Pakistan (M-11 missile launchers and the facilities to produce M-11 missiles, assistance with uranium enrichment, ring magnets and other technologies that could assist a nuclear weapons program), Saudi Arabia (CSS-2 missiles) and North Korea (unspecified weapons and military related programs) as well as other proliferation activities that could not be publicly disclosed.[65]

## The US Administration: yes or no?

There are obvious policy differences on China's proliferation record in the US Administration. On the one hand, there is the Cox Report, above, which US Energy Secretary Bill Richardson, said read like 'a suspense novel' and tended to sensationalise what were mostly allegations, not proven facts. And, despite allegations about Chinese assistance to Iran's nuclear weapons program, President Clinton certified on 12 January 1998 that he was completely convinced by China's assurances on nuclear nonproliferation, whereas just two weeks later George Tenet, the Director of Central Intelligence, testified to Congress that China's relations with some proliferant countries like Iran and Pakistan was longstanding and deep and that China had not promised to stop nuclear cooperation with either country.[66] According to Gary Milhollin, US engagement with China on the nonproliferation of missile and chemicals had 'run out of gas' with the US State Department choosing not to apply sanctions to China and that, therefore, sanctions as a deterrent or punishment, as intended by the US Congress, were not working.[67]

These differences are confusing for anybody trying to work out the extent to which China is being responsible or irresponsible on nonproliferation of WMD.

## Clinton Administration report card

Nonetheless, it is reasonably clear that China is fairly sensitive to US strategic sensitivities, at least whenever it is caught out.

China wants to preserve access to US markets and technology and it is concerned about the anti-China mood in Congress. China's US policy is to seek common ground, find areas of cooperation and avoid confrontation. China has thus been increasingly willing to scrutinise and restrain nuclear exports and cooperation and to address US concerns promptly and seriously.

One would expect the former US Secretary of State, Madeleine Albright to be well-informed by her Department. Speaking in 1997, she said it was 'evident in the last several years that China had 'systematically joined a number of nonproliferation regimes—the NPT, the CTBT, the CWC and the Zangger Committee, and it was generally moving within the regime of control of weapons of mass destruction'. She said that the United States had received assurances that China would not engage in any new nuclear cooperation with Iran and that the existing cooperation—two projects in particular—would end.[68] Specifically, China had

- promulgated for the first time strict national regulations to control exports of nuclear material, equipment and technology
- issued a State Council directive controlling export of dual use items with potential nuclear use
- joined the Zangger Committee, an international group which coordinates international suppliers efforts to control nuclear exports
- agreed not to provide assistance to unsafeguarded nuclear facilities, including through personnel and scientific exchanges
- provided assurances addressing US concerns about nuclear cooperation with Iran
- tightened controls over the export of chemicals that could be used in chemical weapons programs
- agreed to take steps to address US concerns about the provision of advanced conventional weapons to Iran which threaten maritime activities and regional stability.[69]

The United States, which regards nonproliferation as one of its highest priorities, had the following goals in its engagement with China.

- To terminate Chinese assistance to Pakistan's unsafeguarded nuclear facilities and nuclear explosive program.
- To curtail Chinese cooperation with Iran's unsafeguarded nuclear program.
- To establish an effective Chinese nuclear and nuclear-related dual-use export control system.
- To obtain Chinese participation in multilateral nuclear export control efforts.

Significantly, in February 1998, US Deputy Assistant Secretary of State for Nonproliferation, Robert Einhorn acknowledged positive progress by China in most of the sensitive areas mentioned above. He pointed out that

- China had made a commitment on 11 May 1996 not to provide assistance to unsafeguarded nuclear facilities in Pakistan or anywhere else
- China had agreed to phase out its cooperation with Iran
- China is putting in place for the first time a comprehensive nationwide system of nuclear and nuclear-related dual-use export controls
- China had become a member of the NPT Exporters Committee (the Zangger Committee) in 16 October 1997, the first time China has joined a multilateral nonproliferation export control regime.

There are expectations that China will in due course also join the Nuclear Suppliers Group set up to establish tighter controls over nuclear transfers than those specified in the NPT.[70]

It might be argued that China has only become sensitive to US concerns because there are sanctions if it does not, such as withholding trade access and blocking exports of high-technology commercial goods, such as communication satellites. The United States can suspend exports of nuclear materials, facilities and components to China unless the President certifies that China has conformed to US nonproliferation policies in accordance with 'Prerequisites for Implementation of the 1985 US–PRC Agreement for Peaceful Nuclear Cooperation'.

Whatever the reasons may be for China's compliance, as US Deputy Assistant Secretary of State for Nonproliferation, Robert Einhorn stated, the United States was seeing progress beyond mere words, with concrete action in terms of nuclear-related sales to third countries rejected or cancelled, detailed regulations and control lists adopted and publicised and active participation in international regimes initiated.

Einhorn said, however, that the United States wanted to see China make more progress on non-nuclear non-proliferation issues—chemical, missile and advanced conventional arms—where the United States still had serious problems with China's policies and practices.[71]

## Conclusions

In the past, China may have ignored arms control values and sold WMD-related technology for reasons including commercial and diplomatic, keeping Chinese industries in business, accessing technology swaps, gaining strategic advantage or obligations to an ally, as in the case of Pakistan, or it might have been a matter of influence building in zones of importance, such as the Middle East, in deals with Iran, Syria and Algeria.[72]

But the recent record shows that, despite some lapses and a willingness to exploit grey areas, China has, on the whole, been willing and able to uphold its commitments to international arms control regimes.

China wants peace and stability on its borders and in the world generally like any other country with global trading interests, domestic reconstruction priorities and a requirement for stable supplies of key raw materials, such as oil. In this regard, China has geopolitical interests in common with the United States. China also shares with the United States, and the Asia Pacific community, a common interest in stability in the Korean peninsula and avoidance of any excuse that might fuel a Japanese quest to become a 'normal' military power. China has been willing to accept arms control commitments even at some cost to its own narrower self-interest. For example, the freezing of the nuclear weapons technology gap that followed China's signing of the CTBT and the loss of revenue and political influence that followed the suspension of missile sales to the Islamic states.

Why? Because it wants to advance its own security through regional and global peace, and that means, by definition, good relations with the United States, the most important country in the world for China in terms of trade, technology, diplomacy and security. In this context, it is not surprising that China has avoided condemning the United States for breaches of the same rules it seeks to apply to China. For example, the United States has exported dual-use technologies to US friends and allies that are banned under MTCR Category I, such as submarine launched Trident ballistic missiles to the United Kingdom; provision of dual-use technology in the equatorial satellite launches of Russia and Norway, and large solid propellant rocket boosters for Japan's space launch vehicle, the H-2A.

China has had an eye on its public image as a credible, law-abiding member of the international community. But, in my view, that is only one consideration and not the primary one. China is driven by a desire to free itself from the distraction of international tension and the risk of conflict. It wants to follow the Japanese model of minimal defence expenditure and conversely it has learned a lesson from the Soviet mistake of over-expenditure on defence. It wants to focus on domestic economic, social and political reconstruction for 'a long period of time'. That entails an appreciation of the benefits of arms control mechanisms in China's near region and globally.

China's behaviour in supporting arms control processes might be attributed to a concern about its global public relations image, *realpolitik* interests including a mix of commercial advantage, access to advanced technology, reining in the lead of the United States and Russia, securing stable supplies of raw materials, preserving a peaceful world in which to concentrate on its modernisation, and placating its biggest rival and potential enemy in the meantime. Whatever the reason, China's record on arms control is nonetheless primarily one of compliance and broadly shared interests with the United States. In the joint statement issued by

Presidents Jiang Zemin and Bill Clinton in Washington on 29 October 1997, China and the United States agreed that one of their common interests was to prevent the proliferation of weapons of mass destruction.

When one looks at China's record, it is clear, notwithstanding the views of people like Helms, Milhollin and others, that the Chinese government has been positive and responsive to US concerns and is interested in the same nonproliferation goals as the United States.

Of course, China has problems with the US approach. It is unhappy with what it perceives to be

- the discriminatory provisions in MTCR that do not take account of the concerns of third world countries
- the need to promote the concept of cooperative security rather than unilateralism, confrontation, containment and deterrence
- the need to take steps under the NPT to eliminate WMD, including the US nuclear arsenal
- the need to preserve the Anti-Ballistic Missile (ABM) Treaty by not launching into Theatre Missile Defence (TMD) and National Missile Defence (NMD) systems that might lead to an arms race in outer space
- the transfer of responsibility to the UN Security Council for preventing WMD proliferation issues

Nonetheless, China has joined the game and, on the whole, it plays by the rules.

The most telling statistic I came across in preparing this chapter was from Michael Swaine and Alastair Iain Johnston. They point out that in the Maoist period China was negative and dismissive of arms control. In 1970, China had signed about 10 per cent of all arms control agreements that it was eligible to sign. By 1996, this figure had jumped to 90 per cent.[73]

These facts, it was stated in China's first Defence White Paper, demonstrate that 'China is a responsible big country' when it comes to arms control.[74]

This sense of responsibility on China's part may not last long if the United States moves to develop anti-missile defences. China is not a party to the 1972 ABM Treaty but it regards the Treaty as a cornerstone of the strategic arms limitation regime and therefore indispensable to maintaining global strategic stability, preventing an arms race in outer space and ensuring gradual nuclear disarmament. China therefore is aghast at the prospect of TMD and NMD systems, especially while the United States preserves its vastly superior strategic arsenal. It is particularly concerned that a US-designed TMD system will cover Taiwan, which China regards as part of 'one China'.

The Clinton Administration has proposed missile defence systems with a capability of hitting warheads travelling at 5 km/second with a range of about 3000 kilometre. As 80 per cent of Chinese land-based missiles have a range of 3000 kilometre or less, they would be classified as theatre weapons under the US definition.[75] If a TMD system is located in Northeast Asia, China's modest nuclear deterrent and leverage *vis-à-vis* Japan and the United States might be degraded. In China's view, Taiwan's instinct to strike out for independence will inevitably strengthen in such circumstances.

In the absence of some sensitive pre-emptive arms control diplomacy by the United States and credible assurances to China about the aims and limitations of TMD and NMD, China's commitment to arms control processes could quickly evaporate, with increasing pressure on China to modernise and multiply its strategic weapons. This could contribute to a negative spiral in Sino-US relations, a missile and anti-missile arms race, perhaps a new Cold War, and, at the very least, strategic instability in East Asia and the wider Asia Pacific region.

## Acknowledgment

An earlier version of this paper was published in *Journal of East Asian Affairs*, 14, no.1 (Spring/Summer 2000).

## Notes

1 See testimony, James Lilley, 'Proliferation: Chinese case studies', Hearing before the Subcommittee on International Security, Proliferation and Federal Service, Committee on Governmental Affairs, US Senate, USGPO, Washington, 1997.

2 On this, see Alastair Iain Johnston, 'Learning versus adaptation: explaining change in Chinese arms control policy in the 1980s and 1990', *China Journal*, 35 (January 1996), 27, 39.

3 Michael Swaine and Alastair Iain Johnston, 'China and arms control institutions', in E. Economy and M. Oksenberg, *China Joins The World Progress and Prospects* (New York: Council on Foreign Relations, 1999), 90, 93, 105.

4 Robert J. Einhorn, Deputy Assistant Secretary of State for Nonproliferation, 'Proliferation: Chinese case studies', Hearing before the Subcommittee on International Security, Proliferation and Federal Service, Committee on Governmental Affairs, US Senate, USGPO, Washington, 1997, 6.

5 Liu Huaqiu, 'No-first-use and China's security', Electronic Essay, The Henry L. Stimson Centre, 5 October 1999. Available online at http://www.stimson.org/pubs/zeronuke/prefnfu.htm.

6 Senior Colonel Zou Yunhua, 'China and the CTBT negotiations', *Working Paper*, Stanford University, Stanford, 1998.

7 'Beijing envoy lists flaws in nuclear test ban treaty', *Xinhua* (Domestic service), 11 September 1996; and Beijing Central Television, 'Qian Qichen signs Comprehensive Test Ban Treaty', 25 September 1996; 'China calls for flexibility in nuclear test ban talks', *Reuters*, Jakarta, 24 July 1996; 'China makes great concessions, wants early CTBT', *Ming Pao*, Hong Kong, 14 July 1996.

8 Senior Colonel Zou Yunhua, 'China and the CTBT negotiations', 26.

9 Ibid.

10 See Alastair Iain Johnston, 'Learning versus adaptation: explaining change in Chinese arms control policy in the 1980s and 1990', *China Journal*, 35 (January 1996), 27, 31.

11 Zachary S. Davis, 'China's nonproliferation and export control policies', *Asian Survey*, 35, no.6 (June 1995):587, 592. See also Alastair Iain Johnston, 'Learning versus adaptation: explaining change in Chinese arms control policy in the 1980s and 1990', *China Journal*, 35 (January 1996), 27, 51.

12 State Council, *China's National Defence*, Defence White Paper, State Council, Beijing, July 1998.

13 Charles N. Van Doren and Rodney Jones, 'China and nuclear non-proliferation: two perspectives', *Occasional Paper 3*, Program for Promoting Nuclear Non-proliferation, University of Southampton, 1989, 1, 2.

14 'Pakistan denies import of N-weapon technology from Beijing', *Xinhua*, Beijing, 29 February 1996.

15 Senior Colonel Zou Yunhua, 'Chinese perspectives on the South Asian nuclear tests', *Working Paper*, Leland Stanford Junior University, January 1999, 12.

16 US Information Agency, 'US-China joint statement on South Asia', *USIA Washington File EPF403*, Department of State, Washington, DC, 2 July 1998.

17 US Information Agency, 'DAS Susan Shirk worldnet on US–China relations', *USIA Washington File EPF502*, Department of State, Washington, DC, 21 May 1999.

18 See *Jane's Intelligence Review*, 'China's missile sales—few changes for the future', *Jane's Intelligence Review*, 4, no.12 (December 1992), 559.

19 Quoted in 'China helping Algeria build N-reactor: US', *The Japan Times*, 17 April 1991, 2.

20 Andrew J. Nathan and Robert S. Ross, *The Great Wall and the Empty Fortress* (New York: Norton and Co, 1997), 75; 'Opening of second stage of heavy water reactor in Algiers', *Xinhua*, Algiers, 18 January 1994.

21 See Zachary S. Davis, 'China's nonproliferation', 587; and Shirley A. Kan, 'Chinese proliferation of weapons of mass destruction: current policy issues', *CRS Issue Brief 92056*, Congressional Research Service, Washington DC, 1998, available online at http://www.fas.org/spp/starwars/crs/crs92056.htm; accessed 1 August 2001.

22 See Bingham Kennedy, 'Curbing Chinese missile sales: from imposing to negotiating China's adherence to the MTCR', *Journal of Northeast Asian Studies*, 15, no.1 (Spring 1996), 57–68.

23 US Information Agency, 'US satisfied with China's nuclear controls, US officials say', *USIA Washington File EPF508*, Department of State, Washington, DC, 31 October 1997.

24 US Information Agency, 'Lauder says biological weapons threat is growing', *USIA Washington File EPF419*, Department of State, Washington, DC, 4 March 1999.

25 US Information Agency, 'McCurry, Berger Sperling 27 June 1998 Briefing', *USIA Washington File EPF107*, Department of State, Washington, DC, 29 June 1998.

26 Statement by Sha Zukang, China's Disarmament Ambassador in Geneva, 26 June 1997.

27 Swaine and Johnston, 'China and arms control institutions', 90, 111.

28 Office of the Secretary of Defense, *Proliferation: threat and response* (Washington DC: Office of the Secretary of Defense, 1996), 9.

29 Einhorn, Testimony, 16.

30 US State Department Press Briefing, Washington DC, 4 September 1996.

31 US Information Agency, 'Background briefing on nuclear cooperation', *USIA Washington File 404*, Department of State, Washington, DC, 30 October 1997.

32 Gary Milhollin, 'Proliferation: Chinese case studies', Testimony to hearing before the Subcommittee on International Security, Proliferation and Federal Service, Committee on Governmental Affairs, US Senate, USGPO, Washington, 1997, 30.

33 Kan, 'Chinese proliferation of WMD'.

34 US Information Agency, 'McCurry, Berger Sperling 27 June 1998 Briefing', *USIA Washington File EPF107*, Department of State, Washington, DC, 29 June 1998.

35 US Information Agency, *USIA Washington File EPF501*, Department of State, Washington, DC, 13 March 1998.

36 State Council, *China: arms control and disarmament* (Beijing: State Council of the PRC, 1995), 24–25.

37 Swaine and Johnston, 'China and arms control institutions', 118–19.

38 Nazir Kamal, 'China's arms export policy and responses to multilateral restraints', *Contemporary South East Asia*, 14, no.2 (September 1992),121.

39 Alexander Downer, 'China's commitment to prevent ballistic missile proliferation welcomed', Media Release of the Australian Minister for Foreign Affairs, 23 November 2001.

40 US Information Agency, 'Republican policy agenda on US China policy', *USIA Washington File EPF504*, Department of State, Washington, DC, 18 July 1997.

41 *Reuters*, 20 January 1998, cited in Kan, 'Chinese proliferation of WMD', see also US Information Agency, 'National Security Adviser Sandy Berger, briefing on Clinton trip to China', *USIA Washington File EPF303*, Department of State, Washington, DC, 17 June 1998.

42 China has agreed 'to actively study joining the MTCR'. US Information Agency, 'McCurry, Berger Sperling 27 June 1998 Briefing', *USIA Washington File EPF107*, Department of State, Washington, DC, 29 June 1998.

43 Swaine and Johnston, 'China and arms control institutions', 113.

44 See R. Bates Gill, 'Curbing Beijing's arms sales', *Orbis*, 36, no.3 (Summer 1992), 379, 386.

45 Senior Colonel Zou Yunhua, 'Chinese perspectives on the South Asian nuclear tests', *Working Paper*, Leland Stanford Junior University, Stanford, 1999, 13.

46 Milhollin, Testimony, 29.

47 'Report cites China–Pakistan missile links', *The Washington Post*, 13 June 1996.

48 'China denies aiding Pakistan missile plant', *Reuters*, 26 August 1996.

49 See US Information Agency, 'Helms demands US sanction China for missile proliferation', *USIA Washington File EPR507*, Department of State, Washington, DC, 17 September 1999; see also US Information Agency, 'New CIA report assesses future ballistic missile threat', *USIA Washington File EPF507*, Department of State, Washington, DC, 19 September 1999; and Kan, 'Chinese proliferation of WMD'.

50 Senior Colonel Zou Yunhua, 'Chinese perspectives on the South Asian nuclear tests', 12.

51 'China sends nuclear power plant equipment to Pakistan', *Xinhua*, Shanghai, 7 February 1996.

52 Robert J Einhorn, Deputy Assistant Secretary of State for Nonproliferation, Department of State 'Proliferation: Chinese case studies', Hearing before the Subcommittee on International Security, Proliferation and Federal Service, Committee on Governmental Affairs, US Senate, USGPO, Washington, 1997, p.3, 4.

53 Davis, 587.

54 Einhorn Testimony, 13, 18.

55 'US says no sanctions on China in nuclear dispute', *Reuters*, Washington, 11 May 1996.

56 See Kennedy, 'Curbing Chinese missile sales'.

57 'Beijing flouts nuke-sales ban', *The Washington Times*, 9 October 1996, 1.

58 *The Washington Times*, 10 October 1996; and 'US says China did not violate nuclear pledge', *Reuters*, 10 October 1996.

59 'Foreign Minister Tang Jiaxuan: investigations clear PRC firms of involvement in Iraqi air defence upgrades', *Xinhua*, Beijing, 6 March 2001.

60 Mitchel B. Wallerstein 'China and proliferation: a path not taken', *Survival*, 38, no.3 (Autumn 1996), 58, 59.

61 In this context, see Kan, 'Chinese proliferation of WMD'.

62 Milhollin, Testimony, 30.

63 Cited in Kan, 'Chinese proliferation of WMD'.

64 US Information Agency, 'Helsm/Shelby Letter on US–China nuclear agreement', *USIA Washington File EPF204*, Department of State, Washington, DC, 28 October 1997.

65 Select Committee, US House of Representatives, *US National Security and Military Commercial Concerns with the PRC* [The Cox Report] (Washington DC: US House of Representatives, 1999), xxxvii, 78, 198.

66 Cited in Kan, 'Chinese proliferation of WMD'.

67 Milhollin, Testimony.

68 US Information Agency, 'Albright/Berger briefing', *USIA Washington File EPF305*, Department of State, Washington, DC, 29 October 1997.

69 US Information Agency, 'Fact sheet: accomplishments of US–China summit', *USIA Washington File EPF307*, Department of State, Washington, DC, 29 October 1997.

70 According to remarks attributed to Bates Gill in Swaine and Johnston, 'China and arms control institutions', 90.

71 US Information Agency, 'Einhorn statement on nuclear cooperation with China', *USIA Washington File EPF308*, Department of State, Washington, DC, 4 February 1998.

72 For a discussion see Karl W. Eikenberry, 'Explaining and influencing Chinese arms transfers', *Paper Number 36*, National Defense University, Washington DC, 1995.

73 Swaine and Johnston, 'China and arms control institutions', 90, 100–1.

74 *China's National Defence*, State Council, Beijing, July 1998.

75 Alastair Iain Johnston, 'China's nuclear forces: doctrine, modernisation and arms control', conference paper presented in Hong Kong, 13–15 July 1995.

# 10
# China's security problematique: critical reflections

**Yongjin Zhang**

The image of the People's Republic of China as an irresponsible power has been largely, though not exclusively, constructed by examinations and interpretations of what is purported to be China's security behaviour in regional and global international relations. The 'domino theory' associated closely with the threat from Red China in the 1950s and the 1960s and the 'China threat' debates in the last decade are just two primary examples. Issues and incidents such as China's participation in the Korean War, its support of Communist insurgents in Southeast Asia and involvement in the Vietnam War, its border wars with India, the former Soviet Union and Vietnam, its readiness to use force in territorial disputes in the South China Sea and its recalcitrance over the Taiwan issue, and its arms sale and export of nuclear technology to 'rogue' states such as Iran and Iraq, are among the evidence of China's irresponsible behaviour in world politics. This image has become etched in studies of China's international relations.[1]

It is not surprising, perhaps, that the existing literature on regional security in the Asia Pacific has focused on China as the central security concern of the region, particularly with the much trumpeted rise of China's power. What is disconcerting, though, is the severe disproportion between the keen attention to China as a security concern and the intractable neglect of China's security concerns in the current debate.[2] In other words, China is regarded as part of the regional security problematique, but China's security concerns have rarely been problematised. This is true historically and particularly in the post-Cold War discourse on Asia Pacific security, which is dominated largely by the Anglo-American international relations community.[3]

A particularly noticeable void exists, therefore, even in the small cottage industry of the 'China threat' literature.[4] Largely adopting an outside-in perspective, the existing studies have showed very little appreciation of the problems confronting China's security managers. Naturally, a large number of vital questions remain either unanswered or under-appreciated. How have China's conceptions of security, and by the same token, threat, changed over time? What do the Chinese élites perceive as the main problems for China's security and why? Where are China's security concerns generated, and what are generally perceived as China's legitimate security interests? How secure or insecure does China feel at any particular time and under certain circumstances, as for example when the structural changes of the international system take place? An appreciable gap between the security discourse within China and that outside China is therefore discernible.[5] While Chinese scholars find the 'China threat' claims perplexing and incomprehensible, many looking from outside-in find China's behaviour in regional international relations, particularly in the Taiwan Strait and the South China Sea, inexplicable if they are not expressions of China's desire for regional hegemony. Different policy prescriptions, ranging from containment, to constrainment and to engagement, are but a reflection of this perception.

I propose to problematise China's security concerns in this chapter by looking from inside out through a sociological lens. By looking at three integral and transforming social processes in the PRC since 1949—revolution, war and reform—I argue that China's conceptualisation of security has been in constant flux. The irony is that in China revolution, war and reform as domestic political and social processes, which are meant either to guarantee or enhance China's security, have paradoxically accentuated the insecurity and vulnerability of the Chinese state and the regime governing China. That is, an insecurity complex has been both generated and compounded in China by these pervading and penetrating social experiences. This is characteristic of China's security predicament.[6] No Great Power in recent history has had anything approaching this kind of security predicament.

This line of argument shares with realism and neo-realism one common starting point—security (defined more broadly in my discussion) as the central paradigm in understanding the international behaviour of states. It differs significantly, however, from both realism and neo-realism by arguing that it is neither China's national interest, defined in terms of power, nor structural features, such as the distribution of power in the anarchical international system that defines China's security problematique. It also goes beyond the liberalist perspective of internal politics in identifying important internal social processes—integral to China's transformation in the last fifty years—as independent variables that construct and reconstruct China's security conceptualisations and concerns. In a general vein, this is in agreement with claims made by Job and also to a lesser extent Alagappa that Third World states are faced with a particular and peculiar security/insecurity predicament, which emphasises the internal challenges to security and therefore to security conceptions of those states.[7] The difference is China's unparalleled experience in revolution, war and reform. Interacting in their own fashion and intensity with the same processes in the international system, they have resulted in a special social setting within which China's identities have been formed and transformed. As a result, China's security conceptions, and therefore behaviour, have been powerfully affected and sometimes determined by these forces.

## Revolution

By revolution, I refer not just to the transfer of state power but, most importantly, to a political and social process that redefines the political community and remakes the social order. Revolutionary changes in the international system thus refer to a fundamental transformation that redefines the nature and structure of the international order.

It is now a truism to say that the Chinese revolution has profoundly affected the regional and global international order as it has evolved in the second half of the twentieth century. It is, however, still a useful starting point to look first at how the success of the Chinese Communist revolution in 1949 affected China's security. Stephen Walt argues that 'revolutions usually disrupt the international system in important ways' because of the ensuing uncertainty about the balance of power, which results in security competition.[8] From the Chinese perspective, however, the responses of the dominant powers in the international system to the success of the Chinese Communist revolution were the determining factor in New China's security environment. The new regime felt threatened from the very beginning, not because of its weakness but because of the nature of the Chinese revolution and its professed ideological commitment to communism—the basis of New China's identity. Security competition, if any, was therefore defined more in terms of balance of threat than balance of power.[9] Mao clearly saw the Chinese revolution as part of a world revolution started by the Bolsheviks in 1917. Both before and after his proclamation of the PRC, Mao repeatedly warned of the distinct possibility of direct military intervention in the Chinese revolution by US imperialism . The 'lean-to-one-side' policy derived not so much from the weakness of the new regime as from New China's self-understanding of its identity in the Cold War international system as well as its perception of the Other.[10] China's entry into the Korean War was certainly not a step to redress the balance of power, particularly when it lacked explicit full military support from the Soviet Union. Mao's agonies over his decision in October 1950 reflected his uncertainty over the intentions of the Other.[11]

It is commonly argued that the Korean War and its outcome helped spread the Cold War to Asia.[12] The central thrust of US policy towards China—denial of the international legitimacy of the PRC—clearly identified Communist China as the Other, the archenemy of the United States. The containment policy and the military alliances in the Asia Pacific which arose as a result, on the other hand, helped China define itself as a major revolutionary, anti-imperialist force in world politics. The denial of the international legitimacy of the PRC, as embodied in the US policies of non-recognition of the PRC and exclusion of the PRC from the United Nations and nearly all other inter-governmental organisations, solidified such mutual identification for many years. Symbolically, the politically correct reference to the PRC in the United States, and to a lesser extent in the West, was until 1970 'Red China'. Self-understanding on both sides, Revolutionary China and the Other, therefore drew a dividing line of friend and foe in their respective international relations.

The PRC's identity as a revolutionary state in its early years was therefore constructed and reproduced against the implacable hostility of the United States. China and the United States become, in Christensen's words, 'useful adversaries' to each other. At the same time, the survival of the Chinese revolution was threatened by internal subversion of 'reactionaries' inspired and supported by Chiang Kai-shek's rival regime in Taiwan. Political campaigns such as 'three antis' and 'five antis' were waged against attempts to subvert the revolution from within. The coupling of external and internal threat to Revolutionary China's security was cemented by the United States' wholesale military, economic and political support of Chiang Kai-shek. The Chinese revolution was therefore insecure because it constantly faced possible foreign intervention and vicious internal subversion.

China's credentials as an uncompromising revolutionary power were further enhanced by the Sino-Soviet split. To anti-imperialism (the victimisation of China in the hands of imperialism and social imperialism) was now added anti-revisionism (the Chinese Communist Party (CCP) as the only genuine defender of Marxism and Leninism). The threat construction by the Chinese leadership changed accordingly. Now imperialist intervention from without and reactionary subversion from within were not the only serious threat to the Chinese revolution, revisionism and its agents inside the CCP also threatened to undermine the essence of the Chinese revolution. The most dangerous threat to the Chinese revolution was the 'Khrushchevs sleeping beside us'—a rationale that Mao invoked to start the Great Proletarian Cultural Revolution. In the 1960s, Revolutionary China staged open confrontations with both superpowers on several fronts. Many have noted the radicalisation of Chinese foreign policy and domestic politics after 1957. The causal question; namely, the extent to which China's deteriorating international environment contributed to the radicalisation of domestic politics in the PRC; is yet to be comprehensively addressed.

Ironically, the most confrontational period of the PRC's international relations was also the period when the PRC was most vulnerable. Confrontations over the Taiwan Strait in 1955 and 1958 and Sino-Soviet border clashes in 1969 elicited direct and explicit nuclear threats to China by both superpowers. The escalation of the Vietnam War after 1964, which again brought a large-scale war to the borders of the PRC, was justified by the rationale of containing the fanatic and dangerous Communist expansion from China. As the Sino-Soviet contentions intensified and the US containment policy hardened, the PRC, in Richard Nixon's catch phrase, 'lived in angry isolation'.

The Chinese revolution violently transformed China's social order and redefined the political community in China. For this very purpose, many revolutions have taken place within the Chinese revolution.[13] None of them, however, has been as devastating and disastrous (nor, for that matter, as defining) as the Cultural Revolution. Whether the origins of the Cultural Revolution are to be found in Mao's megalomania/paranoia or are more deeply rooted in the CCP's political, economic and cultural experience is beyond the scope of our discussions here.[14] The Cultural Revolution introduced an ultra-revolutionary period in Chinese politics with the construction of a highly militarised state operating according to extremely radical and militant domestic and foreign policies. It destroyed the fragile state apparatus of the PRC, put into the question the legitimacy of the regime, and transmitted an image of a regime dominated by fanatics.

Yet, Revolutionary China's identity was redefined during this period. Pivotal to this development is that, in 1971, on the eve of the breakthrough in Sino-American relations, the PRC was admitted into the United Nations, replacing Taiwan in both the General Assembly and the UN Security Council. The international legitimacy of the PRC was widely recognised for the first time after 1949. Diplomatic recognition of the PRC by many states followed in quick succession. PRC membership in a number of intergovernmental organisations was secured. A revealing indicator of the PRC's transformation from a revolutionary to a 'normal' state is the CCP's efforts throughout the 1970s to downgrade its Party-to-Party relations in order to carry out normal state-to-state relations, particularly with Southeast Asian nations.[15]

The direct military and physical threat posed by the former Soviet Union to China's territorial integrity after the 1969 armed conflicts along the Sino-Soviet borders forced the Chinese leaders to reassess China's major strategic threat. China was forced to acknowledge that the Soviet Union, notwithstanding shared ideology, represented the greatest threat to China's interests. It was also compelled to accept that the United States provided a counterweight to that threat, despite its ideological hostility. This strategic shift was a critical turn in the Chinese leadership's security thinking. Security, and by the same token threat, are now conceptualised in terms of balance of power, not compatibility of ideology. The referent of security is shifting from the Chinese revolution as part of the world revolution to the PRC as a state in the international system. The convergence of US and Chinese strategic thinking at this particular point, the idea that ideological considerations should give way to geopolitical considerations, is not entirely coincidental. Modern China has always been jealously territorial. By redefining Revolutionary China's vital interests, the Sino-Soviet conflicts may have inadvertently helped the formation of the PRC's state identity. Martin Wight once remarked that 'international revolution has never for long maintained itself against national interest. Doctrinal considerations have always within two generations been overridden by raison d'état'.[16] It is clear that by 1969 and within just one generation, raison d'etat for the Chinese state had prevailed over ideological considerations in the security calculus of the Chinese leadership. If the confrontational approaches to international relations adopted by Revolutionary China in the 1950s and the 1960s often confounded realists and neo-realists alike, they must have found China's balance of power behaviour in the 1970s and most of the 1980s pleasingly amenable to their analytical paradigms.

How do revolutionary changes as a social process in the international system affect China's security? Suffice it here to give two examples to illustrate the dynamics of the international systemic changes affecting China's (in)security. One is the anti-colonial revolution, which is sometimes also regarded as part of the 'revolt against the West' in this century.[17] As a revolutionary state, China diligently capitalised on what James Mayall called the 'restructuring of international society'.[18] In this 'revolutionary age', the PRC was able to find allies against the Western domination by identifying itself with anti-colonial revolutions, thus modifying its isolation from both the United States plus its allies and the Soviet-dominated socialist camp. China's revolutionary diplomacy was actively cultivated to serve its national security interests.[19] This systemic change also made it possible for the increased UN membership to vote the PRC into the United Nations in spite of persistent US resistance and maneuvering inside and outside UN fora. China's support for revolutionary violence in national liberation movements throughout the world and its limited, but widely distributed aid to Asian and African countries gave the PRC the semblance of a Great Power with global interests as early as the 1960s. It also projected the image of a revolutionary power bent on world revolution.

If anti-colonial revolutions and China's cultivation of them modified China's security environment, another set of revolutionary changes in the international system—symbolised by the end of the Cold War—has more varied complications for China's security. The disappearance of ideological and military confrontations between the East and the West and the diminishing prospect of an all-out nuclear war have appreciably reduced the structural violence of the international system. As widely acknowledged by even the Chinese leadership, China in the 1990s enjoys an unprecedented degree of security as far as external military threat is concerned. On the other hand, the end of the Cold War also redefines the international political community. With the collapse of the East–West dichotomy, the collective identity of the West, the liberal democracy, is defined in opposition to non-democratic regimes. In civilisational terms, a divide emerges between the West vis-à-vis the rest. Either way, China, as belonging to 'the rest' and as the 'last bastion of Communism' and the 'remaining Leninist state', is certainly the Other. While China is broadly regarded as constituting a threat to liberal democratic values and peace, the Chinese leadership believes that there is a coordinated conspiracy of 'peaceful evolution' that aims to undermine the rule of the CCP and its legitimacy. The revolutionary turn of the post-Cold War international system has increasingly cast Communist China, once a revolutionary state, in the shadow of a counter-revolution. In this way, recent revolutionary changes in the international system have redrawn the enmity–amity line, and have reconstructed threat perceptions between China and the West.[20]

## War

The twentieth century is, as Hannah Arendt once remarked, a century of wars and revolutions.[21] Charles Tilly, in a sweeping review of revolutions through centuries, observed that '[t]he histories of wars and of revolutions have intertwined'.[22] This is truer for China than for most other states in international society. In the second half of the twentieth century, particularly before 1979, the Chinese experience of revolution was closely intertwined with that of war. China's involvement in wars (as in the instances of its involvement in the Korean and Vietnam wars), in armed confrontations (as in the instances of the two Taiwan Strait crises in 1955 and 1958) and in what Johnston called 'militarised inter-state disputes'[23] (as in the instances of its border wars with India in 1962, the Soviet Union in 1969 and Vietnam in 1979) are just part of that experience.[24]

That China has been involved in the use of force in intra-state and inter-state disputes and conflicts more than most other states in the last fifty years there is no doubt; the question is why. Stephen Walt's theory of revolution and war offers partial explanation. His arguments that revolution causes a large shift in the balance of threats and creates spirals of suspicion and misinformation that lead to war sit relatively well in explaining the initial period of hostility between China and the United States and China's eventual participation in the Korean War.[25] Iain Johnston's theory of cultural realism, in particular Mao Zedong's socialisation in that traditional strategic culture, attempts to identify a particular cultural context in which China's war-prone behaviour is made explicable.[26] We may also note Martin Wight's observation that '[a] revolutionary power is morally and psychologically at war with its neighbours all the time, even when legally peace prevails, because it believes that it has a mission to transform international society by conversion or coercion…'.[27]

Three other areas that constitute the specific cultural-institutional context that has conditioned China's social experience in war since 1949, I believe, need to be explored in search for more explanations. First, the PRC has been at the receiving end of collective military operations, threat, or both, first in the Korean War, the containment (of which the Vietnam War was a component), and then in the Soviet-orchestrated encirclement, real or imagined. More significantly, perhaps, China was subjected to repeated explicit nuclear threats in the 1950s and the 1960s by both superpowers, in the wake of war or during military conflicts.[28] War exposes the vulnerability of the PRC and constitutes a constant threat to its security and territorial integrity.

Second, the post-war international system has seen the culmination of what Anthony Giddens calls 'the industrialisation of war',[29] particularly in the advent of nuclear weapons and the eventual nuclearisation of war and peace. The post-war order, as embodied in the Cold War, was highly militarised and driven by an array of warring states. Great Powers, Kal Holsti noted, are 'war prone' in the post-war period.[30] Warfare 'as a virtuous exercise of state power'[31] was not seriously questioned. The Cold War, which represented the institutionalisation of social effects in international society after the end of the Second World War, therefore legitimised an inherently highly violent structural order from balance of terror to mutually assured destruction (MAD). More pertinent to our discussion here is the fact that Revolutionary China was to be socialised into just such an international system in 1949. The PRC, like many other states, acquired its shared knowledge about the nature of this anarchic system, the meaning of power and functions of war, in its social interactions with this system. War therefore not only constitutes a threat to China's security; it is a vital instrument for maintaining China's security and territorial integrity.

Third, exploration of the sociological context must also look at the personal experience of Chinese leaders. China's national experience and the structural character of the post-war international system are, after all, mediated by Chinese leaders—their decisionmaking ultimately determines China's international behaviour. Traditional strategic culture, as Johnston notes, constitutes an important historical-cultural context for Mao's decisionmaking.[32] Equally, we should note that the first generations from Mao Zedong to Zhu De and Deng Xiaoping were all revolutionary warriors in civilian clothes. Fighting guerrilla wars before 1949 was an indispensable and invaluable social experience for them. The Revolutionary War and War of Liberation not only ensured their personal survival but also brought them to power in the first place. Their socialisation in war and the Marxist conception of revolutionary violence, which stayed with them when they became the new ruling élite, undoubtedly shaped their conceptions of war and the *realpolitik* view of power politics in international relations.

The intriguing questions are therefore how much Mao's personal experience of fighting revolutionary wars throughout his life, mostly at the receiving end of militarised violence, influenced his strategic thinking of *parabellum*? In which way did the nature of the highly militarised international system and the industrialisation of war inform Mao's post-1949 thinking about China's security? If definitive answers to these two questions continue to elude us, it is nevertheless clear that both influenced Mao's conception of war, his concerns about China's security, and his construction of the threat to China. Revolutionary violence is therefore an important means of achieving peace. World war is inevitable because of superpower rivalries around the world, which are the ultimate causes of regional conflicts. Military expenditures on building

China's nuclear bomb are therefore justified. It is also natural that 'military imperatives dominate the state in terms of their economic organisation'.[33] The build up of the so-called Third Front deep in China's interior reflects both Mao's acute concerns for China's vulnerability and his appreciation of the destruction that the industrialisation of war might inflict on China. Mao's fear for China's security because of its strategic weakness vis-à-vis the two superpowers, as confided by Zhou Enlai to Kissinger during their first encounter in July 1971, centred on a US-Soviet condominium to destroy China.[34]

One particular aspect of China's social interactions with the militarised order of the post-war international system alluded to earlier can further illustrate China's changing perceptions of war and security. This involves China and nuclear arms control. One simple fact, which is often under-appreciated, is that in the 1950s and the 1960s China was explicitly threatened many times with nuclear attack by the United States. In 1969, following the Sino-Soviet border clashes, the Soviet Union also threatened to carry out 'surgical attacks' on China with its nuclear arsenal.[35] No other Great Power has ever been subjected to so many explicit nuclear blackmails by both superpowers in such a short period. In addition, when the 'nuclear weapons taboo' was institutionalised in the 1960s and the 1970s, China, which became nuclear in 1964, was excluded entirely from the process. In this context, China's insistence on developing its own indigenous nuclear weapons and its denunciation of the 1963 Partial Test Ban Treaty (PTBT) and the 1968 Non-proliferation Treaty (NPT) are not entirely inexplicable. The same logic can also help us make sense of the gradual convergence between China's nuclear arms control behaviour and international norms in the 1990s.

## Reform

China's economic reforms in the last two decades are often regarded as 'China's second revolution'.[36] Radical changes brought about by economic reforms in the social and economic life of China, as noted by many, have reconstituted the socio-economic order of post-Mao China. Much has also been written about the rise of China's economic power, which, it is sometimes argued, has transformed China's international status and augmented China's economic, and therefore military, clout.[37] Economic reforms, however, have had profound impact on China's security in several other important ways. They have induced changed conceptions of security, exposed the vulnerability of the regime and the society, contested the priorities of security, and called for different means to achieve security. Most important of all, these changes have taken place while China is transforming from a revolutionary power to a post-revolutionary developmental state.

The economic reforms in China were launched in the wake of the devastating Cultural Revolution, at a time when the legitimacy of the CCP began to be questioned, if not contested, and when the economy, as acknowledged even by the Chinese government, was on the verge of bankruptcy. China's 'second revolution' was therefore launched to save the Chinese economy as much as to enhance the legitimacy of the regime. The shift of the CCP's central focus from political campaigns to economic construction in 1978 heralded, however, a new phase in the transformation of China as a revolutionary power. For most of the 1980s, 'reformist China' was regarded as 'friendly' by the United States as much because of its strategic value in the global balance of power as its political orientation—in sharp contrast to the Soviet Union and its satellite states in Eastern Europe.

The irony is, however, that the very success of economic reforms poses new threats to the security of the regime. By raising people's aspirations for, and expectations from, the economic reforms, the CCP has tied its claim to legitimacy to economic successes. Any failure to continue to deliver what people expect from economic reforms would cause widespread social discontent, which would in turn challenge the legitimacy of the Party and the government. In other words, the legitimacy of the Party and the regime no longer depends on its revolutionary credentials, but on its ability to deliver what it promises.

Economic reforms do not merely raise people's economic expectations in terms of improved living standards, economic prosperity, and more choices of, and access to, consumer goods.

China's opening up to the world economy and its gradual integration into international society have done more than its share to inform the Chinese people of what they could and should expect from a modern state. More than ever before, the Chinese people have been exposed to what Ayoob calls 'the existence of the modern representative and responsive states in the industrialised world' which, he argues, 'set the standards for effective statehood by their demonstrated success in meeting the basic needs of their populations, protecting their human rights, redistributing income, and promoting and guaranteeing political participation'. As these are increasingly accepted as norms of the standard state behaviour, 'they undermine the legitimacy of Third World states by prescribing standards and yardsticks of statehood in terms of the output functions of political systems that most Third World states will be incapable of meeting for many decades to come'.[38] Rising expectations among the people—economic, political or otherwise—which may lead to a revolutionary situation in China, therefore constitute a serious challenge to the state and regime security.[39]

Economic reforms, more than anything else, represent China's new drive for modernity. They have therefore exposed China's identity as a developmental state. China's catch-up mode has been, among other things, inspired and mobilised by the examples of the four little dragons—Hong Kong, Korea, Singapore and Taiwan. Like many other Third World states, however, the Chinese state now has to deal with the consequences of its march towards modernity. Increased labour force mobility means massive rural–urban migration foreshadowing the existence of an army of 'floating population'. 'To get rich is glorious' inevitably leads to an increasing gap between the wealth of the rich and that of the poor and between interior and coastal China, both of which create tensions that can fragment society. Economic prosperity fosters the emergence of a 'middle class' and the growth of civil society that would demand at least a limited opening of political discourse on democracy. Rampant corruption and other social vices erode the fabric of society. Increased awareness of global risks, such as environmental degradation, narcotics trafficking, and resource shortages, emphasises the vulnerability of China as a developmental state.

Economic reforms, perhaps naturally, have prompted important changes in the Chinese leadership's thinking about security. Coupled with China's re-evaluation of its improved external security situation in the 1980s, Deng Xiaoping deftly replaced Mao's assessment that an imminent world war was inevitable with his claim that peace and development are the two main trends in world politics.[40] During the late 1980s and the 1990s, the new thinking on security has been articulated through the emergence of two new security-related concepts—comprehensive security, and comprehensive national power. Briefly stated, the concept of comprehensive security seeks to emphasise the interface between domestic economic development and national and international security. The new thinking recognises that military security is insufficient; military capabilities alone cannot make China secure. China's security calculus should also incorporate economic, scientific and technological dimensions. Economic development is the key to increasing China's economic, scientific and technological capabilities. But economic development cannot be achieved without political and social stability. Deng's plea that 'China must avoid chaos' (zhongguo buneng luan)—either politically inspired or socially induced—thus smuggles domestic political and social stability onto the security agenda of the Chinese leadership.[41]

The concept of comprehensive national power, on the other hand, refers to 'the totality of a country's economic, military and political power in a given period' and further, 'economic power, including labour power, material resources and financial power, is the determinant and foundation of a country's military and political power'. Level of technological development has underlining importance in economic power.[42] In 1992, Jiang Zemin explicitly stated that competition in world politics in the post-Cold War period is 'in essence, a competition of overall national strength based on economic, scientific and technological capabilities'.[43] In these new formulations, security has become a much more inclusive concept. Accordingly, the perceived threat to China's security is from the external as much as the internal. Second, economic development is now seen as the key to China's security not only because domestic political and social stability is predicated upon it,[44] but also because it enhances China's economic, scientific and technological capability, which is essential to make China secure. Third, non-military dimensions of power are emphasised. Military power is still relevant and important, but is downplayed substantially in favour of non-military power in China's security considerations.[45] Fourth, security concerns have been reprioritised in accordance with changed internal and external circumstances for China. Military security in terms of defending China's borders is no long featured as a top priority. And fifth, naturally, 'the optimal approach to national security is to strengthen all the dimensions of national power—economic, technological, political, social and military', as noted by Wu Xinbo.[46] Recent discourse on China's grand strategy for the twenty-first century places economic and internal security higher than external and military security as conventionally understood.[47]

Finally, one must also consider the implications for China's security conceptualisation of reform that has taken place in the society of states. By reform I mean here in particular recent changing norms in international society. These include human rights norms, the obsolescence of large-scale inter-state wars, the retreat of sovereignty-based international order, and globalisation, among others. As with the structural change in the international system, changing norms in international society redraw the line of enmity and amity. If the former has induced the perception of China as 'the last bastion of Communism' and the 'remaining Leninist state' standing against liberal democracy and democratisation, thus defining China as the 'Other'; the latter stares blankly at China as a 'deviant' in international society, sometimes resisting and more often violating those norms in its behaviour. As Rosemary Foot points out in this volume, China's human rights record falls far short of meeting the new 'standard of civilisation'. Moreover, greater tolerance of, and sympathy for, the claims of ethno-nationalism manifested in the international community constitutes a new challenge to China's management of ethnic conflicts, which threaten the integrity of China. Changing norms of international society make new demands on internal governance of a state, and introduce new yardsticks of legitimacy for any state.

## Conclusion

Peter Katzenstein and others have argued recently that '[h]istory is a process of change that leaves an imprint on state identity'. He further stated that '[d]efinitions of identity that distinguish between self and other imply definitions of threat and interest that have strong effects on national security policies'.[48] All three integral social processes discussed above as China's historical experience have clearly left their imprints on China's identity either as a revolutionary power or a developmental state. By defining and redefining China's identity, revolution, war and reform have created a special set of social relationships between China and other states, and between China and international society as a whole. China's understanding of its own identity and of the Other is instrumental in its threat construction and therefore its security behaviour. This constitutes the social structure in which discussions and evaluation of the security problematique of China should be embedded.

It is beyond dispute that, in its international behaviour, China has often not lived up to the collective expectations of the international community—largely defined by the West. In that sense, China can be said to be irresponsible. But the more important question is why? Here there are several layers of questions that can be asked. First, if norms are no more than 'collective expectations about proper behaviour for a given identity' and if 'models of 'responsible' or 'civilised' states are enacted and validated by upholding specific norms', then inquiries as to how and why China shares and upholds some norms but not others by examining China's changing identity will surely yield necessary insights.[49] Second, if identity matters, then how and why does China assume a certain identity and not share identity with others? What are the domestic and international processes that matter in China's identity formation? Third, if identity construction is mutual, that is, if it is constructed by distinguishing self against the Other, then how does perceiving China as the Other constitute part of China's identity formation? Why should there be such a persistent dichotomy between China and the world (the West writ large)? The debates about whether China is a status quo or revisionist power, and whether China is irresponsible or not, would be futile without an appreciation of the changing purpose and identity of the Chinese state; an appreciation that is shaped fundamentally by dynamic interactions between domestic social processes and those of international society.

## Acknowledgment

A different version of this paper has appeared in *Pacifica Review*, 13, no.3 (2001):241–53. The author is grateful to *Pacifica Review* for permission to publish a revised form of the article in this collection.

## Notes

1 See most recently, Mark Burles and Abram N. Shulsky, *Patterns in China's Use of Force: evidence from history and doctrinal writings* (Santa Monica, California: Rand Corporation, 2000), Thomas Christensen, 'China, the US–Japan alliance and the security dilemma in East Asia', *International Security*, 23, no.4 (1999); Alastair Iain Johnston, 'China's militarised interstate dispute behaviour, 1949–1992: a first cut at the data', *China Quarterly*, no. 153 (1998), and Michael D. Swaine and Ashley J. Tillis, *Interpreting China's Grand Strategy: past, present and future* (Santa Monica, California, Rand, 2000).

2 One important exception is Gurtov and Hwang, *China's Security: the new roles of the military* (Lynne Rienner, London, 1998). See also B. Glaser, 'China's security perceptions: interests and ambitions', *Asian Survey*, 33, no.3 (1993); and D. Shambaugh, 'The insecurity of security: the PLA's evolving doctrine and threat perceptions towards 2000', *Journal of Northeast Asian Studies*, 13, no.1 (1994). These studies suffer, however, from almost exclusive focus on the Chinese military and the PLA. In earlier debates, Gurtov and Hwang argued that studies of Chinese foreign policy need to 'look at the world *as the Chinese leaders do*—with sensitivity to their philosophy of history, their methodology, and their experiences as revolutionary nationalist fighters, liberators, and bureaucrats' and 'we also need studies that interpret China's foreign policy *from the inside out*'. See Melvin Gurtov and Byong-Moo Hwang, *China Under Threat: the politics of strategy and diplomacy* (Baltimore: John Hopkins University Press, 1980), 4.

3 With apologies to my Australian colleagues, I subsume here the Australian IR scholarship largely under the Anglo-side of this community.

4 See Denny Roy, 'Hegemon on the horizon: China's threat to East Asian security', *International Security*, 19, no.1 (1994); Gerald Segal, 'East Asia

and the 'constrainment' of China', *International Security*, 20, no.4 (1996); Robert Ross, 'Beijing as a conservative power', *Foreign Affairs*, 76, no.2 (1997); and Avery Goldstein, 'Great expectations: interpreting China's arrival', *International Security*, 22, no.3 (1997).

5 For a sample of security discourse in China, See Wu, Xinbo, 'China: security practice of a modernizing and ascending power' in Muthiah Alagappa (ed.), *Asian Security Practice: material and ideational influences* (Stanford: Stanford University Press, 1998). Thomas J. Christensen, 'China, the US–Japan alliance and the security dilemma in East Asia', *International Security*, 23, no.4 (1999), Wang Yizhou (ed.), *Quanqiuhua shidai de guoji anquan* [International Security in a Globalised World] (Shanghai: Shanghai People's Press, 1998).

6 I use 'predicament' so that it won't be confused with the security dilemma as conventionally defined. As Alastair Iain Johnston observed recently, China may not understand what a security dilemma is (see Johnstone 'China's militarised interstate dispute behaviour'). There has certainly been little debate within China about the security dilemma and its implications for China in regional and global security.

7 See Brian Job (ed.), *The Insecurity Dilemma: national security of Third World states* (London: Lynne Rienner, 1992), Mohammed Ayoob, *The Third World Security Predicament: state making, regional conflict and the international system* (Boulder, Colorado: Lynne Rienner, 1995) and M. Alagappa (ed.), *Asian Security Practice*.

8 See Stephen Walt, *Revolution and War* (Ithaca: Cornell University Press, 1996), 1–36. Similarly, David Armstrong argues that revolutions have 'a profoundly disordering effect on international society in part because the revolutionary state and the established powers misperceived each other's intentions or because neither could understand the language being used by the other'. David Armstrong, *Revolution and World Order: revolutionary state in international society* (Oxford: Oxford University Press, 1993), 6.

9 For the arguments of balance of threat, see Stephen Walt, *The Origin of Alliances* (Ithaca: Cornell University Press, 1987).

10 For further discussions about Mao's warnings of American intervention, see Yongjin Zhang, *China in International Society since 1949: alienation and beyond* (Basingstoke: Macmillan, 1998), 50–51.

11 For more details, see Chen Jian, *China's Road to the Korean War: the making of the Sino-American confrontation* (New York: Columbia University Press, 1994), and Yufan Hao and Shihai Zhai, 'China's decision to enter the Korean War', *China Quarterly*, no. 121 (1990). For documentary

sources on China's entry into the Korean War, see Zhihua Shen (ed.), *Mao Zedong, Sidalin yu Han Zhan* [Mao Zedong, Stalin and the Korean War] (Hong Kong: Tiandi Tushu Youxian Gongsi, 1998).

12 See Akira Iriye, *The Cold War in Asia: a historical introduction* (Englewood Cliffs, New Jersey: Prentice Hall, 1974); Rosemary Foot, *The Practice of Power: US–China relations since 1949* (Oxford: Oxford University Press, 1995); and Steven Hugh Lee, *Outposts of Empire: Korea, Vietnam and the origins of the Cold War in Asia, 1949–1954* (Montreal: McGill-Queen's University Press, 1995).

13 Volume 15 of *Cambridge History of China* is aptly sub-titled: *Revolutions within a Revolution.*

14 Thomas Robinson argues that Mao's personality, including his 'megalomania and paranoia' informed much of foreign policy making before 1976. Thomas Robinson and David Shambaugh (eds), *Chinese Foreign Policy: theory and practice* (Oxford: Clarendon Press, 1995), 557. See also Roderick MacFarquhar, *The Origins of the Cultural Revolution*, 3 vols., (Oxford: Oxford University Press, 1974–).

15 Zhang, *China in International Society*, 127–38.

16 Martin Wight, *Power Politics* (London: Leicester University Press/Royal Institute of International Affairs, 1978), 92–93.

17 See Hedley Bull, 'The revolt against the West', in H. Bull and A. Watson (eds), *The Expansion of International Society* (Oxford: Clarendon Press, 1984), 217–28.

18 See in particular James Mayall, *Nationalism and International Society* (Cambridge: Cambridge University Press, 1990), particularly chapter 3, 'The Third World and International Society'.

19 See David Armstrong, *Revolutionary Diplomacy—Chinese foreign policy and the United Front doctrine* (London: University of California Press, 1977), Peter Van Ness, *Revolution and Chinese Foreign Policy: Peking's support for wars of national liberation* (Berkeley: University of California Press, 1970).

20 For the construction of threat on the Chinese side, see Sun Geqin and Cui Hongjian, *Erzhi Zhongguo: shenhua yu xianshi* [Containing China: myth and reality] (Beijing: China Yanshi Press, 1996).

21 Hannah Arendt, *On Revolution* (London: Faber and Faber, 1963), 11. Similarly, Giddens, in discussing the consequences of modernity, also claims that 'The twentieth century is a century of wars'.

22 Charles Tilly, 'Changing forms of revolution', in E. E. Rice (ed.), *Revolution and Counter-Revolution* (Oxford: Basil Blackwell, 1990), 10.

23 See Johnston, 'China's militarised interstate dispute behaviour'.

24 One might add also the coercive use of force within China in the instances of putting down Muslim and Tibetan rebellions.

25 See Stephen Walt, *Revolution and War*, 1–39.

26 See Alastair Iain Johnston, *Cultural Realism: strategic culture and grand strategy in Chinese history* (Princeton, New Jersey: Princeton University Press, 1995).

27 Wight, *Power Politics*, 90.

28 For details of covert US nuclear threats to China in 1953, see J.W. Lewis and Xue Litai, *China Builds the Bomb* (Stanford: Stanford University Press, 1988), 13–16; and G.H. Chang, *Friends and Enemies: the United States, China and the Soviet Union, 1948–1972* (Stanford: Stanford University Press, 1990), 88–89.

29 See Anthony Giddens, *The Nation–State and Violence: volume two of a contemporary critique of historical materialism* (Berkeley: University of California Press, 1985), particularly Chapter 9, 'Capitalist development and the industrialisation of war', 222–54.

30 Kal Holsti, 1992. 'International Theory and War in the Third World', in B. Job (ed.), *The Insecurity Dilemma: national security of Third World states* (London: Lynne Rienner 1992), 38.

31 R. Jepperson, A. Wendt and P.J. Katzenstein, 'Norms, identity and culture in national security', in Peter J. Katzenstein (ed.), 1996. *The Culture of National Security: norms and identity in world politics* (New York: Columbia University Press, 1996), 36.

32 see Johnston, *Cultural Realism*.

33 Giddens, *The Nation–State*, 245.

34 Henry Kissinger, *Years of Upheaval* (London: Weidenfeld and Nicholson, 1982), 49.

35 See Zhang, *China in International Society*, 156.

36 See Harry Harding, *China's Second Revolution* (Washington DC: Brookings Institution, 1987) and Nicholas Lardy, *China's Unfinished Economic Revolution* (Washington DC: Brookings Institution, 1998).

37 See for example Susan Shirk, 'Chinese views on Asia-Pacific regional cooperation', *NBR Analysis*, 5, no.5 (Seattle: National Bureau of Asian Research 1994); William H. Overholt, *The Rise of China: how economic reform is creating a new superpower* (New York: W.W. Norton, 1993), and N. Kristof and S. WuDunn, *China Wakes: the struggle for the soul of a rising power* (New York: Times Books, 1995).

38 Mohammed Ayoob, *The Third World Security Predicament: state making, regional conflict and the international system* (Boulder, Colorado: Lynne Rienner, 1995), 38.

39 David Shambaugh in a recent article claims that 'China's rulers face a new revolution—the revolution of rising expectations', *The Independent*, 1 October 1999. My difference with Shambaugh is that rising expectations do not in themselves constitute a revolution. Even if such expectations lead to a revolutionary situation in China, they may not lead to a revolution.

40 For Deng's reassessment of war and peace in world politics, see Zhang, *China in International Society*, 107–13 and Zheng Yongnian, *Discovering Chinese Nationalism: modernisation, identity and international relations* (Cambridge: Cambridge University Press, 1998), 116–19.

41 For more discussions, see Wu Xinbo, 'China security practice', Yan Xuetong, *Zhongguo Guojia Liyi Fenxi* [An Analysis of China's National Interests] (Tianjin: Tianjin People's Press, 1995), and Melvin Gurtov, and Byong-Moo Hwang, *China's Security: the new roles of the military*, 4–12.

42 Zheng, *Discovering Chinese Nationalism*, 114–17. See also Huang, Shuofeng, *Zonghe Guoli Lun* [On Comprehensive National Power] (Beijing: China Social Science Press, 1992).

43 Wu, 'China: security practice', 127.

44 Jiang Zemin was explicit about this when he stated in 1992 that 'If we fail to develop our economy rapidly, it will be difficult for us... to maintain long-term social stability' (quoted in ibid, 127).

45 China's Defence Law of 1993, for example, has stipulated the military role in the 'internal pacification'.

46 Wu 'China: security practice', 140.

47 See Wang Yizhou (ed.), Quanqiuhua shidai de guoji anquan [*International Security in a Globalised World*] (Shanghai: Shanghai People's Press, 1998) and Hu Angang, Yang Fan and Zhu Ning, Daguo Zhanlue: Zhongguo de Liyi yu Shimin [*China's Grand Strategy: missions and interests*] (Shengyang: Liaoning People's Press, 2000). The fact that Hu and other prominent economists are now actively participating in the debates about China's grand strategy is telling evidence of a changing security conceptualisation.

48 Peter J. Katzenstein (ed.), 'Introduction: alternative perspectives on national security', in *The Culture of National Security*, 18–23.

49 Jepperson et al., 53–54.

# References


Alagappa, M. (ed.), 1998. *Asian Security Practice: material and ideational influences*, Stanford University Press, Stanford.

Alderson, K. and Hurrell, A. (eds), 2000. *Hedley Bull on International Society*, Macmillan, Basingstoke.

Almonte, J.T., 1997–98. 'Ensuring security the ASEAN way', *Survival*, 39(4):80–92.

Arendt, H., 1963. *On Revolution*, Faber and Faber, London.

Armstrong, D., 1977. *Revolutionary Diplomacy—Chinese foreign policy and the United Front doctrine*, University of California Press, London.

——, 1993. *Revolution and World Order: revolutionary state in international society*, Oxford University Press, Oxford.

Austin, G., 1995. 'The strategic implications of China's public order crisis', *Survival*, 37(2):7–23.

——, 1998. *China's Ocean Frontier: international law, military force and national development*, Allen and Unwin, Sydney.

——, and Harris, S., 2001. *Japan and Greater China: political economy and military power in the Asian century*, Hurst and University of Hawaii Press, London and Honolulu.

Ayoob, M., 1995. *The Third World Security Predicament: state making, regional conflict and the international system*, Lynne Rienner, Boulder, Colorado.

Bernstein, R. and Munro, R.H., 1997. *The Coming Conflict with China*, A.A. Knopf, New York.

Bhala, R., 2001. 'China's WTO entry in labor surplus and Marxist terms', Paper Delivered at the Conference, 'China and the World Trade Organisation Conference', Faculty of Law, Australian National University, Canberra, 16–17 March.

Blank, S., 1995. 'Energy, economics and security in Central Asia: Russia and its rivals', Strategic Studies Institute, US Army War College, Carlisle, March 1995 (processed).

Bottelier, P., 2001a. 'The impact of WTO membership on China's domestic economy, Part I' *China Online*, 3 January 2001, available online at http://www.chinaonline.com/issues/wto/NewsArchive/secure/2001/January/c01010160.asp.

——, 2001b. 'The impact of WTO membership on China's domestic economy, Part II' *China Online*, 4 January 2001, available online at http://www.chinaonline.com/commentary_analysis/wtocom/NewsArchive/secure/2001/January/c01010260.asp.

Braithwaite, J. and Drahos, P., 2000. *Global Business Regulation*, Cambridge University Press, Cambridge.

Brown, M., Cote, O.R., Lynn-Jones, S.M. and Miller, S.E. (eds), 2000. *The Rise of China*, MIT Press, Cambridge, Massachusetts.

Brownlie, I., 1983. *System of the Law of Nations: state responsibility*, Clarendon Press, Oxford.

Bull, H., 1977. *The Anarchical Society: a study of order in world politics*, Macmillan, London.

——, 1984. 'The revolt against the West', in H. Bull and A. Watson (eds), *The Expansion of International Society*, Clarendon Press, Oxford:217–28.

Burles, M. and Shulsky, A.N., 2000. *Patterns in China's Use of Force: evidence from history and doctrinal writings*, Rand Corporation, Santa Monica, California.

Buzan, B., 1996. 'International society and international security', in R. Fawn and J. Larkins (eds), *International Society after the Cold War*, Macmillan, Basingstoke:262–287.

Calder, K., 1996. *Asia's Deadly Triangle: how arms, energy and growth threaten to destabilize Asia Pacific*, Nicholas Brealey, London.

Chan, G., 1989. *China and International Organisations: participation in non-governmental organisations since 1971*, Oxford University Press, Hong Kong.

——, 1998. 'A comment on an international relations theory with Chinese characteristics', *Asian Review*, 8(Autumn and Winter):176–84 (in Chinese).

——, 1999. *Chinese Perspectives on International Relations: a framework for analysis*, Macmillan, Basingstoke.

——, 2001. Is China a responsible state? Assessing its multilateral engagements. Paper presented at the International Studies Association Convention, Hong Kong, 26–28 July.

Chang, G.H., 1990. *Friends and Enemies: the United States, China and the Soviet Union, 1948–72*, Stanford University Press, Stanford.

Chan, S., 1999. 'Chinese perspectives on world order', in T.V. Paul and J.A. Hall (eds), *International Order and the Future of World Politics*, Cambridge University Press, Cambridge:197–212.

Chayes, A. and Chayes, A., 1995. *The New Sovereignty: compliance with international regulatory agreements*, Harvard University Press, Cambridge, Massachusetts.

Chen Hurng-yu, 1993. 'A comparison between Taipei and Peking in their policies and concepts regarding the South China Sea', *Issues and Studies*, 29(9):22–58.

Chen Jian, 1994. *China's Road to the Korean War: the making of the Sino-American confrontation*, Columbia University Press, New York.

Chen Jie, 1994. 'China's Spratly policy: with special reference to the Philippines and Malaysia', *Asian Survey*, 34(10):893–903.

Chen Quansheng and Liu Jinghua, 2000. 'Quanqiuhua zhong de Zhongguo yu shijie [China and the world under globalisation]', *Zhongguo waijiao* [Chinese Diplomacy], no. 3:4.

Ching, F., 1999. 'UN: sovereignty or rights?', *Far Eastern Economic Review*, 21 October.

Christensen, T.J., 1996a. 'Chinese Realpolitik', *Foreign Affairs*, 75(5):37–52.

——, 1996b. *Useful Adversaries: grand strategy, domestic mobilization, and Sino-American conflict, 1947–1958*, Princeton University Press, Princeton, New Jersey.

——, 1999a. 'China, the US–Japan Alliance and the security dilemma in East Asia', *International Security*, 23(4):49–80.

——, 1999b. 'Pride, pressure, and politics: the roots of China's worldview,' in Deng Yong and Wang Fei-ling (eds), *In the Eyes of the Dragon: China views the world*, Rowman & Littlefield, Lanham:239–256.

Christofferson, G., 1998. 'China's intentions for Russian and Central Asian oil and gas', *NBR Analysis*, 9(2), National Bureau of Asian Research, Seattle.

Clark, A.M., 1995a. 'Non-governmental organizations and their influence on international society', *Journal of International Affairs*, 48(2):507–26.

——, 1995b. Strong principles, strengthening practices: Amnesty International and three cases of change in international human rights standards, Ph.D dissertation, University of Minnesota.

Clinton, W.J., 1999. Speech on US policy toward China, Mayflower Hotel, Washington, DC, 7 April. Available online as *NAPSnet Special Report*, 8 April 1999.

Cold War International History Project, 1995. 'The Cold War in Asia', *Cold War International History Project Bulletin*, Issues 6–7.

Coll, A.R., 2000. 'Introduction: American power and responsibility in a new century', *Ethics and International Affairs*, 14:3–10;

Cooper, R., 1996. *The Post-Modern State and the World Order*, Demos, London.

Cotton, J., 1996. 'China and the Tumen River: Jilin's coastal development', *Asian Survey*, 36(11):1086–101.

Dassel, K., 1996. 'Revolution and war: a critique', *Security Studies*, 6(2):152–73.

Davis, M.C., 1999. 'The case for Chinese federalism', *Journal of Democracy*, 10(2):124–37.

Davis, Z.S., 1995. 'China's nonproliferation and export control policies', *Asian Survey*, 35(6):587–604.

Department of State, 1986a. 'Memorandum of a conversation, Washington, February 1957', *Foreign Relations of the United States, 1995–57: China*, Volume 3, Government Printing Office, Washington DC:481–88.

——, 1986b. 'National Intelligence Estimate (NIE): 'Chinese Communist capabilities and probable courses of action through 1960', *Foreign Relations of the United States, 1995–57: China*, Volume 3, Government Printing Office, Washington DC:230–55.

——, 1996. Press Briefing, US Department of State., Washington, DC, 4 September.

Dibb, P., 1995. *Towards a New Balance of Power in East Asia: what are the risks as the Asian balance of power undergoes a fundamental change?*, Oxford University Press Oxford.

Donnelly, J., 1998. 'Human rights: the new standard of civilisation?', *International Affairs*, 74(1):1–23.

Downer, A., 2001. 'China's commitment to prevent ballistic missile proliferation welcomed', Media Release of the Australian Minister for Foreign Affairs, 23 November.

East Asia Analytical Unit, 1997. *China Embraces the Market: achievements, constraints and opportunities*, East Asia Analytical Unit, Department of Foreign Affairs and Trade, Canberra.

Economy, E. and Oksenberg, M. (eds), 1999. *China Joins the World: progress and prospects*, Council on Foreign Relations Press, New York.

Eikenberry, K.W., 1995. 'Explaining and influencing Chinese arms transfers', *Paper Number 36*, National Defense University, Washington, DC.

Einhorn, R.J., 1997. 'Proliferation: Chinese case studies', Testimony of the Deputy Assistant Secretary of State for Nonproliferation at the hearing before the Subcommittee on International Security, Proliferation and Federal Service, Committee on Governmental Affairs, US Senate, USGPO, Washington, 1997, 6.

Fang Jue, 1998. 'Liberal voices from China II: A program for democratic reform', *The Journal of Democracy*, 9(4):9–19.

Faust, J.R. and Kornberg, J.F., 1995. *China in World Politics*, Lynne Rienner, Boulder.

Feinerman, J.V., 1995. 'Chinese participation in the international legal order: rogue elephant or team player?' *China Quarterly*, 141:186–210.

Fields, P.W. and Stellman, R.G., 1994. *Petrochemicals in China*, Pace Consultants Inc., Houston.

Finer, S., 1988. *The Man on Horseback: the role of the military in politics*, Westview, Boulder, Colorado.

Finnemore, M., 1996. 'Constructing norms of humanitarian intervention', in P. Katzenstein (ed.), *The Culture of National Security: norms and identity in world politics*, Columbia University Press, New York:153–185.

Foot, R., 1995. *The Practice of Power: US–China relations since 1949*, Oxford University Press, Oxford.

——, 1996. 'The study of China's international behaviour: international relations approaches', in Ngaire Woods (ed.), *Explaining International Relations*, Oxford University Press, Oxford:257–79.

——, 2000. *Rights Beyond Borders: the global community and the struggle over human rights in China*, Oxford University Press, Oxford.

Franck, T.M., 1990. *The Power of Legitimacy Among Nations*, Oxford University Press, New York.

——, 1995. *Fairness in International Law and Institutions*, Clarendon Press, Oxford.

Funabashi, Y., Oksenberg, M. and Weiss, H., 1994. *An Emerging China in a World of Interdependence*, The Trilateral Commission, New York.

Fung Yu-lan, 1952. *A History of Chinese Philosophy*, Vol. 1, Princeton University Press, Princeton (trans. by Derk Bodde).

Giddens, A., 1985. *The Nation–State and Violence: volume two of a contemporary critique of historical materialism*, University of California Press, Berkeley, California.

Gill, R.B., 1992. 'Curbing Beijing's arms sales', *Orbis*, 36(3):379–96.

Glaser, B., 1993. 'China's security perceptions: interests and ambitions', *Asian Survey*, 33(3):233–54.

Goldstein, A., 1997. 'Great expectations: interpreting China's arrival', *International Security*, 22(3):36–73

Goldstone, J.A., 1996. 'Revolution, war and security', *Security Studies*, 6(2):127–51.

Gong, G.W., 1984a. *The Standard of 'Civilisation' in International Society*, Clarendon Press, Oxford.

——, 1984b. 'China's entry into international society' in H. Bull and A. Watson (eds), *The Expansion of International Society*, Clarendon Press Oxford:171–84.

Goodman, D.S.G. and Gerald Segal (eds), 1997. *China Rising: nationalism and interdependence*, Routledge, London.

Greenfield, J., 1992. *China's Practice of the Law of the Sea*, Clarendon Press, Oxford.

Guo Yongjun, 1995. 'Fangkong zuozhan ying shuli quanquyu zhengti fangkong de sixian' [Air defence should be guided by the theory of area and integrated defence], *Junshi xueshu*, 11:47–49.

Gurtov, M. and Hwang, Byong-Moo, 1980. *China Under Threat: the politics of strategy and diplomacy*, John Hopkins University Press, Baltimore.

——, 1998. *China's Security: the new roles of the military*, Lynne Rienner, London.

Hamrin, C.L., 1992. 'The Party leadership system', in K.G. Lieberthal and D.M. Lampton (eds), *Bureaucracy, Politics, and Decision Making in Post-Mao China*, University of California Press, Berkeley, California:95–124.

Hao Yufan and Zhai Shihai, 1990. 'China's decision to enter the Korean War', *China Quarterly*, 121:94–113.

Harding, H., 1987. *China's Second Revolution*, Brookings Institution, Washington, DC.

Harris, I., 1993. 'Order and justice in 'The Anarchical Society', *International Affairs*, 69(4):725–41.

Harris, S. and Klintworth, G. (eds), 1995. *China as a Great Power: myths, realities and challenges in the Asia-Pacific region*, St. Martin's Press, New York.

Harvie, C. and Turpin, T., 1997. 'China's market reforms and its new forms of scientific and business alliances', in J.C.H. Chai and C.A. Tisdell (eds), *China's Economic Growth and Transition*, Department of Economics, University of Queensland, Brisbane:481–516.

Hertz, F.O., 1945. *Nationality in History and Politics: a study of the psychology and sociology of national sentiment and character*, Kegan Paul, London.

Hobson, J.M. and Seabrooke, L., 2001. 'Reimagining Weber: constructing international society and the social balance of power', *European Journal of International Relations*, 7(2):239–74.

Hoffmann, S., 1988. 'Political ethics of international relations', Seventh Morgenthau Memorial Lecture on Ethics and Foreign Policy, Carnegie Council on Ethics and Foreign Affairs, New York.

Holsti, K., 1992. 'International theory and war in the Third World', in B. Job (ed.), 1992. *The Insecurity Dilemma: national security of Third World states*, Lynne Rienner, London:119–140.

——, 2001. 'Dealing with dictators: Westphalian and American strategies', *International Relations of the Asia-Pacific*, 1:51–65.

Hu Angang, Yang Fan and Zhu Ning, 2000. *Daguo Zhanlue: Zhongguo de Liyi yu Shimin* [China's Grand Strategy: missions and interests], Liaoning People's Press, Shengyang.

Hu Weixing, 1999. 'Nuclear nonproliferation', in Deng Yong and Wang Fei-ling (eds), *In the Eyes of the Dragon: China views the world*, Rowman & Littlefield, Lanham.

Huan Xiang, 1983. 'Strive to build up New China's science of international law', in Chinese Society of International Law (ed.), *Selected Articles from Chinese Yearbook of International Law*, China Translation and Publishing Company, Beijing:1–5.

Huang, R., 1981. *1587: a year of no significance*, Yale University Press, New Haven.

Huang, S., 1992. *Zonghe Guoli Lun* [On Comprehensive National Power], China Social Science Press, Beijing.

Huntington, S., 1957. *Soldiers and the State*, Belknap, Harvard, Massachusetts.

Iriye, A., 1974. *The Cold War in Asia: a historical introduction*, Prentice Hall, Englewood Cliffs, New Jersey.

Ivanov, V., 2000. 'The energy sector in Northeast Asia: new projects, delivery systems, and prospects for cooperation', *North Pacific Policy Papers 2*, Institute of Asian Research, University of British Columbia, Vancouver.

Jacobson, H.K. and Oksenberg, M., 1990. *China's Participation in the IMF, the World Bank, and GATT*, University of Michigan Press, Ann Arbor.

*Janes Intelligence Review*, 1992. 'China's missile sales—few changes for the future', *Jane's Intelligence Review*, 4(12):559–63.

Jepperson, R., Wendt, A. and Katzenstein, P.J., 1996. 'Norms, identity and culture in national security', in P.J. Katzenstein (ed.), *The Culture of National Security: norms and identity in world politics*, Columbia University Press, New York.

Jia Qingguo, 1996. 'Economic development, political stability and international respect,' *Journal of International Affairs*, 49(2):572–89.

Job, B. (ed.), 1992. *The Insecurity Dilemma: national security of Third World states*, Lynne Rienner, London.

Joffe, E., 1993. 'The PLA and the Succession Question', in R. Yang (ed.), *China's Military: the PLA in 1992/1993*, Chinese Council of Advanced Policy Studies, Taipei:149–59.

Johnston, A.I., 1995a. 'China's nuclear forces: doctrine, modernisation and arms control', unpublished conference paper, Hong Kong, 13–15 July 1995.

——, 1995b. *Cultural Realism: strategic culture and grand strategy in Chinese history*, Princeton University Press, Princeton, New Jersey.

——, 1996a. 'Learning versus adaptation: explaining change in Chinese arms control policy in the 1980s and 1990', *China Journal*, 35:27–62.

——, 1996b. 'Cultural realism and strategy in Maoist China', in P. Katzenstein (ed.), *The Culture of National Security*, Columbia University Press, New York:251–68.

——, 1997. 'Engaging myths: misconceptions about China and its global role', *Harvard Asia Pacific Review*, 2(1):9–12.

——, 1998. 'China's militarised interstate dispute behaviour, 1949–1992: a first cut at the data', *China Quarterly*, 153:1–30.

—— and Evans, P., 1999. 'China's engagement with multilateral security institutions', in A.I. Johnston and R.S. Ross (eds), *Engaging China: the management of an emerging power*, Routledge, London:235–72.

Johnston, A.I. and Ross, R.S. (eds), 1999. *Engaging China: the management of an emerging power*, Routledge, London.

Kamal, N., 1992. 'China's arms export policy and responses to multilateral restraints', *Contemporary South East Asia*, 14(2):112–41.

Kan, S.A., 1998. 'Chinese proliferation of weapons of mass destruction: current policy issues', *CRS Issue Brief 92056*, Congressional Research Service, Washington, DC. Available online at http://www.fas.org/spp/starwars/crs/crs92056.htm; accessed 1 August 2001.

Kanayama, H., 1994. 'The future impact of energy problems in China', *Policy Paper 124E*, International Institute for Peace Studies, Tokyo.

Katzenstein, P.J. (ed.), 1996. *The Culture of National Security: norms and identity in world politics*, Columbia University Press, New York.

Keck, M.E. and Sikkink, K., 1998. *Activists Beyond Borders: advocacy networks in international politics*, Cornell University Press, Ithaca, New York.

Kennedy, B., 1996. 'Curbing Chinese missile sales: from imposing to negotiating China's adherence to the MTCR', *Journal of Northeast Asian Studies*, 15(1):57–68.

Kent, A., 1997. 'China, international organisations and regimes: the ILO as a case study in organisational learning', *Pacific Affairs*, 70(4):517–32.

——, 1999. *China, the United Nations and Human Rights: the limits of compliance*, University of Pennsylvania Press, Philadelphia.

Keohane, R., 1984. *After Hegemony: cooperation and discord in the world political economy*, Princeton University Press, Princeton.

Khalizad, Z.M., Shulsky, A.N., Byman, D.L., Cliff, R., Orletsky, D.T., Shlapak, D. and Tellis, A.J., 1999. *The United States and a Rising China: strategic and military implications*, Rand, Santa Monica, California.

Kim, S.S., 1979. *China, the United Nations and World Order*, Princeton University Press, Princeton.

——, 1990. 'Thinking globally in post-Mao China', *Journal of Peace Research*, 27(2):191–210.

——, 1991. 'China in and out of the changing world order', *Occasional Paper 21*, World Order Studies Program, Centre of International Studies, Princeton University, Princeton.

——, 1994. 'China's international organisational behaviour', in T.W. Robinson and D. Shambaugh (eds), *Chinese Foreign Policy: theory and practice*, Clarendon Press, Oxford:401–34.

——, 1999. 'China and the United Nations', in Economy and Oksenberg (eds), *China Joins the World*, Council on Foreign Relations Press, New York:42–89.

Kissinger, H., 1982. *Years of Upheaval*, Weidenfeld and Nicholson, London.

Klotz, A., 1995. *Norms in International Relations: the struggle against Apartheid*, Cornell University Press, Ithaca, New York.

Koh, H.H., 1997. 'Why do nations obey international law?', *Yale Law Journal*, 106(8):2599–2659.

Kong Qingqiang, 2001. 'Enforcing WTO agreements in China: an illusion or reality?', Paper Delivered at the Conference, 'China and the World Trade Organisation', Faculty of Law, Australian National University Canberra, 16–17 March.

Krasner, S.D., (ed.), 1983. *International Regimes*, Cornell University Press, Ithaca, New York.

Krieger, L., 1967. 'Power and Responsibility: historical assumptions', in L. Krieger and F. Stern (eds), *The Responsibility of Power: historical essays*, Macmillan, London:3–33.

Kristof, N. and Sheryl WuDunn, 1994. *China Wakes: the struggle for the soul of a rising power*, Times Books, New York.

Lampton, D., 1998. 'China', *Foreign Policy*, 110:13–27.

——, 2001. *The Making of Chinese Foreign and Security Policy in the Era of Reform*, Stanford University Press, Stanford.

Lardy, N., 1998. *China's Unfinished Economic Revolution*, Brookings Institution, Washington DC.

Lee, J.C.Y., 1993. 'The exercise of PRC sovereignty: its impact on Hong Kong's governing process in the second half of the political transition', *Issues and Studies*, 29(12):88–111.

Lee, S.H., 1995. *Outposts of Empire: Korea, Vietnam and the origins of the Cold War in Asia, 1949–1954*, McGill-Queen's University Press, Montreal.

Lewis, J.W. and Xue Litai, 1988. *China Builds the Bomb*, Stanford University Press, Stanford.

Li Gang and Wang Qi, 2000. 'Zhengque renshi shijie geju duojihua qushi' [Correctly recognising the multipolarity trend in the world order], *Journal of the PLA National Defence University*, 9:26–30.

Li Lin, 1993. 'Guoji renquan yu guojia zhuquan' [International Human Rights and State Sovereignty], *Chinese Studies of Law*, 1:37–44.

Li Lingjie, 1999. 'Sino-Russian relations in Asia Pacific', in Koji Watanabe (ed.), *Engaging Russia in Asia Pacific*, Japan Centre for International Exchange, Tokyo:54–66.

Lieberthal, K.G., 1992. 'Introduction: the 'fragmented authoritarianism' model and its limitations', in K.G. Lieberthal and D.M. Lampton (eds), *Bureaucracy, Politics, and Decision Making in Post-Mao China*, University of California Press, Berkeley:1–30.

Lilley, J., 1997. 'Proliferation: Chinese case studies', Testimony at the hearing before the Subcommittee on International Security, Proliferation and Federal Service, Committee on Governmental Affairs, US Senate, USGPO, Washington, DC.

Liu Huaqiu, 1998. *No-first-use and China's security*, Electronic Essay, The Henry L. Stimson Centre, Washington, DC. Available online http://www.stimson.org/pubs/zeronuke/prefnfu.htm.

Liu Jinji, Liang Shoude, Yang Huaisheng, et al. (eds), 1994. *Guoji zhengzhi dacidian* [A dictionary of international politics], China Social Sciences Press, Beijing.

Liu Yicang and Ku Guisheng, 1993. *You zhong guo tese de guofang jianshe lilun* [The national defence theory of the Chinese characteristics] (Beijing: the PLA Academy of Military Science Press, 1993), 216.

Lord Howe, 1996. Opening Speech to Amnesty International London Seminar on Human Rights in China, 9 September.

Lu Song, 1997. 'Guojifa zai guoji guanxi zhong de zuoyong' [The role of international law in international relations], *Waijiao xueyuan xuebao*, 1:5–14.

Lukin, A., 2001. 'Russia's image of China and Russian-Chinese relations' *CNAPS Working Paper*, Center for Northeast Asian Policy Studies, Brookings Institution, Washington, DC.

Lynn-Jones, S.M., 2000. 'Preface', in Michael E. Brown et al. (eds), *The Rise of China*, MIT Press, Cambridge, Massachusetts:xi–xxvii.

Ma Zhongshi, 1994. 'China dream in the global 1990s and beyond', *Strategic Digest*, 24(1), reprinted from the Beijing-based journal *Contemporary International Relations*, 3(7).

MacFarquhar, R., 1974. *The Origins of the Cultural Revolution*, 3 vols., Oxford University Press, Oxford.

—— (ed.), 1997. *The Politics of China: the eras of Mao and Deng*, Cambridge University Press, Cambridge.

Mao Zhengfa and Zeng Yan (eds), 1996. *Bianfanglun* [Theory of territorial defence], The PLA Academy of Military Science Press, Beijing.

Mayall, J., 1990. *Nationalism and International Society*, Cambridge University Press, Cambridge.

McGoldrick, D., 1994. *The Human Rights Committee: its role in the development of the International Covenant on Civil and Politics Rights*, Clarendon Paperbacks, Oxford.

Meng Xiangqing, 1999. 'Jiang Zemin's anquanguan chutan' [An initial study on Jiang Zemin's theory of security], *Waijiao xueyuan xuebao*, 2:38–42.

Milhollin, G., 1997. 'Proliferation: Chinese case studies', Testimony at the hearing before the Subcommittee on International Security, Proliferation and Federal Service, Committee on Governmental Affairs, US Senate, USGPO, Washington, DC.

Mooney, P., 2000. 'Post-WTO shocks for China's farmers', *China Online*, 17 January 2000, available online at http://www.chinaonline.com/issues/wto/NewsArchive/secure/2000/january/C00011721.asp, accessed 1 August 2001.

Morphet, S., 2000. 'China as a Permanent Member of the Security Council, October 1971–December 1999', *Security Dialogue*, 31(2):151–66.

Moses, R.L., 2000. 'Chinese views on globalisation', *China Online*, available online at http://www.chinaonline.com/commentary, accessed 26 June 2000.

Munro, R. and Bernstein, R., 1997. 'China I: the coming conflict with America', *Foreign Affairs*, 76(2):18–32.

Mussolini, B., 1973. 'The doctrine of Fascism', in Adrian Lyttelton (ed.), *Italian Fascisms: from Pareto to Gentile*, Jonathon Cape, London.

Nathan, A., 1994. 'Influencing human rights in China', in James R. Lilley and W. L. Willkie (eds), *Beyond MFN: trade with China and American interests*, American Enterprise Institute, Washington DC.

—— and Ross, R.S., 1997. *The Great Wall and the Empty Fortress: China's search for security*, W.W. Norton & Company, New York.

O'Neill, B., 1997. 'Power and satisfaction in the Security Council', in B. Russett (ed.), *The Once and Future Security Council*, St Martin's Press, New York:59–82.

Office of the Secretary of Defense, 1996. *Proliferation: threat and response*, Office of the Secretary of Defense, Washington DC.

Oksenberg, M. and Economy, E., 1999. 'Introduction: China joins the world', in E. Economy and M. Oksenberg (eds), *China Joins the World: progress and prospects*, Council on Foreign Relations Press, New York.

Overholt, W.H., 1993. *China: the next economic superpower*, Weidenfeld and Nicolson, London.

——, 1993. *The Rise of China: how economic reform is creating a new superpower*, W.W. Norton, New York.

Paltiel, J., 1995. 'PLA allegiance on parade: civil–military relations in transition', *China Quarterly*, 143:784–800.

Pang Zhongying, 2000. 'Zai bianhua de shijieshang zhuiqiu Zhongguo de diwei' [To establish China's status in a changing world], *World Economics and Politics*, 1:38

Pearson, M.M., 1999'China's integration into the international trade and investment regime', in E. Economy and M. Oksenberg, (eds), *China Joins the World: progress and prospects*, Council on Foreign Relations Press, New York.

Peng Guangqian, Yao Youzhi et al., 1994. *Deng Xiaoping zhanlue sixianglun* [On Deng Xiaoping's strategic thoughts], The PLA Academy of Military Science Press, Beijing.

Peng Rixuan, Ying Lin and Li Tao, 2000. 'Zhongguo jundui xiandaihua jianshe huigu yu zhanwang' [The review and forecast of the Chinese military modernisation], *Journal of the PLA National Defence University*, 5:8–11.

Potter, P.B., 1997. 'Law reform and China's emerging market economy', in Joint Economic Committee of the United States Congress (ed.), *China's Economic Future: challenges to US policy*, M.E. Sharpe, Armonk, New York:221–42.

Qian Guoliang, 2000. 'Qunmian luoshi [silingbu jianshe gangyao] gaobiaozhun zhuahao silingbu jiguan jianshe' [Comprehensively implementing the Guidelines for the Headquarters Construction], *Journal of the PLA National Defence University*, 6:4–8.

Qin Yaqing, 1998. 'Guoji zhidu yu guoji hezuo—fanxiang xinziyou zhidu zhuyi' [International regimes and international cooperation–neorealism revisited], *Waijiao xueyuan xuebao*, 1:40–47.

Qu Xing, 1994. 'Shilun dongou jubian he suliang jieti hou de zhongguo duiwai zhengce' [China's foreign policy since the radical changes in Eastern Europe and the disintegration of the USSR], *Waijiao xueyuan xuebao*, 4.

Reisman, W.M., 1999. 'The United States and international institutions', *Survival*, 41(4):62–80.

Rice, E. E. (ed.), 1991. *Revolution and counter-revolution*, Blackwell, Oxford.

Roberts, A. and Kingsbury, B. (eds), 1993. *United Nations, Divided World: the UN's roles in international relations*, Clarendon Press, Oxford.

Robinson, T. and Shambaugh, D. (eds), 1995. *Chinese Foreign Policy: theory and practice*, Clarendon Press, Oxford.

Ross, L., 1999. 'China and environmental protection', in E. Economy and M. Oksenberg (eds), *China Joins the World*, Council on Foreign Relations Press, New York:296–325.

Ross, R., 1997. 'Beijing as a conservative power', *Foreign Affairs*, 76(2):33–44.

Roy, D., 1994. 'Hegemon on the horizon: China's threat to East Asian security', *International Security*, 19(1):149–68.

Rozman, G., 1999. 'China's quest for great power identity', *Orbis*, 43(3):383–402.

Scalapino, R., 1999. 'The People's Republic of China at fifty', *NBR Analysis*, 10(4), National Bureau of Asian Research, Seattle.

Segal, G., 1995. 'Tying China into the international system', *Survival*, 37(2):60–73.

——, 1996. 'An un-Pacific Asia', *The Economist*, the special issue on the world in 1996, p. 71.

——, 1996. 'East Asia and the 'constrainment' of China', *International Security*, 20(4):107–35.

——, 1999. 'Does China matter?' *Foreign Affairs*, 78(5):24–36.

Select Committee, US House of Representatives, 1999. *US National Security and Military Commercial Concerns with the PRC* [The Cox Report], US House of Representatives, Washington DC.

Seth, S.P., 1999. 'Potential for trouble ahead as Canberra courts Beijing', *The Free China Journal*, 23 September 1999:6.

Sha Zukang, 1997. Statement of China's Disarmament Ambassador in Geneva, 26 June.

Shambaugh, D., 1994. 'The insecurity of security: the PLA's evolving doctrine and threat perceptions towards 2000', *Journal of Northeast Asian Studies*, 13(1):3–25.

——, 1996. 'Containment or engagement of China? Calculating Beijing's response', *International Security*, 21(2):180–209

——, 1999. 'China's post-Deng military leadership', in J. Lilley and D. Shambaugh (eds), *China's Military Faces the Future*, M.E. Sharpe, Boulder, Colorado.

——, 2000. 'Sino-American strategic relations: from partners to competitors', *Survival*, 42(1):97–115.

Shen Zhihua (ed.), 1998. *Mao Zedong, Stalin and the Korean War* [Mao Zedong, Sidalin yu Han Zhan], Tiandi Tushu Youxian Gongsi, Hong Kong.

Shi Zhigang, 1998. 'Jiji fangyu zhanlue sixiang zai xinshiqi junshi douzheng de tixian' [The application of active defence strategy in the military preparation in the new era], *The Journal of PLA National Defence University*, 8–9:100–104.

Shih Chih-yu, 1993. *China's Just World: the morality of Chinese foreign policy*, Lynne Rienner, Boulder, Colorado.

Shijie zhishi nianjian, 1998. *Shijie zhishi nianjian 1997/1998* [The Yearbook of World Knowledge, 1997–98], *Shjijie zhishi* chubanshe, Beijing.

Shinn, J. (ed.), 1996. *Weaving the Net: conditional engagement of China*, Council on Foreign Relations Press, New York.

Shirk, S.L., 1993. *The Political Logic of Economic Reform in China*, University of California Press, Berkeley California.

——, 1994. 'Chinese views on Asia-Pacific regional cooperation', *NBR Analysis*, 5(5), National Bureau of Asian Research, Seattle.

Sinkule, B.J., 1995. *Implementing Environmental Policy in China*, Praeger, Westport.

Smelser, N.J., 1997. *Problematics of Sociology*, University of California Press, Berkeley, California.

Smith, R.J., 1996. *Chinese Maps: images of 'All Under Heaven'*, Oxford University Press, New York.

Smith, T., 2000. 'Morality and the use of force in a unipolar world: the 'Wilsonian moment'?', *Ethics and International Affairs*, 14:11–22.

State Council, 1995. *China: arms control and disarmament*, State Council of the People's Republic of China, Beijing.

——, 1998. *China's National Defence*, Defence White Paper, State Council, Beijing, July.

*Stratfor Special Report*, 1999. 'Kosovo conflict accelerates formation of Russia–China strategic alliance', *Stratfor Special Report*, 25 June. Available online at http://www.stratfor.com/asia/specialreports.

Sun Geqin and Cui Hongjian, 1996. *Erzhi zhongguo: shenhua yu xianshi* [Containing China: myth and reality], 2 vols., China Yanshi Press, Beijing.

Swaine, M., 1992. *The Military & Political Succession in China*, RAND, Santa Monica.

——, 1996. *The Role of the Chinese Military in National Security Policymaking*, RAND, Santa Monica.

—— and Johnston, A.I., 1999. 'China and arms control institutions', in E. Economy and M. Oksenberg (eds), *China Joins the World: progress and prospects*, Council on Foreign Relations Press, New York:90–135.

Swaine, M.D. and Tellis, A.J., 2000. *Interpreting China's Grand Strategy: past, present and future*, Rand, Santa Monica, California.

Talbott, S., 1995. 'US Deputy Secretary of State Strobe Talbott's speech to the Japan National Press Club on 25 January 1995', Press Release, US Department of State, Washington, DC..

Tao Bojun, 1997. 'Dangde sandai lingdao jiti yu keji qianjun' [The Party's three generation leadership and strengthening the armed forces through technological breakthroughs], *China Military Science*, 3:65–73.

Thalakada, N., 1997. 'China's voting pattern in the Security Council, 1990–1995', in B. Russett (ed.), *The Once and Future Security Council*, St Martin's Press, New York:83–118.

Tilly, C., 1991.'Changing forms of revolution', in E.E. Rice (ed.), *Revolution and Counter-Revolution*, Basil Blackwell, Oxford:1–26.

Toloyan, K., 1995. 'National self-determination and the limits of sovereignty: Armenia, Azerbaijan and the secession of Nagorno-Karabagh', *Nationalism and Ethnic Politics*, 1(1):86–110.

Troner, A. and Milner, S.J., 1995. *Energy and the New China: target of opportunity*, Petroleum Intelligence Weekly Publications, New York.

Union of International Associations (ed.), 1999. *Yearbook of International Organizations 1999/2000*, K.G. Saur, Munich.

——, 2000. *Yearbook of International Organisations 2000/2001*, vol. 2 K.G. Saur, Munich.

United Nations, 1999a. 'Secretary-General presents his annual report to General Assembly', UN Press Release SG/SM/7136 GA/9596, United Nations, Washington, DC, 20 September.

——, 1999b. 'Special session of Commission on Human Rights adopts resolution on East Timor', UN Press Release, United Nations, Washington, DC, 27 September. Available online at http://www0.un.org/News/Press/docs/1999/19990927.hrcn978.doc.html

——, 1999c. 'General Debate', UN document A/54/PV.8, General Assembly, United Nations, Washington, DC, 22 September 1999.

——, 2000. 'Russian Federation, China stress importance of addressing prevention of outer space arms race in disarmament conference', UN Press Release DCF/390, United Nations, Washington, DC, 24 February.

US Information Agency, 1997a. 'Albright/Berger briefing', *USIA Washington File EPF305*, US Information Agency, Department of State, Washington, DC, 29 October.

——, 1997b. 'Background briefing on nuclear cooperation', *USIA Washington File EPF404*, US Information Agency, Department of State, Washington, DC.

——, 1997c. 'Fact sheet: accomplishments of US–China summit', *USIA Washington File EPF307*, US Information Agency, Department of State, Washington, DC, 29 October 1997.

——, 1997d. 'Helms/Shelby Letter on US–China nuclear agreement', *USIA Washington File EPF204*, US Information Agency, Department of State, Washington, DC, 28 October 1997.

——, 1997e. 'US satisfied with China's nuclear controls, US officials say', *USIA Washington File EPF508*, US Information Agency, Department of State, Washington, DC, 31 October 1997.

——, 1998a. *USIA Washington File EPF501*, US Information Agency, Department of State, Washington, DC, 13 March 1998.

——, 1998b. 'Einhorn statement on nuclear cooperation with China', *USIA Washington File EPF308*, US Information Agency, Department of State, Washington, DC, 4 February 1998.

——, 1998c. 'McCurry, Berger Sperling 27 June 1998 Briefing', *USIA Washington File EPF107*, US Information Agency, Department of State, Washington, DC, 29 June 1998.

——, 1998d. 'National Security Adviser Sandy Berger, briefing on Clinton trip to China', *USIA Washington File EPF303*, US Information Agency, Department of State, Washington, DC, 17 June 1998.

——, 1998e. 'US-China joint statement on South Asia', *USIA Washington File EPF403*, US Information Agency, Department of State, Washington, DC, 2 July 1998.

——, 1999a. 'DAS Susan Shirk worldnet on US–China relations', *USIA Washington File EPF502*, US Information Agency, Department of State, Washington, DC, 21 May 1999.

——, 1999b. 'Helms demands US sanction China for missile proliferation', *USIA Washington File EPR507*, US Information Agency, Department of State, Washington, DC, 17 September 1999

——, 1999c. 'Lauder says biological weapons threat is growing', *USIA Washington File EPF419*, US Information Agency, Department of State, Washington, DC, 4 March 1999.

——, 1999d. 'New CIA report assesses future ballistic missile threat', *USIA Washington File EPF507*, US Information Agency, Department of State, Washington, DC, 19 September 1999

——, 1999e. 'Republican policy agenda on US China policy', *USIA Washington File EPF504*, US Information Agency, Department of State, Washington, DC, 18 July 1997.

Van Doren, C.N. and Jones, R., 1989. 'China and nuclear non-proliferation: two perspectives', *Occasional Paper 3*, Program for Promoting Nuclear Non-proliferation, University of Southampton.

Van Kemenade, 1998. *China, Hong Kong, Taiwan Inc.*, Vintage Books, New York (tr. Diane Webb).

Van Ness, P., 1970. *Revolution and Chinese Foreign Policy: Peking's support for wars of national liberation*, University of California Press, Berkeley.

Vogel, E.F. (ed.), 1997. *Living with China: U.S.–China relations in the twenty-first century*, Norton, New York.

Wallerstein, M.B., 1996. 'China and proliferation: a path not taken', *Survival*, 38(3):58–66.

Walt, S., 1987. *The Origin of Alliances*, Cornell University Press, Ithaca.

——, 1996a. 'Rethinking revolution and war', *Security Studies*, 6/2:174–96.

——, 1996b. *Revolution and War*, Cornell University Press, Ithaca.

Wan Ming, 1999. 'Human rights and democracy,' in Deng Yong and Wang Fei-ling (eds), *In the Eyes of the Dragon: China views the world*, Rowman & Littlefield, Lanham:97–118.

Wan Xia, 1999. 'Huigu yu zhanwang–gaige kaifang 20 nian guojifa zai zhongguo de fazhan' [Looking back and ahead: the development of international law in China during twenty years of opening and reform], *Waijiao xueyuan xuebao*, 2:62–66.

Wang Fei-ling, 1999. 'Self-image and strategic intentions: national confidence and political insecurity,' in Deng Yong and Wang Fei-ling (eds), *In the Eyes of the Dragon: China views the world*, Rowman & Littlefield, Lanham:21–46.

Wang Hongying, 1999. 'Multilateralism in Chinese foreign policy: the limits of socialization', in Weixing Hu, Gerald Chan and Daojiong Zha (eds), *China's International Relations in the 21st Century: dynamics of paradigm shifts*, University Press of America, Lanham:71–91.

Wang Jianwei, 1999. 'Managing conflict: Chinese perspectives on multilateral diplomacy and collective security', in Deng Yong and Wang Fei-ling (eds), *In the Eyes of the Dragon: China views the world*, Rowman & Littlefield, Lanham:73–96.

Wang Jisi, 1996. 'International relations theory and the study of Chinese foreign policy: a Chinese perspective', in Robinson and Shambaugh (eds), *Chinese Foreign Policy: theory and practice*, Clarendon Press, Oxford, Oxford University Press, New York:481–505.

Wang Shaoguang, 1996. 'Estimating China's defence expenditure: some evidence from Chinese sources', *The China Quarterly*, 147:889–911.

—— and Hu Angang, 1993. *Guoqing baogao: Jiaqiang zhongyang zhengfu zai shiqiang jingli zhuanxingzhongde zhudao zuoyong; guanyu zhongguo guojia nengli de yanjiu baogao* [Report on the State of the Nation: strengthening the leading role of the central government during the transition to the market economy; Research report concerning the extractive capacity of the state], Beijing and New Haven, Connecticutt.

Wang Xiaodong and Fang Ning, 2000. *China's Road: under the shadow of globalisation*, Chinese Social Sciences Press, Beijing.

Wang Xingfang (ed.), 1995. *Zhongguo yu Lianheguo: jinian Lianheguo chengli wushi zhounian* [China and the United Nations: commemorating the 50th Anniversary of the founding of the United Nations], *Shijie zhishi* chubanshe, Beijing.

Wang Yanjun, 1999. 'Xuexi Jiang Zemin guanyu xianghu yicun de lunshu' [Study Jiang Zemin's remarks on interdependence], in *Waijiao xueyuan xuebao*, 2:36–40.

Wang Yizhou (ed.), 1998. *Quanqiuhua shidai de guoji anquan* [International Security in a Globalised World], Shanghai People's Press, Shanghai.

Warner, D., 1991. *An Ethic of Responsibility in International Relations*, Lynne Rienner, Boulder, Colorado.

Wendt, A. 1995. 'Constructing international politics', *International Security*, 20(1):71–81.

——, 1992. 'Anarchy is what states make of it: the social construction of power politics', *International Organisation*, 4(2):391–425.

White, G., 1993. *Riding the Tiger: the politics of economic reform in post-Mao China*, Macmillan, London.

Whiting, A., 1989. 'Major-Power threats to security in East Asia', in R. Scalapino et al. (eds), *Internal and External Security Issues in Asia*, Institute of East Asian Studies, University of California, Berkeley:26–43.

Wight, M., 1978. *Power Politics*, Leicester University Press/Royal Institute of International Affairs, London.

Wishnick, E., 2000. 'Chinese perspectives on cross-border relations', in S. Garnett (ed.), *Rapprochement or Rivalry: Russia–China relations in a changing era*, Carnegie Endowment For Peace, Washington, DC:227–56.

World Bank, 1994. *Governance: the World Bank's experience*, World Bank, Washington DC.

——, n.d. 'Regions and Countries', *World Bank online*, available at http://www.worldbank.org/html/extdr/regions.htm, accessed 1 August 2001.

Wu Jianhua, 2000. 'Wojun zhonggaoji nianqin zhihui ganbu baiyang de kaocha yu jishi' [The review of promoting young senior officers in our army and its lessons], *Journal of the PLA National Defence University*, 1.

Wu Xinbo, 1998. 'China: security practice of a modernizing and ascending power', in M. Alagappa (ed.), *Asian Security Practice: material and ideational influences*, Stanford University Press, Stanford.

Xie Dajun, 1999. 'Qiantan zhishi jingji jiqi dui junshi gemin de yingxiang yu tiaozhan' [The influence and challenge of knowledge economy to RMA], *The Journal of PLA National Defence University*, (January 1999), 27.

Xu Tao, 2000. 'Ruhe renshi woguo anqun liyi' [How to understand our country's security interest], *Journal of the PLA National Defence University*, 1.

Yahuda, M.B., 1983. *Towards the End of Isolationism: China's foreign policy after Mao*, Macmillan, London.

——, 1999. 'China's foreign relations: the Long March, future uncertain', *The China Quarterly*, 159:650–59.

——, 1999. 'China's search for a global role', *Current History*, 98(629):266–70.

Yan Xuetong, 1996. *Zhongguo guojia liyi fenxi* [Analysis of China's national interest], Tianjin People's Press, Tianjin.

Yao Yanjin and Liu Jixian, 1994. *Deng Xiaoping xinshiqi junshi lilun yanjiu*, [Study of Deng Xiaoping's military theory in the new year], The PLA Academy of Military Science, Beijing:71–76.

Ye Zicheng, 2000. 'Zhongguo shixing deguo waijiao zhanlue shizai bixing' [Strategy of Great Power diplomacy is imperative for China—some problems on China's diplomatic], *Shijie jingji yu zhengzhi* [World Economics and Politics], 1.

You Ji, 1996. 'Jiang Zemin: in struggle for the post-Deng supremacy', in M. Brosseau, S. Pepper and Tsang Shu-ki (eds), *China Review 1996*, The Chinese University of Hong Kong Press, Hong Kong:1–28.

——, 1999.a 'Changing leadership consensus: the domestic context of war games', in Suisheng Zhao (ed.), *Making Sense of the Crisis Across the Taiwan Strait*, Routledge, London:77–98.

——, 1999b. 'Revolution in Military Affairs and the evolution of China's strategic thinking', *Contemporary Southeast Asia*, 21(3):325–45.

——, 1999c. *The Armed Forces of China*, Allen & Unwin, Sydney and I.B. Tauris, London & New York.

——, 1999d. The China challenge in the new millennium, paper presented at the Strategic Update Conference, Parliament House, Canberra, 27 September.

——, 2001. 'China's perceptions on the security of Northeast Asia', Seminar, Department of International Relations, Australian National University, 23 March.

—— and Wilson, I., 1990. 'Leadership by 'lines': China's unresolved succession', *Problems of Communism*, 39(1):28–44.

Yu Bin, 2001. 'NATO's unintended consequence: a deeper strategic partnership…or more', *Comparative Connections*, July 1999, Pacific Forum, Center for Strategic and International Studies. Available online at http://www.csis.org/pacfor/cc/992Qchina-rus.html, accessed 1 August.

Yuan Jing-dong, 1998. 'Sino-Russian confidence building measures: a preliminary analysis', Institute of International Relations, University of British Columbia (processed).

Zhai Qiang, 2000. *China and the Vietnam Wars 1950–1975*, University of North Carolina Press, Chapel Hill.

Zhang Chunjin, 1989. *Renquanlun* [On Human Rights], Tianjin People's Press, Tianjin.

Zhang Yongjin, 1991. *China in the International System, 1918–20: the Middle Kingdom at the periphery*, Macmillan, Basingstoke.

——, 1998. *China in International Society since 1949: alienation and beyond*, Macmillan, Basingstoke.

Zhao Kemin, 1999. 'Duixin shiqi wojun sixiang zhengzhi gongzuo shijian de huigu yu sikao' [The reassessment of and reflection on our army's ideological and political work in the new era], *Journal of the PLA National Defence University*, 10:22–25.

Zhao Wei, 1998. 'China's WTO accession: commitments and prospects', *Journal of World Trade*, 32(1):51–75.

Zheng, Shiping, 1997. *Party vs State in Post-1949 China: the institutional dilemma*, Cambridge University Press, Cambridge.

Zheng Yongnian, 1994. 'Perforated sovereignty: provincial dynamism and China's foreign trade', *The Pacific Review*, 7(3):309–21.

——, 1998. *Discovering Chinese Nationalism in China: modernization, identity, and international relations*, Cambridge University Press, London.

Zou Keyuan, 2000. 'Chinese approach to internation law', in Weixing Hu, Gerald Chan and Daojiong Zha (eds), *China's International Relations in the 21st Century: dynamics of paradigm shifts*, University Press of America, Lanham.

Zou Yunhua, 1998. 'China and the CTBT negotiations', *Working Paper*, Stanford University, Stanford.

——, 1999. 'Chinese perspectives on the South Asian nuclear tests', *Working Paper*, Leland Stanford Junior University, January.

# Index

# Index

# Index

## Index

www.ingramcontent.com/pod-product-compliance
Lightning Source LLC
Chambersburg PA
CBHW040152270326
41928CB00040B/3298
* 9 7 8 1 9 2 5 0 2 1 4 1 7 *